The Benefit of the Doubt

FREDERIC RAPHAEL was born in Chicago in 1931 and educated at Charterhouse and St John's College, Cambridge. His twenty-one novels include *The Glittering Prizes* (1976) and *Coast to Coast* (1998); he has written many short stories, as well as biographies of Somerset Maugham and Byron and a translation of the *Satyricon* of Petronius (2003). Frederic Raphael's early notebooks were published by Carcanet in 2001 as *Personal Terms*; he has also published an autobiography covering his first eighteen years, *A Spoilt Boy* (2003). Frederic Raphael's work includes screenplays for such notable films as *Darling*, *Two for the Road* and Stanley Kubrick's *Eyes Wide Shut*.

FREDERIC RAPHAEL

The Benefits of Doubt

CARCANET

First published in 2003 by
Carcanet Press Limited
Alliance House
Cross Street
Manchester M2 7AQ

A CIP catalogue record for this book
is available from the British Library
ISBN 1 85754 635 0

The publisher acknowledges financial
assistance from the Arts Council of England

Set in Monotype Garamond by XL Publishing Services, Tiverton
Printed and bound in England by SRP Ltd, Exeter

For Beetle and our children and grandchildren, always

Contents

Introduction

When, in May 1968, the frequently garrulous and prolix Jean-Paul Sartre got himself affiliated to the student uprising, he contrived to be called to the Sorbonne podium where Danny the Red and other heralds of the Blissful Dawn 2 had been haranguing grant-assisted Jacobins. On the way to the microphones, old boss-eyes was handed a piece of paper on which was written, 'Sartre, soyez bref' (the new egalitarians did not quite dare to call him Poulou, or even – yet – *tutoyer* him). It would be unwise not to honour their anonymous advice when explaining why I have assembled this bunch of reprinted reviews, lectures and essays.

Who do I think I am to publish my *obiter scripta?* The question recalls the story of when an indignant author said to someone who had not liked his play, 'Who are you to criticise?' To which the unanswerable answer was, 'Who do you have to be?'

It is just forty years since I began reviewing in the *Sunday Times.* To appear on the same pages as Harold Nicolson, Arthur Koestler, Hugh Trevor-Roper, C.P. Snow, Raymond Mortimer and Cyril Connolly was no small promotion. I came of a Cambridge generation that regarded literary criticism as a high calling, though it could never be practised in its most elevated, i.e. Leavisite, style in the Sunday papers. Such perishable journalism was regularly anathematised by 'Frank' and 'Queenie' as Scrutineers called them (at least behind their backs). Yet it had, and has, an irresistible lure. How could it be otherwise when it enabled you both to announce your arrival in literary circles and to vex established vanities with what you hoped, somewhat, was appealing youthful impertinence?

To be offered a place on the *Sunday Times* team was like getting a commission. One might be the merest subaltern, but it was in a crack regiment. Since I completed my formal education before Suez, when the routines of deference were fractured by Eden being put in his passé place, I attached more significance to nods from what seemed on high than any modern *arriviste* can well imagine. Even in the later, libertarian 1960s, I knew my modest place. When Cyril Connolly came into the Literary Department while I was correcting a page hot from the press, I made myself deferentially scarce.

I had hardly got home when Jack Lambert, the literary editor, called to say that Cyril was very upset by the speed of my departure. 'He's afraid he's upset you in some way.'

'Why ever would Cyril imagine that?' I said.

'The way you left the room. He's afraid you think he's getting obsolete.'

That Was The Week That Was had begun the erosive process whereby the old were inferior to the young, and toffs to oiks. Since then, galloping irreverence has established that no one can be better than anyone else, only richer and more famous.

Not many weeks after our first, speechless encounter, I was again in the Literary Department. Again Cyril entered as I was correcting my proof. He sidled up to me and said, 'Hullo. I've got a question to ask you, because I was greatly admiring something you wrote recently.'

'Oh, really?' I said. 'What might that have been?'

'That's my question,' he said.

Youth does not endure; insolence can, even when it grows bald. It becomes wearisome, however, if it fails to mature in any way at all. Coining tart phrases has its enduring lure, but even journalism has its properties: books should always be read on the assumption that they are good until they are seen to be bad. Friends should be accommodated only by being praised when they deserve it; they can always be discreetly ignored when they do not. There is more dignity (and sometimes more feline pleasure) in admiring an enemy's good work than in finding excuses to put the boot in regardless.

Reviewing is still likely to make you more enemies than friends, especially if you tell the unfashionable truth. My ambition in literary journalism has been somewhat A.E. Housmanic: I flatter myself, just a little, by imagining that there is merit in 'saving the sum of things for pay'. The pay is usually poor; nor does the sum add up, necessarily, to anything very much, but intellectual *condottieri* have their uses.

My fuel is less greed, or arrogance, than respect for what Shelley called 'antique courtesies': grammar and honest argument, wit and accuracy are surely among them. Still disposed to deference, I have no notion of being among the scholars, although I like their company; I am perpetually revising for exams I expect to fail. Reviewing is often a form of swotting: in order to be capable of judging a book, one has often to read several others, sometimes more.

Modesty, like gratitude, weakens you in modern eyes. It also makes you unfashionably careful. Craig Raine once accused me, genially, of being the only man in London who still 'puts on a dinner-jacket to write a review'. Incapable of the flippant genius of Sydney Smith, who announced that he never read a book before he reviewed it ('It prejudices a man so'), I read in the expectation of being improved.

I was educated to think that there was merit in being a reasonable man. Addressing some club in Oxford, during the Marxist 1970s, I dared to encourage an understanding of both sides of the Arab–Israeli conflict. When I had finished, a neo-revolutionary from Balliol stood up and called me the worst name he could think of: 'You're nothing,' he said, 'but a middle-class liberal.' Dr Spooner might have said that I should leave Oxford by the town drain.

I have neither a confident political programme nor any consistent scheme for the redemption of men or books. I have called this volume *The Benefits of Doubt*, but doubt is, of course, an insufficient attitude to life. All scepticism is dependent on a measure of credulity, if only in the merits of common decency and civilised values. What we are wise to doubt, as well as the guarantee of their survival, is the wisdom of what Byron once called 'enthusy-musy', an excess of ideological or religious zeal. Beneficial doubt is not a function of being lily-livered but of the refusal to yield to dogma or *apparat*. The prudent sceptic need not doubt everything: what could it be to do so? His general posture is ironic, in the Socratic sense: he wants to know more, but he is wary of ever claiming to be certain that he does. I have always had a soft spot for the men from Laodice whom St Paul derided for 'blowing neither hot nor cold'.

I entitled an earlier volume of essays *The Necessity of Anti-Semitism*. It was flashy, but unwise. Public libraries in America banned my book (unfortunately, without adding markedly to its sales) on the grounds that I must be a politically incorrect crazy. In fact the title was that of a Parkes lecture which I delivered in the School of Jewish Studies at Southampton University. In it, I 'reviewed' an unwritten book which affected to show how anti-Semitism was of the essence of Christendom, and hence of the European genius. My title was evidently a Nabokovian flourish too far (though Frederick Rolfe, Baron Corvo, was the first, I think, to publish reviews of non-existent texts). How could anyone be expected to recognise the wry allusion to Shelley's *The Necessity of Atheism*? I must hope that *The Benefits of Doubt* will not excite anathemas. At least, it sounds unlikely seriously to damage anyone's health or morals.

Frederic Raphael

If This Is a Man

In some respects, Primo Levi needs no introduction. His work has become a classic requiring neither commentary nor explanation. If the style is the man, one might imagine – from its tone and vocabulary – that its author was someone of unassuming appearance and manner. He once said that he modelled his account of life in Auschwitz (or more precisely in Monowitz–Buna, an adjacent *Arbeitslager* or 'work-camp') on 'the weekly report commonly used in factories'. His intention was to write in a language accessible to all. It does not follow that he, personally, was as guileless as his forthright and unadorned narrative. His plain-speaking was calculated to give the world no excuse not to follow every word of what he had to say.

Behind the truthful modesty, which led him to describe his companions more thoroughly than himself, Primo (as his biographer, Myriam Anissimov, among other admirers, impels us to call him) was able to control, although not to hide, his abiding sense of outrage and scandal: Auschwitz, in his view, changed inexorably any assumptions that civilised man might have concerning his fellow men or his God. Primo's candour was as undeceived about himself as it was about others. While he gives the impression of a reasonable man of science ambushed by the monsters of unreason, he was as astute as he contrived to seem artless. If he insisted that chance alone enabled him to survive the camps, it is clear that, in the small areas where it was possible, Levi knew how to make, or at least to improve, his own luck. His survival might be due to chance, but he was never close to becoming a *muselmann*, the term given to those spectral inmates of the camps who, by their listlessness, showed that they had renounced all ambition for survival. Levi was a lover of Dante who refused to abandon hope merely because he had stepped through the gates of hell.

Primo was born in Turin, on 31 July 1919, in the large family apartment where he was to live all his life, save for the time he spent first in the mountains, as a member of a partisan group, and then at Auschwitz, and finally on the perilous, Odyssean journey home which

Introduction to the Folio Society edition of *If This Is a Man*, 2000.

he described in *La Tregua* (*The Truce*). Family tradition says that his birth took place in the room which would later be his study. His ancestors were Sephardic Jews, refugees from the Spanish Inquisition. Their descendants had been in Italy for more than three and a half centuries when Mussolini, under pressure from Hitler, declared them to be aliens and outcasts.

Italian Jews had been, in many respects, the most assimilated in Europe. If they had to endure the usual taunts from Christian schoolfellows, they were rarely victims of systematic discrimination. Before (and often after) the Risorgimento, which unified the country only in 1861, most Italians felt more allegiance to their native cities than to the nation. The Jews' undivided enthusiasm made them, in many ways, exemplary citizens of the new state. Italy had unlocked the gates of the ghetto which, for as long as Rome was still ruled by the Popes, literally enclosed the 'perfidious Jews' (as they were described in Catholic doctrine until Vatican II rescinded the anathema, without quite abolishing the sentiment).

Jews were not, at first, always hostile to the 'anti-Communist' movement which Benito Mussolini founded in the year of Primo's birth. Alexander Stille's *Benevolence and Betrayal* gives memorable accounts of the varying attitudes, and fates, of five Italian Jewish families under Fascism. Not a few continued to be blindly loyal to the Duce even when, in 1938, he betrayed them by promulgating racist laws copied from the Nazis whose barbarity he had earlier derided.

Even those Jews (among them Primo's father) disgusted by the vulgarity of the Fascist parades and speeches had found it almost impossible not to acquiesce in the dominant political and social climate. As Dan Vittorio Segre remarks, in his *Memoirs of a Fortunate Jew*, Fascism became 'the only natural form of existence' for Italians during the inter-war years. When Mussolini opted for alliance with Germany, patriotism demanded acquiescence or silence.

It is tempting to depict Primo as an unworldly science student, of nervous disposition, caught up only by mischance in the hellish machinery of Hitler's war against the Jews. To some extent he fostered this reluctant vision of himself. In fact, although bookish, he was a surprisingly active, decisive young man. If timid with women, he was an amusing companion. As for politics, he was indisposed to fatalism and capable of brave, even reckless decisions. Although of unimpressive physique (thin and fair-haired), he learned to be a resolute mountaineer in the company of close friends, Jewish and Gentile, who were decidedly anti-Fascist, though never Communist.

Primo's father, Cesare, had observed, and been horrified by, Béla Kun's 1919 revolutionary government in Hungary, which he had visited while working as an electrical engineer. He always feared that Jews would attract persecution by becoming identified with Bolshevism. Primo was to remain wary of ideologies, as of metaphysics, but he was soon drawn to the movement Giustizia e Libertà (Justice and Liberty), which had been founded by Carlo Rosselli in 1928. Ten years later, Carlo and his brother were to be murdered in France, in an incident which prompted Alberto Moravia to write *Il Conformista*, later the basis for a film directed by Bernardo Bertolucci which stylishly reconstructs the moral and social vacuousness of Italian Fascism.

Primo dated the criminal insolence of Fascism from an earlier murder, that of the Socialist deputy Giuseppe Matteotti, who was done to death in 1924, on Mussolini's orders. The brazenness with which the Duce denied responsibility, and the facility with which his lies prevailed, was echoed even more savagely by Adolf Hitler, ten years later, on the so-called 'Night of the Long Knives', when he ordered the murders of a number of his enemies, and more of his one-time friends. Europe had entered a time of consciencelessness from which, as Primo was to discover, it proved unwilling to wake.

The phenomenon of 'Holocaust denial', whose authors claim that the gas chambers were a figment of Zionist propaganda, is of a piece with the Fascist dictators' refusal to take responsibility for their crimes, or to see them as criminal. Primo Levi's later years were bedevilled by the fear that, for all the candour of his narrative, his evidence had not been believed.

If, as a Socialist group, Giustizia e Libertà was not avowedly extremist, its partisans did not flinch from extreme means. There were sporadic, sometimes spectacular, acts of defiance: for instance, the dropping of leaflets over Milan in 1930. Most of their plans, however, proved as abortive as the plot to assassinate Mussolini. By the late 1930s, nearly all the leaders of the movement had been arrested. Only those in Turin, led by Carlo Levi (the author of *Christ Stopped at Eboli*) avoided detection for a while. Hence Primo's native city became, by elimination, the centre of anti-Fascist intellectual activity. The philosopher Benedetto Croce, who had recanted from his early endorsement of the Duce, was its inspiration.

The outbreak of war brought about no immediate or marked change in Primo's life. The anti-Jewish laws did not yet impinge cruelly on a community which somewhat gloried in its now hermetic separateness: Jews were obliged to the endogamous, inward-looking caution which not a few of the elders found more congenial than the fear of assimilation and apostasy. Unlike in Germany, where state-sponsored brutality was eagerly adopted, there were only rare incidents of enthusiastic anti-Semitism in Italy after the passing of the race laws. Even among members of the Fascist Party, who in 1938 were formally instructed to interest themselves in 'the Jewish question', a mere 864 out of a membership of 400,000 answered the call to dutiful malice. Jews were, however, abruptly excluded both from the armed forces (though expert engineers had sometimes to be recalled, in mufti, to solve difficult problems) and from national educational establishments. One not wholly unhappy consequence was that many of the best teachers were forced to teach small classes in private Jewish schools.

In 1940, Primo received the top mark in the quantitative analysis examination at the Chemical Institute. This result was not unexpected, nor unmerited, but it was achieved thanks, in part, to his having gained secret access to the room where the practical quizzes were being prepared. A quick sight of the apparatus was enough for an astute young man to guess the nature of the imminent tests. He tipped off two of his closest friends, who later received the same high mark.

It was one thing for Primo to pass examinations, another to find a reputable supervisor for his thesis. Most of the qualified academic scientists were either active Fascists or wary trimmers. Fearful of rejection, he steeled himself to approach a Gentile professor, Nicola Dallaporta, in the street one night. As he tried, stammeringly, to make his case to be allowed to pursue his research, in spite of the laws, Professor Dallaporta said simply, in the words of Jesus, 'Follow me'.

In private, Dallaporta was briskly encouraging: 'Listen,' he said, 'Do your thesis. Who gives a damn about the laws?' The same teacher was to come and see Primo soon after his return from Auschwitz. He told him that he had been chosen to survive in order to write *If This Is a Man*. Never doubting Dallaporta's good intentions, Primo took his remarks to be 'like a blasphemy': it would entail that God had granted privileges, by saving some and condemning others. 'I am obliged to say,' he later told Ferdinando Camon, a Catholic friend, 'that the experience of Auschwitz hit me so hard that it drove out any remnant of religious education that I might have received.'

Although the author of *Memoirs of a Fortunate Jew*, Dan Vittorio Segre, observed after meeting him in 1982 that Levi was 'a stranger to Jewish culture' and that he had 'landed on a Jewish planet in Auschwitz with no preparation and no Jewish upbringing', Primo had certainly learnt something of Judaism when studying for his *Barmitzvah*, the ritual admission into manhood, during his early teens. As he recounts in his memorable autobiography, Segre had escaped the Nazis and served in the British army before emigrating to Israel. Zionism no more inspired Primo than did Orthodoxy. At the same time, if confirmed in his lack of religious faith, he was by no means unfaithful to his origins. He appears to have become 'more Jewish' as time went by. In his later, anguished years, he was known to frequent the synagogue in Turin, albeit self-effacingly. His loyalty to what he could not believe was strengthened by what he had endured. Belief in God, if he ever had it, had been quenched forever. Such credulity is not essential to Jewish identity, which is more to do with conduct, and community, than with creed.

That Primo Levi was not sent to Auschwitz until 1944 was, as he says with truthful irony, a piece of 'good fortune'. The massive deportations and murders of most of European Jewry were already well advanced, but the German war-machine had become so overstretched that physically strong or professionally useful Jews, in particular scientists, were not immediately murdered: it was their privilege to be worked to death, rather than to be slaughtered.

Italian Jews, who were not numerous, had remained largely inaccessible to the exterminatory efficiency of the Nazis until the collapse of Mussolini's tyranny in 1943. Even after the Germans occupied the country, and began to treat their erstwhile allies with vindictive contempt, Jews were often sheltered by compatriots whose dislike of the Germans greatly exceeded any distaste for Jews. On the other hand, in the so-called 'Republic of Salò', a Fascist enclave in the north of the country, where Mussolini continued to rule a petty fiefdom under the aegis of the Germans, the hard core of his followers – conscious that their last days were at hand – conducted themselves with redoubled arrogance.

Hannah Arendt, in her *Eichmann in Jerusalem*, famously and recklessly suggested that European Jews went docilely into the gas chambers. She represents them as submissive and without the will or leadership to resist. This charge has proved as adhesive as it is tendentious. There were many instances of resistance against odds infinitely less favourable than those under which the fully armed forces of many countries of Europe, great and small, surrendered to Hitler. In any event, as Elie Wiesel remarked, the supposed sheep-like behaviour of the Jews was nothing compared to the sheep-like obedience of their murderers.

Primo's family continued to live in anxious safety in Turin throughout the war. He himself might never have been deported had he had not been captured, late in 1943, after a company of Fascist militiamen stumbled by chance on the mountain hideout where he and some of his friends had formed a group of partisans. Although of pacific manner and scholarly appearance, he had decided to take up arms and was sleeping with a pistol under his pillow. He managed to hide it in the ashes of the stove before he was arrested or he might well have been shot on the spot.

As it was, he had a choice when he was interrogated. If he confessed to being a partisan, he faced summary execution; if he posed as a Jew in hiding, he would be less offensive to his captors. In fact he was promised by them that if he would admit to being Jewish, 'We'll send you to a concentration camp and you'll stay there for the rest of the war. In Italy we don't hand anybody over to the Germans.' In the light of this assurance, Primo elected to camouflage himself as the Jew that he really was.

No disparagement is intended in remarking that the strength of Primo Levi, in the camps and afterwards, was of a piece with a certain duplicity which enabled him to be both himself and what others did not suspect: an observer as alert, and aloof, as he was unblinking. The Italians have a disobliging saying 'Piedmontese, fals' e cortese' (the Piedmontese deceitful and courteous); Primo did not, I think, lack a deceptive side. Scrupulous in the honesty of his account, and in his personal behaviour, he made a quiet point of being less naïve than he appeared: he was both what he seemed *and* something more. Instead of the self-pity which introspection can provoke, he made a habit of dispassionate self-regard: as he entered the nightmare of the camps, he noticed his own reactions and conduct as if he were a specimen in an experiment.

He watched his fellow-inmates with equal attention and, in many cases, with courteous coldness. In 1986, he told Philip Roth:

> I had an intense wish to understand, I was constantly pervaded by a curiosity that somebody afterwards did, in fact, deem nothing less than cynical, the curiosity of the naturalist who finds himself trans-planted onto an environment that is monstrous, but new, monstrously new.

It was this novelty which led him later to say that his time in Auschwitz had been an 'adventure'. In some respects, *the* experience of his life had been his season in the inner circle of a man-made inferno.

There were those, like his friend Alberto and the noble Lorenzo, a civilian worker who for six months brought him the remains of his rations, for whom his love is unequivocal, but his attitude to others, notably the young Frenchman whom he calls 'Henri', comes close to censure. He says of him, with a palpable wince of distaste, that he admired the resourcefulness which procured his survival, but that he would not care to meet him again.

'Henri''s real name was Paul Steinberg. As he told Myriam Anissimov:

> I had to be very clever, and from the start I watched my subjects [those in power] coldly... Their intrinsic instability, in fact a genuine madness was a constant danger... whose violent symptoms were utterly unpredictable even to those who knew them best... I practised all the circus arts – animal tamer, tightrope walker, and even conjuror. And at this game, I made rapid strides.

There was, it seems, a blatancy about Steinberg's calculations which gave him, at least in Primo's eyes, something of the allure of a prostitute. He was, at the time, not yet twenty years old (Primo was only a few years his senior). If Steinberg was shameless in his seductions of those in authority, he did not, so far as we are told, betray his fellow-inmates, still less behave towards them with the callousness of the *Kapo*s. What is sometimes missed in Primo's account of the horrors he endured, and observed, is that they did not impel him to abandon, or much alter, the moral standards with which he arrived. He does say that 'If the *Lager* had lasted longer, a new, hard language would have been born', a language in which it might be possible to denote exactly what it felt like to suffer beyond endurance. As it was, however, Primo had to use the old language, with its civilised nuances and moral undertones, with which to convey what we, the fortunate, can never know in our flesh.

When he speaks of a 'degenerate German engineer' giving warm water from the train engine to a father and mother so that they could bathe the little girl whom the same engineer knew that he was taking to her death, the fastidious disgust with which the adjective is weighted seems to saturate it with a new dimension of revulsion. Early in the narrative, we get a sense of the moral finesse of which, like his literary and scientific culture, the naked, shivering, tattooed Jew, *Häftling* 174517, cannot, and will not, be stripped.

Not the least of Primo's chilling accuracies is that with which he concedes that, for all his suffering, he never really reached 'the bottom'. The true witnesses, he remarks in his late book, *The Drowned and the Saved*, were 'those who breathed their last in the gas trucks and gas chambers, or died under machinegun fire in Babi Yar, Riga, Minsk or Ponary…'

By virtue of his B.Sc. (Turin), and a capacity to speak German, Primo was able to pass crucial weeks in the warmth of the laboratory; because he was lucky enough to get scarlet fever in time to be consigned to the camp hospital, he avoided the death march away from the camp on which so many of his fitter companions died. Whatever the monstrosity of what he witnessed, he knew, in the words of Goya, 'Eso no es lo peor': that is not the worst of it. Perhaps, for Primo, that *was* the worst of it.

He repeatedly emphasised one important, and often missed, point: that Auschwitz (and the other camps) 'had nothing to do with the war'. The constant use of the term 'war crime' has done more than anything else to obscure and falsify the nature of what was done to Primo Levi and to those even less fortunate than he. The mystification of a crime, like the allegation that it is unique, both dignifies and obscures what happened. Neither Primo nor anyone else has been able rationally to explain what drove the Germans specifically to a crime which may have been without parallel, but was scarcely without precedent. What would it be, after all, to give a reasonable account of the irrational? Primo realised that unfaltering description of the facts was as close as he, or anyone, was likely to come to an explanation of them. He regretted the obscurantism of, for particular instance, Paul Celan, but he would not, I think, have failed to nod grimly at the poet's famous line: 'Der Tod ist ein Meister aus Deutschland' (Death is sovereign in Germany).

The history of European anti-Semitism does not account for the Nazi cult of mass murder, but it is not irrelevant to it. What happened at Auschwitz was not *caused* by a centuries-old tradition of disparagement and humiliation, nor by the example of pious murders by the first Crusaders, especially the Germans, who rehearsed what they hoped to do to the Saracen armies in the Holy Land by massacring unarmed Jews in the Rhineland. However, as Ferdinando Camon mentioned, to Primo's surprise:

There is something in Christian culture that recommends relations with 'the other' with the sole purpose of achieving his conversion... The fate of 'the other' is considered as nothing compared to his conversion. If you look into this assertion, at the end of a certain time you can see extermination.

Martin Luther's change of attitude, from geniality to scatological abuse, after the German Jews failed to rally to his new version of Christianity, does something to confirm Camon's notion. Luther's splenetic expression of his frustration supplied a fundamental warrant for German anti-Semitism.

What Alphonse Dupront called 'the myth of the Crusades' did not die with the last Crusader. When the Popes granted dispensation from normal Christian morality in order to confound the Heathen, they inaugurated a kind of ruthlessness which has licensed the betrayal of civilisation, in civilisation's name. This finds its iniquitous echo in Himmler's speech to his extermination squads. In it, the Reichsführer SS cloaks the unspeakable in the lineaments of a sacred mission.

After the war, Primo lived a peacefully tormented life in Turin until 1987. His book had not at first found a wide public, and only reluctant publishers, but by the end of his life he had become the venerated voice of those who had been to hell, and back. His books eventually enjoyed the kind of success, and he the kind of renown, which might have filled another author with complacency. In fact, Primo's dismay at human cruelty, and the fear that he could never make his message sufficiently credible, filled his old age with unappeasable demons. The past came back in palpable form when he was diagnosed with prostate cancer. It was probably due to the effect of the chemicals he had to manhandle, without any protective clothing, in the *Lager*.

His dignity and his irony armed him with a terrible, wilful calmness, but he was never at ease. Knowing all the time that there was much that he could never express in words, he kept his voice down the better to make it carry. He had admired the solidarity of the Greek Jews in Auschwitz who never allowed themselves, as most national groups did, to be fractured into selfishness. If the Greeks were pious, they were also ruthless in their struggle (mostly vain) to survive. They were never resigned; no more was Primo.

It is clear, from many studies, that belief in some ideology, religious or political, helped inmates to rise above despair. Reason alone was Primo's crutch. He was sustained by the abstract, entirely human discipline of a scientific training. He willed himself to be the sane man to whom rage and hatred were futile, if understandable, responses to savagery. He resisted accusing all Germans of some kind of ethnic taint, since that would have been to lapse into a racism hardly distinguishable from Nazism. Nevertheless, he declared *If This Is a Man* to be 'aimed at the Germans like a loaded weapon'.

It is widely believed that, like his fellow-survivor Jean Améry before him, Primo committed suicide when he fell from the third-floor landing of his flat to the hallway below. David Mendel, a retired consultant cardiologist, shrewd admirer and personal friend of Primo, is not so sure. He told me that the medication which Levi was taking *might* have caused dizziness and could have unbalanced him into falling. What is certain is that Primo *was* a man, and a rare one, and that he left behind a testament which will live as long as civilisation and barbarism continue their battle to master humanity.

Primo Inter Pares

Can we assume that it is generally known that Primo Levi was the most articulate of concentration camp survivors? *If This Is a Man*, his account of Auschwitz, and *The Truce*, the story of his tortuous, Odysseus-like return journey to Turin in the chaos of 'liberated' Europe, are classics: school texts (in Italy, at least) and, as Thucydides said of his own history, a *ktema es aei*: baggage for eternity.

Born in 1919, Levi's early life was that of a pampered, shy Jewish middle-class prodigy (top of the class, both in literature and in his chosen vocation, chemistry). Neither Thomson nor Angier mentions the story, told by Myriam Anissimov (who is not cited in either bibliogaphy), of Primo's 'cheating' in a final exam by drawing quick inferences from a crafty look at the equipment set up for a practical question.

In the untypical Italian city of Turin, reticence was a common characteristic, carried to endogamous extremes by the large Jewish population, many of whose ancestors had been Sephardic refugees from the Spanish Inquisition. Jews were welcomed in partly Protestant Piedmont with a tolerance rare in the rest of Italy. In Rome, they continued to be ghettoised (literally), until after the Risorgimento in which Italian Jews were eager *Garibaldini*. Even then, though no longer locked in, they were confined to the same insalubrious quarter.

Jews proved more enthusiastic citizens of the united Italy than many Romans, Milanese and Neapolitans, for whom the city, not the nation, was the focus of loyalty (cf. Giovanni Bologna's terracotta of the triumph of Florence over Pisa). Jews were also among Mussolini's earliest adherents. Mussolini's Fascism may have been militant mountebankery, but (like the Mafia it suppressed) it was only casually murderous and not programmatically racist until 1937/8.

Primo's father, the somewhat louche Cesare, offered scornful passive resistance to Fascism, but – as Dan Vittorio Segre remarked in his *Memoirs of a Fortunate Jew* – it was 'the only natural form of exis-

Review of Carole Angier, *The Double Bond: Primo Levi, a biography*, and Ian Thomson, *Primo Levi*, in *The Spectator*, 2002.

tence' for Italians between the wars. Mussolini had a Jewish mistress, Margherita Sarfatti, and – until the late 1930s – affected to despise the racist mania of the Nazis. He then betrayed the Jews, and Italy itself, by his fatal, infatuated alliance with Hitler. Even so, not until the Duce was overthrown, in 1943, and the German army, followed by the SS, became the masters of Italy, did deportations begin. By then the Nazi killing frenzy had somewhat abated. Only thousands and thousands of women and children and old men were immediately despatched. A doctor of chemistry had his uses, as one of Primo's quick-witted comrades realised on arrival. 'Alberto mi ha salvato la vita', Primo said. He could not do as much for Alberto, who survived only to be murdered, at the end of the war, on a death march in which Primo was too prostrate with scarlet fever to take part.

Levi wrote, with obsessed objectivity, about what came to be called (not to his approval) the Holocaust. Like a naturalist, he tabulated varieties of individual responses to 'the horror, the horror' (he was a keen reader of English, and not least of Joseph Conrad). Then, in *The Periodic Table*, he composed a sequence of 'scientific' fables, often fantastic but always aware of the heartless ingenuities of nature. Levi remained a practising Jew, of a kind, but he ceased to believe in God. On arrival in Auschwitz, he asked 'Warum?' (Why?) when forbidden to slake his thirst on an icicle. The *Kapo* replied, 'Here there is no "why?"'. Primo came to take the same view of the world at large.

Much has already been written about a man with whom his biographers tend very soon to be on intimate terms. Now we are blessed with two more damn fat books: Carole Angier's weighs in at nearly 900 pages; Ian Thomson's at a more modest 600 plus. In the light of such exhaustiveness, it may be assumed that few stones remain unturned, or indeed unthrown.

Carole Angier – eager to be fetchingly original – adopts a searching, sometimes scathing, and passionate (as opposed to dispassionate) approach. Ian Thomson is self-effacing and historico-journalistic: he gives us a lot of facts, and background, but stays discreetly out of the frame, from which Angier too regularly pops out to wave hello.

Her mastery of Levi's writings is exemplary, though she is too prompt to accuse him of 'lying' when he tailors fact to furnish a better or more telling story. Since, especially in what are avowedly fictional or fabulous tales, he changes names and conflates characters, such reproaches smack of self-righteousness. However, the recent publication of Paul Steinberg's *Speak You Also*, suggests that Levi's 'objectivity' contained a fiercely moralising, and sometimes complacent, element. Levi portrayed Steinberg as 'Henri', the survivor-at-all-costs whose endurance he recognised but whom he said he would never wish to see again, as he did – almost as if they had been at school together – a number of old Auschwitzians, and the rare 'decent' German. 'Henri', Angier says, was as clever as Primo, and Primo didn't like it. He doubted his body; he was proud of his mind.

The greatest grief of his post-war life was probably the death of Lorenzo, the Italian 'guest-worker' billeted adjacent to Birkenau, who – at the risk of his life – supplied Primo with food, comradeship and even the means of communicating with his family. He could not support the memory of what others had suffered and drank himself to death when he got home. Yet Primo's putative suicide is somehow made to seem the result of some innate weakness of character. In fact, his endurance was astonishing.

Angier's scolding eulogy derives from an advertised scheme:

> this book is on two levels: a rationally tested, known or knowable one; and the other. Perhaps I needn't say that the felt and imagined level seems to me equally true and even more important. But I would have liked to say so to Primo Levi. For these two, the rational and the irrational, were also his own two sides; but he chose to live in only the rational half of himself... That was his armour, but also the gap in it.

The author thus appoints herself the sententious pathologist who will dissect and evaluate Primo's merits and mentality. Unlike Thomson, she never had access to Levi in person, but she has put herself about his circle like the busiest tangent in the world. Sure of her right to probe, and speculate, she intrudes the word 'perhaps' less to indicate self-doubt than to remind us all of her intuitive presence.

All sorts of women are paraded to testify to Levi's roving eye, and inhibited manner, quite as if leaving his wife Lucia (the shrewd editor of his masterpiece) and playing the Latin lover would have averted his depressions and prevented his death. Since the overriding reason for his strained conjugal relations was an obsessive concern with his mother 'Rina', who outlived him by four years, is it credible that another woman would have persuaded a man doubly bonded to filial duty (Italians, no less than Jews, have mothers) to leave the apartment where he lived with both Rina and Lucia (not to mention his children)?

Angier suggests that Primo's 'rationalism' was a defective and –

she implies – unmanly response to life. At the same time, she remarks the apparent artlessness of his work, and praises the elaboration of its simplicities. Aesthetically she admires what she deplores ethically. This is a flawed rationale and yields predetermined readings.

The Double Bond remains an immensely useful source of intelligence and detailed fact. The shooting of Sandro Delmastro, for instance, is much more poignantly described by Angier than by Thomson, but I suspect that he is right in saying that Cesare Pavese (a famous novelist and suicide) was never one of Primo's *liceo* professors, whereas Angier maintains that he was. She, on the other hand, seems more reliably specific about a number of other matters: Lello Perugia, the wily trader who helped Primo survive on the homeward journey, is said by Angier to have *eaten* a cigar, in order to feign a needed sickness, where Thomson says he only put one under his arm (Angier has him, convincingly, doing both). Fräulein Dreschel, the German bitch whom Levi tried to infect with scarlet fever (the only 'bad thing' he concedes having done), does not get a mention in Thomson.

One only wishes that Angier had had the principled modesty to adopt Primo's despised, 'factory-report' methodology and ventured less into the limitless world of 'perhaps'. Her book might then have had definitive authority. As for Thomson, he gives us a lot of interesting background, not least the painful truth (I assume) that the young Antonioni admired *Jew Süss* when it was shown in Italy in 1943. Say it ain't so, Michelangelo!

On the heart of the matter, and notably Auschwitz, Thomson is tick-tockingly chronological: too many later, mundane events (about failure and success) are given the same weight. However, I should not want to have missed Thomson's story of Levi, in the Soviet Union after the war, when Fiat had a factory there, overhearing an Italian worker complaining that Russian condoms were 'like lorry tarpaulins'.

Levi *was* a man and, like any man, he fell short of divinity. Only hagiographers will be dismayed to find that he liked talking to attractive women, disliked nasty reviews and revelled in good ones, even those as platitudinous as John Gross's sales-enhancing eulogy of *The Periodic Table*: 'true writer… fine gift for narrative… subtle insight into character'. Who will be surprised that Saul Bellow was jealous of his unassertive charisma, though he saluted his work? There are Jews who feel belittled, even deprived, by not having been in a camp. Bruno Bettelheim vaunted himself on surviving pre-war Belsen – which was vile, but never exterminatory – and created a taxonomy of the qualities that marked survivors. He did not include luck; Primo always did. Levi was a witness who too many people wished had *not* survived. Holocaust-denial came to fill him with despair. Did not Jesus warn of the dubious credibility of one who came back from the dead? Levi detested all forms of oppression and mystico-fustian (if he loved H.G.Wells, he despised Tolkien) and he was no wholehearted supporter of any domineering and ruthless creed, not least Zionism: in 1982, he was horrified by Menachem Begin, whom Thomson continually calls 'President' of Israel. In fact, he was Prime Minister.

Levi was a chronic depressive, an important writer, and an industrial chemist (his work-life was spent in a paint factory, as was that of another great Italian Jewish writer, Italo Svevo). When he went to Germany on business after the war, and was asked how he came to speak the language so well, Levi told his hosts, 'I learnt it in Auschwitz.' Banquo's polite tone whispered home the metaphorical stiletto.

Levi came to believe that – the cruellest of all ironies – Auschwitz had been *the* great adventure of his life. His children were alienated and embarrassed when he spoke of it. It remains the indelible writing on all our walls, not excepting Ariel Sharon's.

The Stage and the Stagyrite

The root meaning of 'drama' is simply a deed, a thing done. Thanks (if thanks are due) to Aristotle, Greek poetry – a general term for all forms of artistic fabrication, including tragedy – was categorised according to retrospective rules. After the *Poetics* were rediscovered by the Renaissance, the done thing for Western playwrights was to aspire to compositions which conformed to Aristotle's putative recipe. The now derided 'well-made play' of boulevard theatre was the vestigial, terminal fruit of this tradition. So are the 'three acts' beloved, alas, of movie executives. The notion that 'creative writing' can be taught also originates with the *Poetics*, although Aristotle's didacticism was more philosophical than banausic: art was not a socially elevating activity in ancient Greece, though elevated persons such as Sophocles – priest and general – might practise it.

Oedipus Tyrannus was Aristotle's golden instance of the complex play, properly dignified with the ingredients of *peripeteia* (surprise or twist) and *anagnorisis* (recognition). *Antigone* was another; its confrontation of two incompatible but equally valid notions of righteous behaviour – Creon's and Antigone's – seemed to Hegel (if only to Hegel) to validate his vision of sublime synthesis. George Steiner has tabulated how many Antigones the same myth has spawned. The *Poetics* have been scarcely less seminal: Horace's *Ars Poetica* was, for centuries, the most influential recension of a short book which has cast a very long shadow.

As Alfred Gudeman pointed out over sixty years ago, Aristotle's conclusions about drama were drawn from the evidence of the 300 plays by the great trio of Attic tragedians available to him. We can check his acumen against only a tenth as many. However, he often cites texts known to us. This may suggest that conscious choice, no less than chance (the unpredictable machinery of the gods), has something to do with the quality of what has come down to us.

Our attenuated canon proves that Aristotle was both sharp and fallible. Taxonomic tidiness could lead him to press exceptions into

Review of Aristotle, *Poetics, A New Translation* by Kenneth McLeish, in the *Times Literary Supplement*, 1999.

being proofs of the rule. In his philosophy, everything – including drama – had a natural form. Its growth was determined by an innate need to reach the fullest expression of its form. On achieving maturity, it had no further prospects of development: essence determined existence, both in nature and in the evolution of art.

In A.J. Ayer's sense, Aristotle was the great journeyman: the most brilliant philosopher who cannot quite be accused of genius. His master, Plato, the prime pundit, saw everything as subordinate elements of a coherent whole; hence, in his ideal polity, Art could not be privileged above the official vision of divine order. The service of virtue required that the gods be depicted as moral. If poets would not honour that line, they had no place in the city. Iris Murdoch's 'Sovereignty of the Good' may be necessarily benign; by the same token, it can never be tolerant.

Aristotle's systematic pluralism was that of a biologist. In his vision, everything on earth was in some sense alive and subject to its evolutionary destiny. He took a more relaxed (and subtle) view than Plato of what artists did. 'Homer,' he says in the *Poetics*, 'has above all taught the rest how to speak falsehoods as a poet ought.' This wise paradox came more easily to an outsider than to one who, like Plato, had been shaken by the decline and fall of Athens. Plato wanted to staunch and reverse what d'Annunzio would call 'this grey flood of democratic mud' which the theatrical audience impersonated. Aristotle preferred to conduct a dispassionate autopsy.

The son of the court physician to Amyntas, king of Macedonia, Aristotle could take a visiting professor's view of Greek politics. His anatomical methods, like the vexed concept of *katharsis*, may derive from his father's professional practice. A habit of vigilant aloofness disposed him, like a physician, to investigate phenomena with more care than emotion. Although he succeeded Plato as head of the academy, he was never consumed by the little local difficulty of what had gone wrong with Athens or its morals.

The *Poetics* is the first extant treatise to attempt a general account of the arts. Poetry, Aristotle argued, should help us to perceive patterns of coherence in human life. Tragic characters had to rise above mundane specifics and, as Stephen Halliwell puts it, 'elevate human action to a higher degree of intelligibility so that it acquires something which even the philosopher might recognise as significant'. As Aristotle said, in his *Metaphysics*, 'all men by nature desire knowledge'. Tragedy – on his studied account – offered a painful, vertiginous ladder to the dispassionate knowledge of human prospects.

The *Poetics* started with, and maintained, a commanding lead as a manual of practice and, perhaps, of instruction. Jonathan Barnes still sees the text as prescriptive. Halliwell – probably the most authoritative contemporary analyst of the *Poetics* – maintains that '… a young Athenian dramatist [might] come away with material for reflection, but he would have had to develop his craft elsewhere'. Is it so certain that sound principles of construction are irrelevant to artistic practice? Does the still touted notion of the avant-garde not depend on an Aristotelian notion of artistic evolution? Genius leads us on a march towards an inevitable destination. Without theoretical backing, *some* art (not least Conceptualism) would be unthinkable. Whether we should miss it is another question.

The *Poetics* certainly had practical effects on the course of written poetry. In Renaissance England in particular, Aristotle's advocates and critics squabbled over his corpus. Some – notably Sir Philip Sidney and John Dennis (who called the Stagyrite 'the legislator of Parnassus') – were eager to clothe themselves in his armour. Others found it a poor, or limiting, fit: John Dryden observed ''Tis not enough that Aristotle has said so; for Aristotle drew his models of tragedy from Sophocles and Euripides; and, if he had seen ours, might have changed his mind'. Dryden also resented Aristotle's promotion of tragedy over epic 'because it turns in a shorter compass; the whole action being circumscribed within the space of four-and-twenty hours. He might prove as well that a mushroom is to be preferred before a peach because it shoots up in the compass of a night'.

Aristotle's rules were made exaggeratedly constricting because of tendentious readings. The tradition of inadequate translation began early. Roger Bacon attacked Hermannus Alemannus 'quem non ausus fuit interpres Hermannus transferre in Latinum propter metrorum difficultatem, quam non intellexit.' Scholars have wrangled regularly for 500 years over the proper meaning of key terms such as *katharsis*. This debate was described by Henry Morley as 'a grotesque monument to sterility'.

Thomas Gray observed more than two centuries ago that 'Aristotle is the hardest author by far I ever meddled with; then he has a dry conciseness that makes one imagine one is perusing a Table of Contents rather than a book'. The received wisdom is that Aristotle must have unpacked his ideas more explicitly in a seminar. His lack of Athenian *parti pris* seems at times calculated to pique his pupils in the Academy. He points out, for instance, that drama – from *dran* (to do or act) – is probably a term of Dorian origin; the Athenians normally used the synonymous *prattein*. Not even comedy, he tells the class, was an autochthonous Attic genre: sixth-century Megarian democrats got there first. One hears the chorus of 'Oh, sir, *surely...*'

Aristotle's commodious mind, and the speed with which he saw links between one department of it and another, makes him both an invaluable source and, at times, a gabbling guide. His condensed obscurity is a function of how much he has to tell us. When he is not obscure, he is not always revealing. Is it an observation of the greatest subtlety to point out that a composition must have a beginning, a middle and an end? This seeming truism has been repeated without end, and with didactic solemnity. Even the iconoclastic Jean-Luc Godard conceded that films too had to have a beginning, a middle and an end, before adding the kicker: 'though not necessarily in that order'.

The Stagyrite seemed incontrovertible because his aesthetics struck a scientific attitude. As Alexander Pope said, 'Poets.../ Receiv'd his laws, and stood convinc'd 't was fit/ Who conquered nature should preside o'er Wit'. The *Poetics* have been influential not least on account of the misconstructions put upon them. Some of these are due to Aristotle's failure to elucidate his own terseness. As often they result from tendentious and/or anachronistic translations, and translations of translations (during the early Renaissance, an Arabic version was the prime source). Posterior analysts and critics often sought to dignify their own theories with Aristotelian laurels. As Kenneth McLeish points out, Christian moralists elaborated the concept of *hamartia* in order that it seem to prefigure, or even embody, unGreek notions of sin and possible redemption. *Hamartia* means more an error than a 'flaw' in any moral sense. McLeish compares it to a dropped stitch which damages the pattern of stability and leads to disaster until it is repaired, by whatever terrible means. *Hubris* did violence to due process; it might involve, but did not exclusively *mean*, arrogance.

This new, typically lucid and demystifying version of the *Poetics* was the last completed work of the outstanding translator of his generation. I was lucky in having Kenneth McLeish as one of my closest friends. Over a period of twenty-five harmonious years, I worked with him on several translations of Greek tragedy and Latin poetry. I was always excited, and instructed, by the accuracy of his passion for the classics. All his versions of drama, whether from Greek, Norwegian, or French, comic or tragic, were sublimely modest; he served his authors, never his vanity.

When McLeish died, at the end of 1997, he had just succeeded in translating the entire works of the great Athenian dramatists. Having already written an excellent, extremely practical, handbook on *The Theatre of Aristophanes*, he was well advanced on a comprehensive study of Attic drama. This plain-spoken version of the *Poetics* was undertaken as a prelude to the monograph on Aristotle's dramatic theory which he wrote for the Great Philosophers series. That essay should be read as a copious supplement to the unfailingly helpful but brief notes in the present translation. McLeish's glosses shine without flashiness:

> The concept of *mimesis* is at the heart of Aristotle's analysis of the aesthetics not merely of drama but of all arts. Predictably, the word defies translation. It means setting up in someone's mind, by an act of artistic presentation, ideas that will lead that person to associate what is being presented with his or her previous experience. The pleasure we take in the arts is related to our cognitive faculty: recognition is a function of cognition. Our knowledge is reinforced and extended by what the arts reveal to us and in us: they extend our human experience and awareness and make us more human.

Despite his respect for the text (no Gilbert Murrayish excesses or Faglesian flourishes) McLeish's piety was never obsequious. The text was sacred, but not unquestionable. He argued sharply, but cogently, against Aristotle's overview of tragedy and, in particular, against his conception of the gods:

> Aristotle's metaphysical writings, following Plato, find an echo in the Judaeo-Christian notion that God is unique and unchanging, that the divine is by nature not devious. But absolutism of this kind was no part of the Greek dramatists' armoury... they treated their immortal characters like any others, often deviating wildly from the original myth-stereotypes... Aeschylus shows us a... Prometheus who snarls and rails at Zeus like a rock-bound Thersites, an Athene and Apollo who bicker like jealous mortal siblings... Euripides' gallery of gods includes a sun-princess tormented because she chooses [?] to take on mortal feelings... a devious and sexually ambivalent Dionysos... This kind of plurality, so bizarre to Christian readers... is absolutely consistent with the everyday Greek view that the gods were everywhere and could be anything they chose. It must have startled, intrigued, amused and edified the original audiences, but in a way entirely to do with

popular entertainment and religious sentiment and foreign to the austerities of philosophy and metaphysical enquiry.

Like Halliwell, but much more accessibly, McLeish maintained that the *Poetics* underestimated the religious aspect of Greek drama. Aristotle was insulated from it both by his temperament and by the likelihood that he studied plays in the library rather than saw them in the theatre. Wincing at the vulgarity of *opsis* (spectacle), Aristotle related poetics to rhetoric without remarking on how deeply the theatrical mode had affected – Plato might say *in*fected – Athenian life.

The parade of weeping children and wives, in criminal trials, was a spectacle which Socrates deplored, but such things clearly affected juries whom – as theatre-goers – Euripides' *Trojan Women*, for instance, had schooled in pity and terror. The Athenian *demos* came to delight in dramatic peripeties: for instance, they reversed their verdict in the case of the revolt of Mytilene and rewrote the death sentences with a happier, if hardly amiable, ending.

Aristotle's predilection for private reading set a dubious example to subsequent scholars who scarcely admitted the importance of *performance* in classical drama (Oliver Taplin's study of Aeschylus' stagecraft broke the mould). In his protracted treatment of the *Poetics*, Stephen Halliwell never mentions the significance of masks and buskins in concealing – if not eliminating – the individuality of dramatic characters. There was a generalising and alienating dimension to tragedy which was calculated to turn the *muthos* (story, plot-line) into what used indeed to be called an 'argument': a logical sequence of events from which knowledge – not merely emotional consternation – might follow. It was said of a Greek playwright that he 'taught' his cast; and the cast its audience. Wisdom, Aeschylus said, came through suffering; and through drawing the right conclusions from it.

Unfortunately, McLeish did not find time here to deal in any way with the vexed issue of *katharsis*. Halliwell suggests, plausibly, that Aristotle analogised the experience of tragedy with preparation for initiation in the mysteries. At Eleusis, 'cleansing' – literal and metaphorical – was a prelude to revelation.

McLeish and Halliwell agree that it was part of the theatrical experience, but not its purpose, to excite 'pity and terror' (Samuel Butler – rather Britishly – disparaged these sentiments as 'these two maggots'). *Katharsis* cleared the mind for a calmly disillusioned perception of human possibilities and limitations. In *Samson Agonistes* (perhaps the most Greek play in English), Milton signalled the moment of quietus as one in which all passion was spent.

It is usually said that the cathartic affectations of psychoanalysis have nothing in common with Aristotelian *katharsis*, but is that so? Freud's *idea* was to enable a patient, by dramatic re-presentation, to come through his or her fears (and self-pity) and to reach a stage where reason could influence and civilise the mind. Whatever the great tragedians themselves thought they were doing, was their effect – on Aristotle's account – very different? It was, as the Marxists say, no accident that Freud chose Oedipus as a motif. His method of obliging neurotics to 'surface' their hidden histories was also of dramatic consequence. While the demandingly nuanced, and musically punctuated, texts of Greek drama allowed little individual licence to their performers, the Freud-inspired spontaneities of Stanislavsky's 'method' and – in particular – of the American, psycho-analytically driven, Actors' Studio, added a new, unscripted dimension to the theatre, and then to the cinema. Whether substituting the 'authenticity' of actors for the facticiousness of authors represents the last flower of Aristotle's aesthetic teleology is another question.

The derivatives of the Greek world seem endless, quite as if we knew exactly what it meant to us. Yet Arnaldo Momigliano confessed, after half a century of scholarship, that he still did not know what the Greeks expected of their gods or their gods of them. Should we not say the same of their culture, and its effect on us? The glory of Greece lies in the elasticity of its myths (and morals) and in the ingenuity with which they have been revised and even travestied. No one loved the Attic theatre and ancient Hellas with more ardent accuracy or unpretentious clarity than Kenneth McLeish; few have served them better.

Breton and His Slaves

Surrealism was a game of three halves. It kicked off during the Great War, rose to a thunderous *diminuendo* as the 1930s turned out to be too sombre to be amused by chic shocks, and flowered again in New York during the war when the loudest of its malodorous blooms was the scatological frivolity of Salvador Dali. Dali's appetite for fame and – more particularly – fortune led André Breton (a founding father) to call him 'Avida Dollars' (punning was always part of the Surrealist idea of fun).

One of the greatest problems for Ruth Brandon must have been the plethora of, as she would say, protagonists. The turnover of prima donnas during the thirty years of Surrealism's facetious solemnity requires the deft management of entrances and exits. Ms Brandon's sources are often excellent, though (in the Surrealist tradition?) she takes some liberties with French grammar.

The term 'Surrealism' was coined by the poet Guillaume Apollinaire (actually an illegitimate Pole called Wilhelm Apollinaris de Kostrowitzky). In 1917, he applied it to his avant-garde play *Les Mamelles de Tirésias* (*Tiresias' Tits*). This extravaganza began two hours late, or it would have been even further ahead of its time. As the curtain failed to rise (there wasn't one), a fat woman came on stage and unbuttoned her blouse, revealing two gas-filled balloons which she threw at the audience. Yes, it was that kind of a show, folks.

Who knows how it might have ended? It never did because, so legend insists, suddenly 'a young man in English uniform entered the stalls... pulled out his revolver and prepared to discharge it into the audience'. However, as Ruth Brandon tells us, 'In the nick of time [when else?], a studious-looking fellow, with thick auburn hair, dashed up and dissuaded his friend... from his murderous intentions'. If it ever happened, the whole thing was probably a set-up within a send-up.

The officer was not English, but part-Irish, and his name was Jacques Vaché. The dissuasive twenty-year-old was André Breton, medical student and ambitious poet who was to say, more than once,

Review of Ruth Brandon, *Surreal Lives*, in the *Sunday Times*, 1999.

that only the word 'Liberté' really gave him a lift. Breton venerated Vaché's regular refusal to be cowed. So far from deploring his threat to open fire on the audience, Breton would later decree that the fundamental Surrealist act was 'going into the street, revolver in hand, and shooting at random into the crowd'. This has, of course, since become a commonplace of life in civilised societies.

Vaché had something of the doomed allure of Sebastian Flyte, in Evelyn Waugh's *Brideshead Revisited*. His entrancing lack of moral restraint appealed to the squeamish Breton who – like Waugh – was embarrassed by his own middle-class provenance. Breton was to spend his life trying to prove that he had shaken off his bourgeois shadow. He did this first by toadying to established literary figures such as Paul Valéry, Apollinaire and André Gide, who gave him a generous welcome. Despite his novelistic advocacy of *actes gratuits* – deliberately scandalous happenings – which were to be the hallmarks of Surrealism, Gide was soon blacklisted for unBohemian respectability. Gratitude was not in Breton's repertoire, though demanding autocracy became his habit. Early on, he recruited Tristan Tzara, the unpossessive proprietor of Dadaism, whose anti-art was very much his style, but soon relegated him to the periphery.

Breton was the very type of the literary hermit crab who sidles into fancy company and makes himself at home there. When Apollinaire was badly wounded in the war and died of flu soon after it, Breton acquired Surrealism's estate and made himself the infallible Pope of artistic impropriety. If he was unfeeling over Apollinaire (who had actually been square enough to go into the trenches), Breton was stunned by the early death of Vaché. In 1919, that dandyish scapegrace committed suicide (always a glamorously Surreal way to go) by taking an opium overdose in a Nantes hotel bedroom with another young man. 'I'll die when I want to,' he had told a chum, 'but I'll die with someone else. To die alone is boring.'

Despite the Surrealists' reputation for erotic outrage (three in a bed was never a crowd), Breton was a prim public homophobe. If Vaché was the love of his life, he never spoke its name. He winced with disgust when taken on a fact-finding mission to a brothel. Despite his friends' ideologically licensed debauches (Paul Eluard and Francis Picabia were the Surrealists' most promiscuous goal-scorers), Breton always retained a romantic attitude to hetero-sex.

He was, however, hostile to reproduction. He proposed to imitate Rousseau and give away any children he was 'sloppy' enough to father. When he did have a daughter in middle age, we are not told what became of her. He soon divorced the mother. Women were supportable as acolytes to the group, but not as leading lights, even though a female invented perhaps its most famous artefact, the fur teacup and saucer.

The great problem is how to reconcile the centrality of Breton in the Surrealists' world with the fact that he seems to have been humourless, domineering and without convincing talent. 'Possibly the best poem he ever wrote' is said to be:

My wife whose buttocks are sandstone and asbestos
Whose buttocks are the back of a swan and the spring
      My wife with the sex of an iris
      A mine and a platypus
With the sex of an alga and old-fashioned candies
      My wife with the sex of a mirror
      My wife with eyes full of tears...

We have to believe that much has been lost in the translation, and that there was much to lose. Breton was so embarrassed by his lines that he published them anonymously. Louis Aragon saw through the anonymity at once. When challenged, Breton said, 'You recognised me?' Aragon replied, 'No, but I recognised the woman.'

Ms Brandon does not mention the echoes of Breton to be found in Edith Sitwell (and in George Seferis) nor does she mention that *Façade*, the stage show which made (and marred) the Sitwells' group identity was clearly a belated tribute to what had already been done by Apollinaire.

Louis Aragon is said, by Julia Kristeva (one of today's Parisian cultural commissars), to have written 'one of the great masterpieces' of the French language in a section of one of his novels entitled *Le Con d'Irène* which supposedly contains the following 'close-up description of Irène's orgasm [*sic*]':

So tiny and so large! Here you are at home, man finally worthy of that name... This is the place, bring your face close, already your gossiping tongue is loosened, this is the place of shadowy delights, this ardent patio... O crack, sweet humid crack, dear vertiginous abyss...

It sounds like the close-up more of an organ than of an orgasm, but who will deny that it is one of the unquestionable glories of French friction?

Aragon and Breton were inseparable until they separated. Then, like so many of the huge cast in the Surrealists' world, they stopped speaking to each other. Together with his forever smiling wife, Elsa, Aragon became a contemptible and long-lived sacred monster of French intellectual life. Born illegitimate and obliged to live with a mother who had to be said to be his sister and a grandmother who had, accordingly, to be devalued to motherhood, he spent his life looking for the stern father he never had. He found him in Breton and then, more lastingly, in the French Communist Party, whose prize literary lackey he became. After years of uxorious bliss, Elsa died, whereupon Aragon confessed that he had always been gay.

For a while, in the late 1920s, he and Breton believed that the Surrealist revolution was reconcilable with Communism. As long as Trotsky was still in power in Russia, this was at least conceivable. However, when Socialist Realism became the dogmatic rule in Stalinist aesthetics, Aragon clenched his fist and turned hard left.

Breton too had joined the Party, but it never joined him. He had to endure solemn interrogation by members of the Central Committee whom he lacked the nerve to deride. In 1934, when Salvador Dali turned out to be – in John Lenin's phrase – a 'Spaniard in the works', Breton himself convoked a Surrealists' court martial to arraign Dali on a charge of glorifying Hitler. Since Dali could claim that he had depicted the Führer as a 'wetnurse with four testicles and four foreskins', he had some grounds for repudiating the charge. He promptly turned the proceedings into brilliant farce:

> Dali makes a spectacular entry, dressed in a huge camel coat. He stumbles along in shoes without laces… His lips grip something that might be a pencil. He takes it out, consults it, replaces it, and explains that it is a thermometer… He will keep [it] under his tongue during the entire meeting, checking his temperature at each stage of the discussion…

It would need the soul of a Jesuitical Robespierre to take such grotesqueries seriously. Breton had one, and the treason trial continued. He was determined to be implacable, even when Dali stripped off the camel coat to reveal a series of sweaters, which he then discarded. Naked to the waist, he went on his knees to assure Breton of his unconditional Surrealism by saying 'if I dream of you tonight, if I dream I'm fucking you in some erotic position, I shan't hesitate to paint the scene tomorrow…'

'I don't advise it, my friend', was all that Breton could find to say.

By the end of the 1930s, Dali had hijacked Surrealism and taken it to New York. He never gave it back. In the 1920s, when he and Luis Buñuel made *Un Chien Andalou,* a preposterously influential avant-garde silent moviette, the two Iberians had already proved that the cinema was an ideal vehicle for the collage of dream-images and illogical logic which Breton had tried to capture in his automatic writing sessions. Buñuel later fell out with Dali (over credit on their anarchic movies) and was denied financial support by Avida Dollars, even though the latter was rolling in it like a pig in the shit which, Dali swore, was his favourite diet.

Perhaps the most memorable, and durable, of the Surrealists was the taciturn Marcel Duchamp, inventor of readymades: he pseudonymously signed the notorious urinal which was his contribution to a New York art show and defied the selection committee to refuse it. He later gave up art for chess. Despite his death, he proved that he could rise again in the form of soon-to-be-Lord Damien Hurst, who was the first to have invented his earlier incarnation's ideas and has been duly saluted by English reputation-makers who lack intellectual affectations, know nothing of France and will never, never, never be slaves of Breton.

Why Write Movies?

Not long ago I was invited to Oxford to give a lecture in a series on aesthetics to a collection of philosophy students. My allotted subject was 'Film, Truth and the Subjective View'. Just the kind of catchy title to have them queuing around the Taylorian Institute. I first cited Jean-Luc Godard's famous remark, that film was 'the truth at twenty-four frames a second'. This, I suggested, was a reliable indication that the cinema was an excellent medium for lying. What French intellectual ever asserts anything to be the case unless it isn't? Would the impudent claim that film directors are *auteurs* ever have been made, if François Truffaut and his editorial friends at *Cahiers du Cinéma* had not known very well that there was rarely any truth in it? Do novelists go around claiming in a challenging voice that they are authors? *Auteur*-theorists make exceptions – directors such as Welles, Chaplin, Buñuel, Antonioni – into evidence for the rule that any petty tyrant can be crowned king of the world and pose as the sole true creator of the twentieth century's typical artform.

Unlike Bach or Proust, films rarely prove durable; let alone a joy forever. Roger Fry, Bloomsbury's foremost critic, once remarked that even the greatest paintings are seldom worth looking at more than three times. Yet who, given easy opportunity, would not go again *and* again to see Goya's black paintings or even to refuel at one of Edward Hopper's gas stations? On the other hand, the films which made the greatest impression in my youth are the ones I now avoid. *Odd Man Out*, *Edouard et Caroline*, *The Scoundrel*, *Open City*, *A Matter of Life and Death*, *Rashomon*: which will not have aged into a mere curiosity? Even *Citizen Kane* no longer pulls me urgently from my book. Sorry, Jedediah.

'If only,' my headmaster once wrote in my report, 'he would criticise himself with half the ruthlessness he applies to the films shown by Film Society...' Good point; fat chance. Printed fiction might have been pronounced dead, I told my Oxonians, but at least it was dead and *kicking*; today's movies astound and excite and amuse, but no one should confound artfulness with art. I preached aesthetic virtue with all the earnestness of duplicity. If I could deter these bright young persons from the debasing temptations of peonage in 'the business', my time would not have been wasted. Questions? The first was from a young philosopher: 'Can you tell me how I can become a screenwriter?'

How did I become one? As a young man, I was all set to be a starving novelist. My ambition was to be the author of the writing on the wall that denounced social injustice, racial prejudice and the public schools, especially Charterhouse. In 1955, however, soon after settling to married life in a Chelsea basement where the sun never shone, I was offered a two-picture deal by the Rank Organisation. Leslie '*Stop the World I Want to Get Off*' Bricusse and I were recruited on the strength of our material for a Cambridge undergraduate show, *Out of the Blue*, which had been the brief talk of London a year earlier.

I knew the cautionary tale of Scott Fitzgerald's (largely deserved) humiliations in Hollywood, but Sylvia and I had to eat while I wrote important novels. With Rank's money we could even drive around in a Ford Anglia. The weeks, and months, went by, and no Rank producer ever called, though my salary was regularly paid while I wrote a novel. It seemed an excellent arrangement.

When the year was up, Leslie and I were immediately recruited by a Rank producer to script *Bachelor of Hearts*, a 'Cambridge comedy' based on *Love's Labours Lost*. When they came to shoot it, I was too busy writing a new novel to go to the set. Had I really wanted to master screenwriting, should I not have jumped at the chance to observe film-making at first hand? I lacked the vocation to go traipsing out to Pinewood and endure hours of tedium while 'barn-doors' were opened and shut, make-up freshened, fuses changed and hammers wielded by fully-paid-up members of the appropriate unions.

What I did study, happily alone, was the layout and form of screenplays. In basic ways, screenwriting is as formal as musical or verse composition. The 'beats', as Stanley Kubrick called them, have to be right. Film must accelerate (not *always* but generally) towards its end. As with a skier in a giant slalom, there has to be a final, if possible thrilling, dash for the line.

Before *Bachelor of Hearts* came out, I was asked to rewrite another Rank movie, entitled *The Big Money*. It was to star Ian Carmichael (who was flush and flash enough to turn up to a conference driving a Ford Consul convertible). Jo Janni was the producer. Years later, after I had written *Darling* for him and John Schlesinger, he asked whether I remembered the first thing I ever said to him when I went to see him about *The Big Money*. 'It wasn't "Good morning, sir", was it?' I said. 'No,' Jo said, 'it was not. What you said was, "What do you want to make this piece of shit for?"'

It remains a tempting, if tactless, question. If there was little else to make in the 1950s, things changed in the 1960s. My late friend David Deutsch commissioned me to write *Nothing But the Best*, which starred Alan Bates and Denholm Elliott. Its success led to the (happily) notorious *Darling*, which affected to denounce the 'cult of the easy lay' and, thanks to Julie Christie's miniskirted seductiveness, did much to encourage it.

In those days, we all thought that film could be a means of social revolution. Nudity was a form of political outspokenness (we said). The bourgeois queued up to be shocked. British films were in demand. Hollywood lost its nerve and came shopping for talent in Europe. We sold it dearly, and readily. In no time, it seemed, I ceased to be a struggling novelist and became an in-demand screenwriter. When I won the Oscar for *Darling*, Jack Lambert, then the literary editor of the *Sunday Times* said to me, 'Well, Freddie, from now on you can cease to expect to have your fiction reviewed on its merits.'

At the time it hardly seemed to matter. When Sylvia and I were flown to New York for the première of *Far From the Madding Crowd*, we were shown into a huge suite at the Plaza. The MGM greeter looked round and suddenly seemed embarrassed. 'Oh, oh, oh, I'm *so* sorry...'

I said, 'That's OK. I understand. This is John Schlesinger's suite and we shouldn't be here.'

'Not at *all*,' he said. 'This is your suite all right. But what happened to the *flowers?*'

Cellophaned bouquets soon arrived, with warm messages of executive welcome. After the movie's première, they took on a funereal significance. Plans for a big opening in California were scrapped. So what? I had had four feature movies made in three years (Stanley Donen's *Two for the Road*, in which Audrey Hepburn was sublime, remains my favourite, though English critics gave it a good biffing). I could always – perhaps *should* always – go away and write books. 'I wish I were in mine island', Byron used to say when the going got rough. A screenwriter too is wise to have a life elsewhere.

By the end of the 1960s, *auteur* cinema had proved a costly indulgence. Hollywood had been suckered; the movies slid towards what seemed an irretrievable slump. I had just written a movie called *Guilt*, which I was slated to direct, with Faye Dunaway. Faye was hot from *Bonnie and Clyde*, the film which more than any other would help

Hollywood recover its nerve. Jo Janni and I were flown to Los Angeles and found 20th Century Fox all but bankrupt. However, they still made a chauffeured limousine available to me twenty-four hours a day. It seemed that the green light was still on.

When I was sent to see the Head of Production at the inactive studio, he asked grimly if I could use thirty Zero fighters in my movie. They were going cheap after the expensive failure of *Tora, Tora, Tora*, a costly re-enactment of Pearl Harbor. As the playwright Phrynichus learnt in ancient Athens, when they fined him for drawing attention to an Athenian humiliation, it is rarely profitable to remind audiences of embarrassing disasters. By the time Jo Janni and I were back in London, *Guilt* had been cancelled. Jo tried by all available means to raise the money. He was sufficiently frustrated in his devious negotiations to say, 'Fred, in the last resort we do it honestly.' In the event, we couldn't even do it that way.

In the 1970s and 1980s, American movies thrived again when Americans, or Arnold Schwarzenegger, resumed blowing away the bad guys, beginning with the ravenous mechanical whale that gave Steven Spielberg the keys of the kingdom over which he now reigns. He and George Lucas and their gang had and have no hangups about art, though they all crave awards. They set out to make hits (and fortunes) and they have been so hugely successful that no one out there ever wants to do anything else. Modest successes are better known as failures.

I have been lucky enough to go on working both sides of the street. Like Tennyson's Sir Galahad, faith unfaithful keeps me falsely true to prose fiction. At the same time, the possibility of doing something 'different' in the movies keeps one ear cocked to the Coast. In spite of the triumph of special effects and neanderthal dialogue, film still sets puzzles of an addictive (and well-paid) kind. Kubrick's secret skill was playing chess; creating a movie is more like problem-solving than it is like painting the Sistine Chapel (even though Pope Julius II was a prototype of the interfering producer). The screenplay may yet turn out to be a form which allows the writer to unroll imaginary movies for his readers without the hassle of raising the budget or luring the stars. In my short novellas *All His Sons* and *Life and Loves*, I use the script form as a literary device, inciting the reader to *perform* as well as to read, to *hear* the dialogue and impersonate the characters. The only genuine *auteur* film is a script which the reader can project in his imagination.

Whether or not film is a high art, it defined and transformed the twentieth century, though not in the (mainly political) ways that anyone intended. No one went from the movies to storm the Winter Palace; as soon as they could, they went from storming the Winter Palace to the movies. Costa-Gavras' *Z* did not overthrow the Greek colonels and Gillo Pontecorvo's *Battle of Algiers* utterly failed to hint that independent Algeria might become a nightmare. Kubrick's *Paths of Glory*, Milestone's *A Walk in the Sun* and Spielberg's *Saving Private Ryan* may warn the audience to keep its head down (and count its lucky stars), but they have done nothing to stop wars. However gory or gruesome, film is not good at pain. It evokes passions and, sometimes, both pity and terror, but rarely *thought*. Film characters may be memorable, but how often are they *deep*?

In his autobiography, Jean-Paul Sartre remarked that his grandfather's character was ruined by the advent of the still camera. The old man became self-conscious in presenting his better profile to the world's eye. He began to pose. The movie camera has had an incomparably more thorough, perhaps even more narcissistic, effect on human behaviour. Who drives home after a thriller without glancing in the mirror for the guys in the grey sedan? Lovers learned to kiss longer, once they saw how the stars did it. Nowadays sex is a spectator sport which – who knows? – may soon have a World Cup. When footballers roll in agony, French commentators call it *cinéma*. Sincerity, honesty, wisdom are what *look* sincere, honest and wise. The Buddha got it right: appearances are reality, at twenty-four frames a second.

Who now reads novels as a guide to life and love? Everyone wants to star in his or her own movie. Who doesn't try to look like Bruce or Brad or Roberto, Gwyneth or Julia or the miraculously unfading Julie? We walk along accompanied by a soundtrack and expecting a zooming close-up. It is more important for politicians to look and sound right (Blair) or wrong (Hague) than to be right or wrong. Presidents and tycoons can be crooks and liars and get away with murder, as long as they are cute enough. Historical truth has been replaced by tell-them-anything fantasy: in James Cameron's *Titanic*, the rich are all selfish cowards even though dull old documentation shows that the crew was often more cowardly than those in first class (where Cameron and his stars always travel).

The audience and the electorate have merged into a mass of whom tycoons and politicians alike are deferentially contemptuous. In 1984, Orwell foresaw a society narcotised by eroticism and supine under printed pap. The public is now only a massive audience. The lucky end of the global village, where we live, is a theme park in which people imagine that they are really living but in which we are fed, amused and taxed by a whole new race of Our Betters: the manipulative producers of entertainment and news. They all speak of the 'quality of life' but they care only for the quantity of punters or voters. By 2084, the individual artist may well be furtively scratching his own unsponsored work in obscure caves or cellars into which Arts Council inspectors and 'simplicity police' (Disney actually employs them) disdain to follow them and improve their work by making it worse.

Judge Not?

In a 1999 interview in *Poetry Nation Review*, Philip Hobsbaum said that
the greatest man he ever met was Frank Leavis. There was something
so sweetly anachronistic about this assertion that I was reminded of
the lost decades in which one might have had a hat to take off to it.
Today, no pundit seems more terminally dated than Dr Leavis. Who
shares his notion of the 'common pursuit' of valid judgements in literature and, by extension, in life? We are all swing-wing pluralists now,
aren't we? We wallow in a publicity-led media-world in which the
notion of one book, or work of art, being better than another is either
naïve or élitist, unless it means that it sells more widely or at a higher
price. Our *fin de siècle* is a hierarchy of preferences, not of values.
Punctuation and grammar are dusty relics and nothing that anyone
writes is wrong, only different (which is better, as long as you don't
mean *morally* better).

Yeah, yeah, so? Curiously enough, the paladins of The Culture (a
conveniently vapid expression, implying distinction but void of
judgement) cannot quite abandon the notion of ranking, any more
than the government can quite give up lordliness, even if it wants to
'modernise' the Upper House by substituting placemen for those
dignified by the accident of birth. Perhaps the top prize in the lottery
will soon include a dukedom. Why not? In the literary world, we have
a surfeit of awards which seem to certify the winners who then, very
often, become the judges who beckon others to their rank and dignity.
The self-promoting are themselves promoters, pursuing domination
over artists where they cannot pretend to art. Bill Buford was the first
postmodern opportunist in this style: by acquiring *Granta* and setting
himself up as the selector of The Best of British, he turned writing
into a sport where he was the manager who said, or did not say, 'The
lad done well', which clearly entailed adopting a style of play
subservient to the gaffer's requirements.

Making lists – a habit first practised by Hellenistic Alexandrians –
remains a fast-track route by which the ambitious can establish themselves not only as arbiters of elegance, but also as the commissioning

editors to whom to look for advancement. What is advanced is less often the cause of art than the fame of the selectors. The latest artful instance of self-importance is the list of 'seminal artistic works of the twentieth century', drawn up by the usual judges who can afford the time and crave the bench.

The wetness of the qualifying adjective, 'seminal', is nicely suited to the times. It avoids the question of worth in favour of progenitive *puissance* and renders the judges more or less immune to judgement. Less, in my opinion; since even eclecticism can involve stupid or ignorant choices. As a leading instance of parochial triviality and social climbing of the most recent jury of pundits, they chose Harold Pinter's *The Caretaker* but neglected Ionesco, whose Theatre of the Absurd supplied the semen which fertilised Harold's and many other egg-heads. They put Ezra Pound's sprawling *Cantos* (awful warnings against poetic elephantiasis) in the same category as Cavafy's single poem, *Waiting for The Barbarians*, when the whole of Cavafy's *oeuvre* merits inclusion. Lorca's *The Poet in New York* is a piece of cosmopolitan ostentation by comparison with the same writer's *Blood Wedding*. Toadying to the feminists, they choose Sylvia Plath's *Ariel* (who cares to remember much about it except that she hated daddy whom she called a Nazi because he died on her?) and ignore Ginsberg, Berryman, Bob Dylan and Gerard Manley Hopkins. They include Updike's post-Euphuistic *Couples* and omit Arthur Koestler's *Darkness At Noon*; they give two-thumbs-up to Ingmar Bergman's *The Seventh Seal*, as if it were either good or influential. *On The Town*, for casual example, was far more important to the history of the cinema (as was *On The Waterfront* or *Odd Man Out* or Cocteau's *Orphée*, whose semen probably helped to generate *The Seventh Seal*). The presence of *A bout de souffle* and the omission of *L'Avventura*, the key 'art' film of our time, show how little the panel knew about anything except what was expected of it: obvious surprises. *Rear Window* was a dud Hitchcock; a better choice, if Hitch really had to be included, would be *Strangers on a Train*. *For Whom The Bell Tolls* was a great *title*, but *A Farewell To Arms* was Hemingway's best novel, even if *In Our Time* was his most influential work.

Is it not odd that, in an exercise prompted by the BBC, not a single television or radio programme makes the list? *Cathie Come Home* was surely as influential (and as good?) as *Snow White*. *The Goon Show* spawned a whole shoal of comic inventions, while Orson Welles' radio version of *The War of the Worlds* was crucial to the development of radio drama *and*, one might say, 'factual' news programmes. And since when did Stanislavsky become the author of *A Month in the Country*? Here is a prime instance of the now pandemic disease/crime of directors supplanting the author. How nice that it is Turgenev who gets bumped off the credits for his own play! Ivan always was a softy, and notoriously slow in the seminal department.

Am I taking a parlour game too seriously? After all, Antonia Byatt and co. knew that they were being naughty and, pluckily at their age, provocative. However, what matters about the rented bigwigs' larky choices is the contempt they display for their audience. They are dons who have turned their backs on education and who no longer dare to be intelligent or accurate or – *absit omen* – highbrow in patronising the public.

In the literary world, the most obvious and regular opportunity for self-importance is the choice of Books of the Year. Since I have long contributed, briefly, to such listings, I shall not pretend that it is easy (or even necessary) to avoid favouring one's friends or choosing the last recent book which one found tolerable. Such lists are recommendations, not final judgements on the basis of all the annual evidence.

Nevertheless, there is a temptation to take certain critics' choices seriously, especially when they are backed by strenuous sententiousness. How can one not feel intellectually dowdy at not yet having read a novel recommended by Lady Antonia Fraser *and* George Steiner *and* Neal Ascherson? It was in a spirit of humility that I ordered a copy of Bernhard Schlink's *The Reader*, as translated by Carol Brown Janeway (perfectly competently, or at least grammatically). It was also saluted by Jorge Semprun (whose experience of the savage politics of the century gives his endorsement a certain gravity) and deemed 'superb', by *Le Monde*. Ruth Rendell – an authority not to be cast aside lightly – promises 'a very fine novel, as far above a holocaust genre' (excuse me?) 'as *Crime and Punishment* is above the average thriller' (she ought to know) 'a sensitive, daring, deeply moving' (ah, that touch of adjectival originality!) 'book about the tragic results of fear and the redemptive power of understanding'. Stamp that order RUSH.

The Reader turns out to be a short novel; brevity usually commends itself to those in a hurry to endorse new work. Its *donnée*, like its style, is very simple. A *Bildungsroman* of stunted growth, its first-person narrator is the son of a lawyer (its author *is* a lawyer) who grows up in post-war Germany. When he is fifteen (always a dangerously sensitive age for Thomas Mann's countrymen), he is taken ill on the way to school outside some low-price housing. His vomit is sluiced away by a woman called Hanna who calls him 'Kid' and, when she sees him crying, takes him in her arms.

> I could feel her breasts against my chest. I smelled the sourness of my own breath and felt a sudden sweat as she held me, and didn't know where to look. I stopped crying.

You can pretty well guess what's coming; and it comes. When young Michael recovers from his hepatitis, he goes to the building on Bahnhofstrasse to thank the breasty woman with flowers. When she offers to walk him home, she has to change her clothes, and guess what. Here's what:

> I waited in the hall while she changed her clothes in the kitchen. The door was open a crack. She took off the smock and stood there in a bright green petticoat. Two stockings were hanging over the back of the chair. Picking one up, she gathered it into a roll using one hand, then the other, then balanced on one leg as she rested the heel of her other foot against her knee, leaned forward, slipped the rolled-up stocking over her toes, put her foot on the chair as she smoothed the stocking up over her calf, knee, and thigh, then bent to one side as she fastened the stocking to the garter belt...
>
> As she was reaching for the other stocking, she paused, turned towards the door and looked straight at me. I can't describe what kind of look it was – surprised, sceptical, knowing, reproachful. I turned red. For a fraction of a second I stood there, my face burning. Then I couldn't take it any more. I fled out of the flat, down the stairs, and into the street.

This is a passage from a novel of just over 200 short pages and what does it tell us? In one trite image after another, we are invited to share an adolescent's first vision of a woman putting on her stockings. The description is entirely banal, and so is his response. The scene is trite, but promising: what it promises is further slo-mo accounts of Hanna's anatomy and, we need not doubt for a second, young Michael's initiation into it. And that is exactly what we get.

On his next visit, he has some comic difficulties with the coal scuttle, while replenishing Hanna's home fire, and gets so dirty that guess what. You're brilliant: he has to have a bath in her proletarian tub. After which, what? How can you *possibly* guess? But you are right again: Hanna comes with a towel and says 'Come' as she wraps him in it, 'from head to foot' (ah sweet details!), and rubs him dry. Then... Are you ready for this?

she let the towel fall to the floor. I didn't dare move. She came so close to me that I could feel her breasts against my back and her stomach against my behind. She was naked too. She put her arms around me, one hand on my chest and the other on my erection. 'That's why you're here!'

Can you fill in the next few paragraphs without going wrong? Believe me, you can: nothing happens that you would not expect to have happen and – surprise! – Michael now finds himself in love with Hanna, who is considerably older than he, but not *old*.

I feel no great outrage when I read or see pornography and I was not scandalised by the adolescent activities of young Michael: better to go into Hanna than into the Hitler Youth, as his father might have said (but didn't, it seems, since he turns out to be a solemnly moral old stick). What is shocking in *The Reader* is the almost comic absence of any *specific* or alert detail; there is not one description, whether of events or feelings, which is not platitudinous.

Who can be sure that Herr Schlinck did not experience every single thing which is depicted in *The Reader*? The whole story may be completely true; it is still false, *as fiction*. As a work of the literary imagination – in terms of vocabulary, character, tone, narrative – it is trite, catchpenny, trivial and witless. Its source may be 'genuine', but its models are German sex films and those countless stories of The Young Man and the Older Woman (ah *Chéri*!) with which continental fiction is crammed. At best, there is a whiff of Alberto Moravia, but none of his humour, none of that sense of inhabited place and lived time (and political decadence) which render the prostitute in *La Romana* so memorable and which make *Gli Indifferenti* as seminal a novel as any parochial panel might ignore in favour of *The Waves*, whose showy surf I cannot prefer to, say, Svevo's *Memoirs of Zeno* or even to Maugham's *Of Human Bondage*.

How come Schlink's novel is called *The Reader*? There was a neat film with the divine Miou-Miou called *La Lectrice*, but Michael's readings are given to only one audience: Hanna. She likes his voice; she envies his education; he gets in the habit of satisfying her first physically and then with *Emilia Galotti* and stuff in that classy range (some curriculum these German schools have!). This simple lady, who works as a tram conductor, also asks to hear the *Odyssey* and 'the speeches against Cataline [*sic*]' in the original languages. Does she want to better herself or *what*? She gives Michael a sexual education and, after tutorials, he comes back with Hemingway and Homer.

Hanna soon becomes a critic and calls out 'Unbelievable', quite as if she were reading *The Reader*.

Why does Hanna so much like having Michael read to her? Yes, you *can* guess: despite the enviable scholastic system which turned out Heidegger (*vot* a reader *he* was!) and Himmler, she *never learnt to read*. Imagine! Born 1922, she is a simple working-class girl who never enjoyed the full benefits of the Third Reich. Hanna is someone you have to feel for.

The first part of Michael's story ends when Hanna abruptly resigns from being a tram conductor (after being offered promotion) and disappears. The next Michael hears of her, his innocent, generous mistress has been arraigned *as a war criminal*. Unlucky! Some insistent victims, who 'by rights' (the narrator's *ipsissima verba*) ought to be dead, have filed suits against her and other SS ladies who were guards at Auschwitz and on the death marches which followed the Russian advance toward the camps.

At the outbreak of the war, it seems, Hanna was so badly needed for factory work that no one ever noticed that she was illiterate. At Siemens (a magisterial novelistic touch that, to specify employers who actually *exist*), she was so industrious that she was offered promotion to foreman. It was at that point, in the autumn of 1943, that she dumped electrical assembly and... joined the SS, with the 'tragic' result that she selected female victims for the gas chambers, but only – it turns out – after doing what she could to keep them in her personal custody for as long as possible, during which time she fed and, it seems, had sex with them, so that they could have something nice to remember while they choked to death. The girl is some kind of a *saint* right? (Lord Longford would have been in there for her like *that*!) And now the bastards are putting her on trial because she helped to murder people. Is this justice, *mein dammen und herren*?

Michael, whose marriage has foundered as a result of his surreptitious memories of and longing for his initiatrix, attends the court as an acute and legally informed observer. Hanna proves incapable of cunning, or prudence (she talks back to the judge in a what-would-you-do-chummy way). The gallantly uncomplaining scapegoat of the other women in the dock, she soon confesses to being the author of a 'report' which admits that a number of death marchers were locked into a church when allied bombers came over. The church burned and the guards did not unlock the doors to let the prisoners out (the two surviving witnesses, who 'by rights' should have died, got lucky in the organ loft).

When Hanna is convicted and sentenced to life imprisonment, Michael feels (and wants us to feel) that she has been victimised. Over the years, he sends her tapes of his readings, though he cannot summon up the humanity, or the love or lust, actually to visit her. On the eve of her parole, Hanna hangs herself, leaving Michael with feelings of inadequacy and an opportunity for moral musings about the fugitive nature of history and our inability to judge others and ballocks of that familiar kind.

By the same token, readers of *The Reader* are supposed, by Rendell and other experts in blood sports, to have gained important insight into love, horror, mercy (Neal Ascherson's noun, which describes nothing that I read about), ambivalence, contempt, and understanding.

Who would still dare to insist that the novel is confected junk from beginning to end? OK, I would. Even if every incident described is part of the author's autobiographical stockpot, this is neither a true book nor a work of art. Fiction is not a form of heightened transcript; novels cannot be validated by *sincerity* (not that I am imputing anything so jejune to this book).

Schlink's whole sly performance reeks of contrivance, special pleading, Germanic self-pity and – as Larry Durrell's Scobie would say – 'la grande bogue'. Consider one simple, crucial element in the story, the idea that Hanna 'joined the SS' to conceal her illiteracy. That organisation – which is made to sound like an undemanding alternative source of employment – may have been short of men, as it was of humanity, but are we seriously to believe that Hanna could have been recruited (it did, after all, pass itself off as an *élite* formation) without having to so much as fill in an entry form, if only to validate her Aryan lineage? Did she have no apprentice period of written work – an essaylet on consciencelessness perhaps – before going to whip up the inmates at Auschwitz?

The premiss of the entire book – the *innocence* of Nazism's rank and file (pitilessly hounded by post-war trials whose hedonistic judges, according to Schlink, turned fact-finding missions to Israel into junkets) – is an insolent imposture. Note the clumsy subtlety which turns the women for whose deaths Hanna is tried into victims of an *allied* air raid: the RAF couldn't hit the camps, or the railway lines which served them, but they managed to destroy *churches*. You can hear the slop of the same old whitewash, accompanied by a chorus of 'We are all guilty.' It needs no Orwellian wit to respond 'And some of you are a lot guiltier than we are.'

If space allowed, I could discourse in detail on the manipulative falseness of a novel without novelty, honour or invention. *The Reader* lacks even the solemn phoneyness of the moral debate in *Sophie's Choice* or the candid calculation of Spielberg's *Schindler's List.* It confuses writing fiction with telling lies and selling fakes. The come-buy-me froth of sexuality (straight and lesbian) covers a confection whose 'seriousness' is of a piece with that of Nazi apologists and historical revisionists. Schlink *pretends* to be a novelist just as his voyeurism *pretends* to be an unblinking look at moral issues.

As for those who recommended *The Reader,* they can always claim that they are entitled to their opinions. So they are, so they are. But if they have the right to enthuse, others have the duty to denounce their want of literary taste and moral honesty. It is for this reason that Hobsbaum's nostalgia for Frank Leavis seemed so pertinent. Perhaps, after all, it *does* make sense to maintain that there can, and should, be standards in literature and that it is possible, and urgent, not to defer to reckless relativists and byline hogs. No one could recommend *The Reader* without having a tin ear for fiction and a blind eye for evil. Such are today's guiding lights. Shame on them.

*

In reply to a friendly personal letter from Cynthia Ozick.

14 June 1999

Dear Cynthia,

Since even hostile movie executives whom one has never met now make bold with what used to be called Christian names, will you forgive me if I use your first name?

Since we are in large agreement, we may bask in mutual recognition of our just view of *The Reader.* Enough said by you and me on the subject of its many delinquencies. I wasn't *all that* displeased by Styron's work, though I suspect that his depression (which is, of course, not his 'fault') may have had something to do with the steadiness of his impersonation of a *serious* writer, grappling with *Issues.* He has no vernacular register at all, in any of his work; melodrama is, I suspect, the addictive form of writers who have to gee themselves up with what the French call, in erotic circumstances, *sensations fortes* (up close and fucking). The best Styron, I think, was *The Long March,* which made its bloody imprint on the imagination because it was so understated. Somehow he could not stay with the pained liberal, *heautotimoroumenos*, and moved on to the Big Book. Bellow, though none may say so, made the same, I believe, wrong, premeditated move when he did *Augie March/Henderson/ Humboldt's Gift* (which I did not enjoy unwrapping). Immodesty of scale is essential to fame and fortune in the US and *un peu partout*, no doubt. Schlink's cleverness lay in playing the opposite trick, which is to write briefly on a grand theme, thus enabling busy persons to enthuse without delay.

How do we explain Steiner, Fraser and Ascherson? The hard truth – not easy to establish without specific attention to cases – may be that they are instances of people corrupted by vanity, the adulatory solicitations of publishers and friends. I do not think that true artists should have friends, in the *professional* sense, but perhaps that is a romantic and/or self-serving view, since we live in isolation and my award-free life is evidence of a want of sponsors/*clientela*. Steiner is, in my personal acquaintance, a man who is torn between the desire to make brave and exceptional stands and the wish to associate with success and fame. I should confess, if confession it is, that I was once in regular correspondence with George and often visited him in Cambridge before he did something unforgivable (depend upon it, it did not involve the seduction of my wife, who never liked him *one bit*). George is obsessed with status and with demonstrations of cosmopolitan range: he advertises all his languages, quite as if the merest Alexandrian functionary was not once at home in Greek, French, English, Arabic and still took home only a tram-conductor's stipend. I think poor George is motivated by the wish both to startle and to please; he has many attitudes but no genuineness. He thinks he can write fiction, and often told me so; he actually got an *award* (wow!) for some portentous 'fables' which he called short stories: the sort of stuff André Gide confected when he had been bitten by the Classics. You've guessed: I do not love George Steiner, though (because?) I once pretended to.

Antonia Fraser is not someone I know except *very* slightly and by reputation. I do not doubt that she is a woman who knows her way around, up and down also. She is not a bad writer, but she is not a *writer*. She has decided to find fame through writing (mostly histor-ical biography in the Philip Guedalla tradition, but also girly-thrillers about a sleuth called Jemima, I believe) as well as through the diligent cultivation of the social main chance. Why not? Whether this has been accompanied by literary taste, I am not so sure.

Neal Ascherson I do not know at all, although I believe that we were contemporaries at Cambridge. He is a grand journalist of long date and, perhaps more pertinently, a historian of Poland. He prides himself on understanding the middle European mind/ soul/whatever. Since *The Reader* is a sort of opportunist journalism, affecting to be a work of the imagination, it may seem to be the kind of novel he might write (oh those 'ideas!' with which the ungifted for fiction spruce their narratives) if he had, as they always say, time. You can add (Dame) Antonia Byatt to your list of admirers of Schlink; she has such a grand idea of herself that she affected, in public, not to have read my article to which her own was published, subsequently, as a 'rebuttal'. She later confessed to me personally that she *had* read it but did not like public controversy. Apparently, she prefers humbug. Her prose has very thick ankles, which perhaps disposes her to admire a dainty dancer on thin ice such as Herr S.

Of course, *de gustibus* etc., but as Nietzsche said, 'You say there can be no argument about matters of taste? All life is an argument about matters of taste.' Good one, Friedrich. Our common literary agent, David Miller, *did* at first say that he liked the book, but – as a good Cambridge man – he allowed reason to influence first impressions and, without twisted ligaments, came to see that I had a point or two. It is counter-cultural with a vengeance to suppose that it is weakness later to be led to perceive that a work one admired is flawed, false or futile. I rather liked *The White Hotel*, but it went grey on me (without pressure). I am sure that much too much time is spent teaching criticism, but that is all the more reason to practise it as a form of civility, not a form of correctness. Without the possibility that you understand a book better than I (or worse), what sense is there in reading? I am more admiring of David Miller for seeing where I/we happen to be right than I am of the lettered intransigence of Steiner and *la* Byatt.

A Propos Arthur Koestler

In the thoroughness of its research, David Cesarani's biography of Koestler has much in common with the same author's *Justice Delayed*, an accusingly accurate account of the sainted Attlee government's recruitment (and concealment) of part of an SS division, mostly Balts, in order to work in English mines immediately after the war. *Justice Delayed* was both brave and – if what is overdue can be – timely. *Arthur Koestler* is a no less accusing analysis of a key witness of our time, but it has a somewhat different thrust.

Koestler was a hallowed figure in my young literary pantheon, not only for *Darkness at Noon* but also for *Thieves in the Night* and, in particular, *Scum of the Earth* and *Dialogue with Death*. How lucky to have had such frightfully memorable experiences and how adult both to have been in the Party and to have seen through it, all before he was thirty-five!

My only personal contact with Koestler was when I edited *Bookmarks*, a volume of essays compiled to raise funds to campaign for Public Lending Right. Already shaken by Parkinson's disease, he contributed punctually, although he had warned that writing in English was still a labour. This unsexual act of altruistic solidarity was, of course, too trivial to warrant mention by his biographer.

Cesarani's important and, I fear, definitive study has been copiously, if not always adequately, reviewed. The central issue has often been missed, or ducked. Michael Shelden, for instance, contrived to avoid using the embarrassing word 'Jew' in his lengthy *TLS* piece (unless he was being *clever*, like Georges Perec when he avoided employing the vowel 'e' in a whole novel). Yet Cesarani tells us specifically that *The Homeless Mind*, as he subtitles his work, began as a study of 'a Jew who exemplified the Jewish experience in Europe during the twentieth century'.

Shelden's reticence suggests either that the author failed to deliver on his initial scheme (he did not) or that insistence on Koestler's Jewishness struck his critic as beside the point, which surely merited remark. The mordant biographer of Graham Greene also neglected

Review of David Cesarani, *Arthur Koestler*, in *Prospect*, 1999.

to observe the manifest affinity between Koestler's depiction of the brutally sympathetic interrogation of Rubashov, in *Darkness at Noon* – note the anglophile homage to Milton in the title – and the quizzing of Greene's whisky priest by the idealistic atheist lieutenant, in *The Power and the Glory*, which was published almost simultaneously, in 1940.

Perhaps it has been felt that Koestler was *such* a rampant Jew that it would be disobliging to mention what were so obviously typical characteristics. The curiosity of Jewishness lies precisely in the imprecision of what defines it. Yet there remains the conviction – shared by Jews and their enemies – that *something* must. Does this oddly ineradicable identity derive from racial, religious or social staining? Or is Jewishness inescapable, if it is, in Some Other Way? Jean-Paul Sartre, who believed that every man should define his own essence if he is not to be a *salaud*, made an exception only for Jews: they were advised to 'assume' the identity they were accused of possessing and to carry their shame proudly. Does that take care of the problem? Or was calling it a problem the problem?

Before the foundation of the State of Israel, it was rarely for complimentary reasons that men were called Jews. At English public schools 'jewing' was (is?) slang for swindling. Orwell was amazed when an Indian volunteered that he was a Jew. 'Est-il – pardon! – juif?' they used to ask in Eastern Europe, as if apologising for an obscene suggestion. Assimilation was the frequent hope of those impatient with antique rituals and narrow communities. Success in the big world required matching Gentiles for wit, energy and inventiveness. If the Jew could expect no easy welcome – he had, as they used to say, to do twice as much to get half as far – high ambition was the fuel of the smart *arriviste*. Disraeli set the encouraging mark in England; in France, the fate of Dreyfus prompted Theodor Herzl to Zionism. Assimilation or exit were the choices which confronted Koestler all his life.

In pre-war continental Europe, there were two main avenues to fame and fortune: the arts (if we include journalism and politics) and science (including medicine, mathematics and philosophy). The first category required individual brilliance; the second did too, but it also entailed collegiality. A man might be accused, in Nazi rhetoric, of doing 'Jewish science', which meant something bogus or alchemical, but those in their right mind knew very well that people may race to solve equations, but equations do not have a race. If Einstein had not discovered relativity, a Gentile might well have done so. By recruiting the Gentile Jung as co-adjutor, Freud sought to have psychoanalysis recognised as a science, rather than as a cabal headed by a Jewish 'witch-doctor', as the pro-Semitic Vladimir Nabokov once labelled Freud. If the latter never quite procured scientific respectability, it was less on account of prejudice than because of doubts whether his 'science' is indeed scientific. Jung celebrated his emancipation from Freud's polluting aegis by hailing the Nazis as mythical messengers.

It could be argued that exclusion has inspired Jews in particular to what D.H. Lawrence called 'disinterested speculation'. They have stood outside local logics, surveying the world from an Archimedean platform which allowed them to put a lever to it. This has resulted in general theories of varying merit and use: Marxism and psycho-analysis are modern(ish) examples, but Spinozan philosophy is another, Christianity another (Paul was a proto-diasporite). We need not, *a priori*, repudiate Cesarani's claim that Koestler's ideas and obsessions were largely the consequence of Jewishness. But the strands of his competence, as of his ambition, need to be distinguished.

There were at least two Koestlers. One wrote self-effacing (if never modest) work like *The Sleepwalkers*, a study of scientific genius which emphasised its illogicality and haphazardness; another wrote *Thieves in the Night* and *Darkness at Noon*. Koestler the journalist, the fact-finder, the inquirer and inquisitor, was the servant of both talents. Arthur I, the scientific journalist, although sometimes extravagant in his claims and hypotheses (as scientists, no less than Jews, can be), had a Gentile agenda and style: in a blind tasting, it would be weird to declare that *The Case of the Midwife Toad*, say, had a Jewish bouquet. I labour this point because Cesarani more or less ignores it. Convinced that 'Jewishness' explains Koestler in pretty well every regard, he makes small distinction between Arthur I, who seeks acceptance, if not quite anonymity, in the scientific and academic community and Arthur II, the 'unapologetic Jew', who wants to be the king of the world (and have the run of its harem). *Janus – a Summing Up* acknowledged Koestler's – and human – duplicity, to which he offered a dolefully deterministic explanation, based on cerebral anatomy.

In distinguishing between science (impersonal) and art (personal), we need not concede – still less insist – that art created by Jews always, and of necessity, has a distinct flavour. Does Camille Pissarro paint more Jewishly than Sisley or Renoir? The question of *motivation* is altogether different: *why* a person paints is one thing, *what* is painted has to be another. Otherwise artists would be as good, or as bad, as their motives, which – alas for the well-intentioned! – is absurd. Hot for hidden explanations, Cesarani probes the sub-text and springs locked closets. He seeks scandalous skeletons in the many cupboards of the perigrinatory Koestler's many homes. A.K.'s sexual habits and (often) appalling behaviour towards women begin to obsess the author; finally they become his overwhelming topic.

This whole scheme relies on passing off as discovery what is wished for *a priori*. Cesarani declares Koestler's fundamental Jewishness and then reads the evidence in such a way as to prove his case. He regards sexual intemperance as repugnant and is duly shocked by what he hears. The shadow of the portraitist falls darkly into frame; and, in my view, the shadow of the shadow of Stalin falls on Cesarani. This interesting and impressive biography is also something of a show trial.

Cesarani trails what is coming in his preface. The first thing he tells us is that *Darkness at Noon* was chosen by a 'distinguished panel of writers and intellectuals, including Maya Angelou, A.S. Byatt, Arthur Schlesinger Jr, William Styron and Gore Vidal... as the eighth best novel of the century.' If there were even a tincture of irony in his proclamation of this estimate, it might excite hopes of refreshing scorn for the ordinal fetish of neo-bourgeois society. Or, if he showed any awareness of the comedy of modern celebrity, which makes Arthur Schlesinger Jr – the house toady of the Kennedys – into a Lord Justice of Fiction and which promotes the author of *Sophie's Choice* (once described as what 'happens when *Playboy* magazine meets Auschwitz') to the bench beside him, there might be some prospect of hilarity at the conceit of minnows affecting to rank as sharks. Instead, Cesarani relies on his posh sources to certify literary qualities to which he himself is tone-deaf (notice 'vice-like grip' on his opening page). It was surely convenient for him to regard Koestler as a rootless 'journalist'.

Cesarani's consciousness is shaped by academic procedures and prudential deference: his preface is a red carpet unrolling before a train of notable helpers. This parade of kind chums is a standard warning to critics that the author is *not alone*. Even novelists, such as Martin Amis, in *Time's Arrow*, and Ian McEwan, in *Enduring Love*, use forewords and postfaces in order to remind the reader of their sponsored eminence. We Are Many, and Famous, they tell us; awards and rewards are my friends' to bestow. Applaud or die.

If *Darkness at Noon* is indeed a masterpiece and a supreme anatomy of Leninist–Stalinist procedures, Victor Serge's *The Case of Comrade Tulayev* may well be its equal, despite our not knowing what seeding Angelou, Byatt and company were gracious enough to accord it (or, offhand, whether Serge was a Jew). Since *The Case of Comrade Tulayev* can stand on its own as a dramatisation of Soviet institutional mania after the murder of Kirov, might it not be argued that the illuminating brilliance of *Darkness at Noon* should excuse its author from the invasive intuitions of what Henry James called 'publishing scoundrels'? Why is it not enough to earn abiding respect by having written a *roman à thèse* with a durability that transcends journalism and which, more than any text before *One Day in the Life of Ivan Denisovitch*, blew the whistle on Communist Russia with devastating audibility, even if there were those who refused to hear it?

Oh, oh, oh! Am I claiming that, if their books are good enough, authors' private lives should be closed to the curious? No. But to relish and retail the shortcomings of the famous (who seldom lack them) differs categorically from accurate appreciation of their work, and hence of what makes them interesting. After the revelations about Wittgenstein's alleged appetite for rough trade, a man once wrote to me from Newcastle volunteering information about the public lavatories Wittgenstein attended, after work as a hospital porter during the war, and what happened in them. So much for the author of *Philosophical Investigations*. The price of marketable secrets has made eager rag-and-bone men (and women, and women) of those who clamber onto every pedestal in the hope of finding clay feet, and other parts.

Even without malign intentions, the consequence of the biographical itch is to have us read all art in the light of the human-all-too-human failings of its creators. 'Celia – Celia – Celia *shits*!' said Swift, and could not love her for it. Dishing the dirt is lots of fun, but it is also ruinous fun, leading finally to the tabloid 'culture' in which the cult of celebrity is the only art and denunciation is the reward of achievement. Kirov would not be assassinated today; he would have an assiduous researcher assigned to his biography. Even the BBC is now known to incite those who make programmes to dig out sexual dirt if they hope to have them aired. This will be denied; it is true.

Cesarani harps on Koestler's personal vanities and faults, especially his – as George Mikes called it – Hungarian conduct towards women. He accuses him of at least one serious crime. When Koestler sets out to denounce Communism, at the height of the cold war, more attention is paid by his biographer to how pissed he was before the event, or how boorishly he behaved to hangers-on afterwards, than to the substance of his address. The content of his work is scamped or patronised. For instance, much play is made of the pretentious claim (not *printed* in Koestler's main texts) that his scientific theories, or theories about science, might render him 'a second Darwin'. What writers do not have ridiculous dreams of eminence? Nabokov made solemn fun of his own conviction that he would be *aere perennius*, which was wise of him, but did not mark a want of vanity. The treatment of Koestler's final obsession with the paranormal implies that he was both ga-ga and megalomaniac in imagining that there was some 'invisible writing' for which he alone had eyes. Well, Newton wasted a lot of time on alchemy, and so what?

Cesarani's censoriousness is validated, I suspect, by that accusing cousinship, typical of some Jews, which mixes a certain pride in 'our' exceptional achievements with a reminding wag of the finger that indicates, 'Don't think I don't know what you *really* are!' It is said that when the young Freud was practising medicine, he was called to a certain Countess, of Jewish origin, who was about to give birth, 'any minute'. Freud said, 'How do you know that?' The servant said, 'The countess is crying out, "Oh, Oh, Oh!"' Freud said, 'Let me know when she starts saying "Oy, oy, oy!" and I'll be there right away.' Jews hate the one who think he's got away, so they claim that none can (*whether* they can, or should, is another issue): some Jews vie with some homosexuals when it comes to the outing itch. Shall we ask, *should* we investigate what makes Cesarani so eager, or simply so disposed, to heap odium on his subject? Can biographers not have motives, and secrets? Cannot they too be deconstructed?

Cesarani is regularly (if sometimes anachronistically) shocked by Koestler's sexual conduct. I am not referring only to the putative rape of Jill Craigie (Mrs Michael Foot), which so scandalised (some of) the female students of Edinburgh University that the author's statue has been banished from their sight, on the grounds, apparently, that it eyed them in a brazen way and deserved defenestration. The chaste Cesarani winces for us at Koestler's recourse to prostitutes, which was quite usual in waltzing Vienna (who was shocked by Schnitzler's *Blue Room* recently, if it was Schnitzler's?). Cesarani is particularly put off by Koestler's penchant for treble acts. Such squeamishness may establish a man's suitability for a mortgage with Scottish Widows, but how helpful is it when seeking to empathise with a lifelong *dragueur*? Cesarani deplores his subject's phallocratic behaviour towards women, just as we might the acquiescence of the noblest Romans and

Athenians in slavery. Do we not therefore admire the Parthenon or read Catullus? The abuse of women *was* (if it is not still) a certificate of virility in many great men, of whom Bertrand Russell is, in many respects, a more lurid and despicable instance. If we are to dispraise famous men, who is to be spared?

As for the rape of Jill Craigie, which made all the headlines, we need not doubt that force was used or that understandable shame explains why the facts took so long to come out. I daresay that fear and embarrassment and even a sort of generosity led Jill Craigie to file no loud immediate complaint. But the limitations of biography are obvious here. Perhaps only a novelist (or the director of *Rashomon*) could bring the right kind of imagination to bear on such a case. We may have the facts; we do not, and cannot, have them all.

Both Ms Craigie and Jane Howard, whom Koestler is said to have treated callously after making her pregnant, have a right to their grievances, but both were ambitious and experienced women, who liked the company of the powerful and the famous. Both had enough intelligence to read Koestler for a dangerous man. Is it any disparagement to suggest that they might, at the time, have been excited by the risks they were taking? They did not *deserve* what he did, or is said to have done, but they were not foolish virgins and knew Koestler's character. We are entitled to do what Cesarani did not, but should have: wonder what they were doing with him.

The vilification of Koestler, egocentric as he may have been, has been altogether too gleefully undertaken. A biographer who looks to Simone de Beauvoir for reliable testimony should be reminded that she and Sartre were liars, fabricators and calumniators *de longue date*. *Darkness at Noon* had said everything which they should have, but dared not, say. Koestler constantly and accurately announced the truth which the cowardly Sartrean duo denied. What kind of reliable judges were they of his character? Would anyone dare to cite a Nazi's opinion of Koestler, even if he were not a Jew, after he had been (as he was) the first intellectual to write in England about the Final Solution and the death trains, in Cyril Connolly's *Horizon*?

Oh but there's a difference! Oh but is there? Read carefully the passage at the end of his preface where Cesarani is very candid in saying that 'Both my parents had been involved with the Communist Party in the Pink Decade'. It is piously filial to declare this (though it is not made clear which decade was 'Pink': the 1930s or the 1940s) but isn't there something a little too cosy about the suggestion that Mr and Mrs Cesarani were only doing what everybody, pretty well, was doing by being a little pinker than most? More significant, however, is the peroration:

My father's faith was more durable and gently decayed into stoical support for socialism and its parliamentary vessels in the United Kingdom. His life story made me wary of those who dismiss the youthful adherents of the CP in the 1930s and 1940s as gullible, naïve or ludicrously idealistic. To him the likes of Koestler would always remain 'renegades', but he sedulously tracked down Koestleriana... He made me realise how Koestler's writing had electrified those to whose experience it spoke. Koestler hoped that by writing books he would influence future generations. If it was necessary to avoid having children and the trivia of family life, that great end justified the means. Perhaps. By taking the responsibility of parenthood my father had a profound influence on at least one person: unobtrusively he taught me what justice means and what it is to live decently. He has not written any books, but this one is his all the same.

This is a handsome and touching tribute. It also says more than may have been intended. Here too is a closet, and skeletons. Cesarani is a nice Jewish boy; he has been taught family values. His father, we are incited to believe, was exemplary in raising a son, whereas Koestler was vaingloriously pretentious in preferring a life of childless promiscuity which left him free to write for the ages. Well, with all faults, he *did* write for the ages, however perishable some of his stuff may be. Meanwhile, that Cesarani *père* refused to face the facts of Communist practice is ascribed to the durability of his 'faith'. Why not to blindness? Why not to moral dishonesty? Why not to Jewishness? What would Cesarani say of anyone who advertised equally durable loyalty to Nazism, before 'gently decaying' into a member of the Christian Democrats (or the SPD)? And why is 'stoical' an appropriate adjective here, as if it were a form of noble suffering to collapse into acceptance of democracy?

In the recent *Le Livre Noir du Communisme* (Robert Laffont, 1998), there is an 800-page factual compilation of the murders committed and deaths procured by Communists: something of the order of 100 million, if we include those who died of organised famine, something which, in the twentieth century, happened *only* in countries dominated by Marxists. Anyone with honest eyes could have known, from 1918 onwards, that the Bolsheviks wilfully created a system of concentration camps, torturers and state terrorists. Nor was it impossible, or necessary, merely to guess such things: Bertrand Russell wrote, with horror, of the murderous glee with which Lenin spoke to him about summary executions. Less famous witnesses of brutality, fraud and sadism were hounded, often to death, by the lackeys and dupes of Utopia.

As with the Holocaust, clear proof and declarations of murderous intent were ignored by fools or decried by scoundrels. Foot-soldiers in the Party kept the faith by persecuting the truth-tellers. Conniving intellectuals relativised, and still relativise, the facts (see *Un Pavé dans l'Histoire* (Laffont) for recent nuanced responses to *Le Livre Noir*). Not a few of the rank and file CP members were, I daresay, good family men; so, we are promised, were many Mozart-loving concentration camp guards who kept their faith in Adolf. Decent Communists were also tools or fools. 'Innocently', they endorsed a conspiracy no less pitilessly dedicated to the systematic extermination of millions of human beings, whether because of their ethnic origin (the Cossacks) or on account of their putative class (kulaks, bourgeois, etc.). Many Communists no doubt imagined – and taught their children – that justice was something that existed (only) in the Soviet Union. Now bring on those nice misguided Nazis.

It is not the least of Koestler's achievements – and one that may well have driven him mad – that he saw the horrors Left and Right and fearlessly proclaimed both. In both cases he did it before almost anyone else and in the face of abuse, hatred and intimidation. Thanks to Cesarani, he will now he remembered as the lowlife crackpot sex maniac who banged a film director's head on the kitchen floor and refused to use a contraceptive when making love to Jane Howard. Now think again about 'He [Cesarani *père*] has not written any books, but this one is his all the same'. Indeed.

A Long Storey Long

On his arrival in London, D.H. Lawrence was praised and faintly damned by being called 'the provincial genius'. Like Thomas Hardy before him, he suffered from condescending applause; T.S. Eliot accused him of being uneducated. The genuine charge was that Lawrence was more alive, and less sly, than the St Louis man who concealed his provincialism well enough to pass for a metropolitan mandarin.

From the beginning of his long literary career, David Storey has been a consciously embattled heir to Lawrence's mantle. *This Sporting Life* – a prime instance of the novel as contact sport – was instantly important in 1960. Storey, like Lawrence, was the son of a miner, a provincial who tore himself from his roots in order to flourish as an artist. His scholarship to the Slade had to be supplemented by commuting to Leeds in order to play professional Rugby League. If he has always refused to assimilate to London sophistication, he has also denounced the artless Philistinism of middle England. His integrity has isolated him.

The vocation of Art sanctioned his secession and ensured his alienation. His heroes are typically lonely, and unhappy, forked between the spiritual and the physical. Whether or not he wholly shares their alienation, he has certainly dwelt on it as a theme. *This Sporting Life* glorifies physical courage and, in the same breath, declares the futility of its satisfactions. Thirty-eight years and eight novels later, *A Serious Man* breaks old ground with the same fatalism which matched Arthur Machin to his bone-crunching career.

The first-person narrator this time is Richard Fenchurch, who announces himself – with more than a hint of authorial endorsement – as a genius. He is also a man wrestling with manic demons; he spends a lot of time under doctors, though he is always eager to get on top of them intellectually.

Fenchurch is said to have been born in 1934, but he is unsure whether it might not have been '33 or '35. Since he is declared to be sixty-nine in the present, the story takes place, it seems, beyond the

Review of David Storey, *A Serious Man*, in the *Times Literary Supplement*, 1998.

millennium, unless Fenchurch is suffering from arithmetic delusions. The difficulty with novels about supposedly mentally disturbed people, when told in the first person, is that the writer can defend himself against charges of inconsistency, no less than tedium, by insisting that the bedevilled hero is acting in unfortunate character. This can be fair enough in dialogue, and even in cases where the narrative is clearly meant to drift on the stream of thought of a deranged person, but it is less impressive when, as here, the form of the novel is, to a great degree, routine in its alternations of dialogue and prose, even though it does, without any remarkable surprises or invention, cut nervily between past and present.

Richard Fenchurch's life echoes Storey's in that he is working class and wins a scholarship to the Drayburgh, a London art school very like the Slade, after which he becomes a full Renaissance man: painter, sculptor, successful dramatist, important novelist. Nor is this all: like the D.H. Lawrence who wrote *Fantasia of the Unconscious*, he has a prophetic side: 'You must have heard,' he tells the working-class woman who now lives in his childhood home, 'of *New Mind Theory* or *The Narrative or Pentadic Theory of the Mind*'. The lady is less certain, even when he glosses his remarks with: 'By "mind", of course, I mean the psyche.' Earlier he has told a consultant psychiatrist called Maidstone:

> I am visited by a vacuity of mind… which I can never explain nor wholly describe… It gives an insight, on the other hand, into the structure of the mind. How, under stress, it comes apart. *The Quinary or Pentadic Theory*. When I've written the book, I'll ask you to check it. Once published, assimilated, and understood, it will revolutionise psychiatry.

This may sound like delusional babble, but later the whole theory is spelt out, which suggests that Storey imagines that its elaboration is either revealing or even, perhaps, significant. Fenchurch's egotistic genius excites small irony from the writer, and is rarely challenged, except by the vexed patience of his daughter, Etty, who has become responsible for taking her father from his insanitary London lodgings back to the large country house which once belonged to the rich local family into which Richard married. Many memories are stored there and are presently unlocked.

The hero's now ex-wife, Bea, has abandoned him for a younger lover, who is characterised only by having one arm and being a 'parliamentary private secretary' in the Ministry of Health. This job is said to be likely to lead to a high position in the Home Office, which suggests that Storey imagines that the man is a civil servant not an MP, as PPSs tend to be. This detail exemplifies a propensity to flash dubious worldly credentials. For further instance, is it necessary for the otherwise indistinct Bea to be dignified into being a candidate for the Nobel Prize on the verge of finding a cure for cancer? Hardly less improbably, a psychiatrist is alleged to have bought a house in Belsize Park 'from the sales of *The Phenomenology of Experience*', which plagiarises, of course, our hero's *The Logic of Grief*. An eye specialist charges 200 guineas to say that there is nothing he can do for Fenchurch's actress friend, who later kills herself. It all proves how beastly the bourgeois is.

Fenchurch's 'mature' life has been haunted or graced (or both) by a long love affair with his mother-in-law, Isabella, whose hybridised beauty comes from Lebanon and Connemara. This adulterous passion for a woman more than thirty years his senior is depicted as insatiably sexual, but is also meant to be something more: the true love which renders Fenchurch's marriage, although fecund, a secondary relationship (which does not inhibit him from expecting from Bea the loyalty he does not supply). The novel might be subtitled *Sons-in-law and Lovers*.

Fenchurch's belief in his own genius is presumed to warrant the domination of all around him. In this sense, Storey remains an unreformed romantic, for whom, as the Dadaist said, 'when an artist spits, that's art'. Fenchurch's saintly daughter panders to his revolutionary notions:

> 'If anyone's work has been produced by a place like this – and by these conditions – and from amongst these people,' she further exclaimed, 'it's yours!'
>
> 'I think you're a couple of vowels out,' I said. 'Revolution returns at any point on a circumference to where it was before. You don't think I'd waste time on that? It's not revolution,' I went on, 'but revelation you're on about. Unless hypocrisy can be described as a phenomenon with a dynamic all its own, neither religious nor political sentiment affects or has affected anything at all. Both are based on appetites which are undeclared, and not merely undeclared but dishonestly perceived. I, for one, have always believed in a true revolution – of the individual spirit which prefers not to put its faith in authority, but to disseminate the authority of faith.'
>
> 'Feathering your own nest is a better description. Faith,' she went on, 'like love, is only achieved through others.'

'Not through destroying them by political and religious bigotry,' I said.

What are we to make of the many pages of similar dialogue, in which pretentiousness and incoherence create an impression of hectic naïveté in a novelist whose achievements have won important prizes and whose *alter ego* has made a fortune (Fenchurch is said to have given away half a million quid) with plays that, to be staged at all, must have contained less psyche-numbing exchanges?

This novel is sad as well as serious. It affects to be written by an '*uomo serioso*' (*sic*) who like Sartre, he thinks, sides with the workers 'pour ne [*sic*] désespérer Billancourt'. We can all make mistakes, of a kind which used to be picked up by diligent editors, but the writing in *A Serious Man* is of a portentous ineptitude which only comic intent could excuse. It offers us a literary genius, now pitched on the cultural scrapheap of a decadent Britain, who – after all those years, however many they are – regularly says 'between Bea and I', 'between he and I', 'between her and I' and 'as for she and I', etc.

Infelicity is matched by inelegance: not even Elizabeth Bowen, doing her mannered worst, ever split her dialogue with 'he said' etc. in more inappropriate places: e.g. '"He owns," she said, "a lot of lorries"' which calls for the reader to pause where the character would not. The prose contains repeated peculiarities and Hardyesque coinages such as 'transcendity', 'robosity' and 'dispiration' (used three times on a single page), until even the most deferential critic must feel dispiritated.

We also have Maidstone, the psychiatrist, planning a book 'of which the provisional title was... *The Morassic Ingenitive*' (eh?) and using the word 'nosomania', more than once, as a synonym for nostalgia, a wildly implausible error for a medical man. A character who has just been identified by name (Harris) is declared to be 'anonymous' and 'metabolism' is taken to be something that can be tormented, just as 'embolismic' is alleged to be an English word; cars are said to be 'dilapidated' (did they once belong to the Flintstones?) and gardens 'decimated'.

There is a lot of sensitive and protracted description of the Midlands countryside, in the closely observed style of a Lawrencian sensibility in love with his native heath. Yet who has ever *twice* seen beech trees with 'coiling branches', which happen, by the way, to be 'flecked with cicatricial scars'? These scarry scars match, in redundancy, 'stunted dwarfs' and 'luminous light'.

Halfway through this long, lugubrious trudge, the author speaks, I fear, for the reader:

'What,' I enquired, 'is the point of it all?'

'Isn't the point of the point,' he [Maidstone] ingenuously persisted, 'that the point of the point is a circle?'

A Serious Man may become, like Fenchurch's painting, '*de rigueur* with aficionados'. In the world of the morassic ingenitive, who knows?

Notes Towards a Definition of Culturelessness

There is a standard embargo on reviewing the same novel in two places, and I do not mean to breach it. I have, however, been thinking about David Storey's *A Serious Man*, even though I recently wrote quite a long piece about it. Since what I said there, and what I mean to say here, is unlikely to please the author, it may be tempting to suppose that I am pursuing some kind of vendetta. In truth, I have never met and am not jealous of David Storey. It is, however, not quite true that I have had no contact with him. Over thirty years ago, I made bold to say that a continental novel which I was reviewing, set during the Holocaust, proved that there were 'greater tragedies in modern history' than getting your teeth bashed in playing Rugby League. Was there, at that time, a measure of envy in my remark? I hoped that I was also saying something about English parochialism and the 1960s inflation of local grievances which looked silly, not to say ignoble, in the face of incomparably more terrible cruelties in faraway lands of which Neville Chamberlain was not alone in being ignorant.

I should not have chosen to recall my antique jibe, had it not provoked from the then aggressively famous Mr Storey an angry letter telling me that I was, among other things, impotent and sterile, hectic charges – implying his own potency and fecundity – which recalled the furious, but more accurate, terms in which D.H. Lawrence once attacked the astounded (and devastated) Bertrand Russell. I cannot recall if I responded to Storey's letter; I mention the dusty episode only to declare whatever residual animus he might impute to me. My purpose here is not to reopen old scratches, but to look more closely, and also more generally, at the culture of which *A Serious Man* may well be – who would be surprised? – an award-winning instance.

A Serious Man affects to be the autobiographical novel of Richard Fenchurch, whose career as painter, writer and playwright tracks that of his author. Like Storey, Fenchurch was born in 1934 or '33 or '35 (in his fragile fictional mental state, he is not sure); like Storey, he was the son of a miner, found Art as a vocation, went to London on a scholarship, became a success and suffered from the alienation of those who lose one community without finding another. As to be expected in a fictional character, Fenchurch's life has its idiosyncrasies, not least that his emotional memories are dominated by the great love of his life, who happens to have been his mother-in-law, an exotic woman more than thirty years his senior.

What concerns me is less the specific quality of the novel than its significance as the latest (culminating?) work of a novelist who has, once or twice, been described as 'the leading novelist of his generation'. As the very exemplar of an autochthonous genius, sprung from the same soil as D.H. Lawrence and consciously echoing many of his qualities, Storey was a providential, even messianic, figure in the 1960s. *This Sporting Life* was published at the beginning of that happy decade; the film version, starring Richard Harris and directed by Lindsay Anderson (an eminently bourgeois champion of the coming revolution and a founding father of 'Free Cinema', at least until he began to get well paid), was immediately successful. A watchable work of cinematic art that also said 'Watch out', *This Sporting Life* both spoke for the inarticulate and clenched the exploited fist of the working class at the beastly bourgeoisie, who bought the book and went to the movie.

The 1960s cant that the public arts should be weapons in the social struggle was not new: André Bazin had made solemn claims for the educational and socially liberating force of the cinema; the Group Theatre in the pre-war USA and the Berliner Ensemble in post-war East Germany based their style and policy on the assumption that, as in ancient Athens, the theatre was a central cultural locus that could, and should, shape and change the consciousness of an audience well advised, again and again, to wait for Lefty.

After he had veered from camp Oxford aestheticism to what he called 'Socialism' (and Tom Wolfe would term Radical Chic), Ken Tynan became the trumpeter for a new kind of theatre in which ballsy John Osborne replaced chintzy N.C. Hunter and prosaic Harold Pinter dumped versifying Christopher Fry. Language and gesture were soon liberated from the Lord Chamberlain's repressive and reactionary control. At pretty well the same time, Richard Hoggart's and others' po-faced evidence at the Lady Chatterley case helped D.H. Lawrence's worst book to achieve enormous sales. It was, apparently, worth paying good money just to see a word which everyone had heard many times printed in a text which, if one believed the tendentious witnesses, approximated to Holy Writ. The myth of Lady Chatterley was largely delusive: it suggested, on wishful evidence, that the sexually uninhibited and earthy gamekeeper, Mellors, gave his employer's wife orgasmic delight which could not be supplied by her effete upper-class husband, a paraplegic privileged to have been wounded in the war which had so shell-shocked the non-combatant Lawrence. The idea that three-star erotic pleasure was available only from real men who worked in the woods, or the pits, was a wilful (or apprehensive?) imposture on the part of an unrobust author whose own wife was notoriously, and without losing faith in his genius, inclined to look elsewhere for orgasms.

Lawrence's frenzied youthful reaction both to the morals of Bloomsbury and to the habits of Bertrand Russell (whom he accused of being 'all disembodied mind') suggests that he was more embarrassed by the polymorphous activities of the upper class than alerted to their want of virility. A small instance of the degree to which, even in today's erotically surfeited England, working-class men (and women) can be disconcerted by sexual *behaviour*, though their language may be full of obscenities, is to be found in *The Full Monty*, where the fat husband tries, with touching witlessness, to make love to his wife by climbing on top of her. And she, though she loves him, has no idea of how to contribute to his resurrection by more active means than by lying there waiting for the electricity, so to say, to be connected.

What Lawrence could not admit – that erotic effectiveness is (usually) not a function of primitive desire or muscular authority, but of intelligence and *knowledge* as well – culminated in the hero of *The Plumed Serpent* telling his mistress that she should not expect to *enjoy* it with him. Sex, in the later Lawrence, becomes a form of stabbing which, in *The Woman Who Rode Away*, becomes sacrificial and murderous, although the ultra-masochistic heroine is alleged to crave the killing stroke.

Storey does not make Lawrence's mistake in *A Serious Man*: the young Fenchurch may be full of passion, but he is depicted as a clumsy lover who has to be instructed, with female tolerance, by the exotic Isabella, the mother-in-law with Levantine blood who, we are told, 'vouchsafes' herself to him. The use of this obsolete Biblical term is a nice example of Storey's defiant refusal to avoid the callow. His novelistic investigations of the boyhood and early manhood of his heroes are often disarming, though they may bear, and merit, another interpretation: like the playwright Arnold Wesker, Storey's work is regularly – Derrida-speak has its uses – *past-oral*. Where he and Wesker catch the accents of the now vanished worlds from which they came – the Jewish East End or the mining regions of the English provinces – both can have a freshness of recall, an elegaic and regretful tenderness which, especially in dialogue, is moving and cautionary. Something goes wrong, it seems, in both writers when they seek to be grownup or to find broader, deeper topics of the kind on which, given their promotion to cultural priority, they assume a duty, and competence, to express themselves.

A Serious Man is not, so far as I can see, an ironical title. When Fenchurch claims, repeatedly, to be a genius, his author does not subvert his self-esteem: his self-mockery is self-important too. The novel is, in a way, a recension of Orwell's undistinguished *Coming Up For Air*, in which a man goes back to his rural roots and finds them covered in suburban tarmac. Fenchurch returns to the mining village where he was born and finds it full of unemployed men and drug addicts. The few who do have jobs commute to them. The lineaments of old England are superficially in place (he can still recognise the landscape and the prettified spoil heaps), but the vitality is gone.

Fenchurch has come home not to *be* at home but – if he is not shipped off to a 'Home' first – to die there. Not yet seventy, he is a self-confessedly senile neurotic, the artist as slippered pantaloon, at the end of a tether which is more or less firmly held by his patiently exasperated daughter, whose husband, Charlie, is a genially condescending bigshot in the unrevolutionary local Labour Party. Charlie is a chairman who presides less because of the depth of his Socialist convictions than because he has a deepish purse.

Although he is portrayed as a cultural giant to match Michelangelo, Fenchurch is a prophet literally unrecognised in his country: no one in a large cast seems to have seen him on telly, still less on a book jacket. He has spilled his genius, as he once spilled his seed on merely seeing his beloved mother-in-law, without anyone on his native heath being aware of it. His art has had no impact on those whom it should have revived and excited. He has earned a fortune (we are told that he has given away half a million), but for all the difference he has made socially, he might as well as saved his breath. If we are to take him as seriously as do the author and the character himself, we have to believe that, for his life not to be a mockery, Fenchurch has been doing art: something timeless, self-validating, valuable, whether anyone likes it or not. Has he? Has David Storey? And if not, what have they been doing?

Since the 1960s, when Tom Maschler's ardent and brave belief in the importance of new writing made Jonathan Cape into the home for a variety of emerging talents, the English novel has, supposedly, been as vigorous as it was once feared to be moribund. Maschler's sponsorship of the Booker Prize, which he hoped would give at least one novel a year the same *réclame* that the Goncourt bestows, was central to his promotion of the form. When, in the mid-1960s, Maschler was asked to name the writers who would endure, he chose David Storey, Robert Shaw and Alan Sillitoe. Shaw's early death and distraction by the movies mean that, in fact, he bequeathed little or nothing to the ages; Sillitoe – the grittiness of whose early work and whose working-class origins shadow Storey's – has worked with admirable, prolific integrity, expanding his scope but, to some degree, losing his fame and, with it, the centrality he seemed to have won with *Saturday Night and Sunday Morning*. His later work may not, I suspect, fulfil Maschler's hopes, although it is the thoughtful product of a man who, however ruefully, has moved on into maturity.

Storey is a different case. His success has been greater than Sillitoe's: his plays have been applauded throughout the world, and performed by great actors; his novels have won all the available prizes; he has had every encouraging opportunity to achieve the greatness which Maschler foresaw. And yet he now writes *A Serious Man*, which, if it were submitted by an unknown, would be regarded as unpublishable. No, I do not mean to go back on my early promise: this is not a vendetta. Nor is it an instance of hitting a man one has already knocked down. It is to confront a demanding puzzle: what has happened?

Perhaps we have to go back to the 1960s in order to understand where and why things went wrong. I am not among those who wish to dismiss an 'ignominious decade' or who want to believe that there are signally wicked witches to be hunted among those who denounced the Greek colonels or opposed Uncle Sam in Vietnam or grew their hair, scuffed skiffle-boards, smoked pot and fucked a lot. Let us pretend that we are interested in literature and art and ask simply, what has happened to writing in the last thirty years? Good things? Why not? Prize-winning things, award-winning things? Tons of them. But? But along with the convenient and sentimental idea that Socialism could be procured by bringing art to the workers (cf. the quixotic vanity of Centre 42 and its unappreciated attempts to thrust folksinging, for unwanted instance, down the toilers' ear-holes) came the notion that art, although A Good Thing in itself, had to be progressive, experimental, accessible and, of course, non-élitist.

Journalistic talk of 'leadership' and the growth of the ranking game, which graded writers in terms of their popularity and charm, aimed to wrest judgement from Establishment critics and prim grammarians and lodge it in the hands of TV suits, publicists, odds-shouters and agitprop *vanguardistas*. Ken Tynan was the stammeringly verbose spokesman for the new journalism which would rate artists according to their capacity to excite quasi-erotic spasms: he could not, he said, love anyone who did not like *Look Back in Anger*, a text which – in the mid-1950s! – could claim sulkily that there were no good brave causes left. Tynan was unalert to the parochialism of Osborne's anger, which was more like petulance, perhaps because the conquest of London seemed to both of them to be the greatest imaginable victory. English Art was becoming entirely subjective and self-expressive: neither grammar nor draughtsmanship mattered any more than good manners or creased trousers.

When D.H. Lawrence came to London, before the Great War, he confronted a cultural centre whose dominating personalities had something of the confidence that went with empire. Even an iconoclast like H.G. Wells, famously impatient with Henry James's art of the novel, derived his cockiness from being English and imagined that Fabianism could be exported to a world market like Sheffield steel. Could G.B. Shaw ever have been Portuguese? Why did Conrad learn English? The Grand Fleet made English writers, and writers in English, important. Lawrence was obliged to match himself with and against a prevailing world of letters in which a certain erudition (at least about wild flowers) and grammatical nicety were conditions of entry. The English Bible, Shakespeare, Milton, Hazlitt, supplied the building blocks of literature. Lawrence discovered that a matrix for writing novels was to compare and contrast the fortunes of two couples and, for all his urgent desire to tear down the walls of the bourgeoisie, he proceeded to do so with a certain stylistic deference: both *The Rainbow* and *Women in Love* more or less honour the discovered formula.

The emerging writers of the 1960s confronted no society sure of its primacy. They would not, perhaps, have emerged at all, still less to dominance, had it not been for the eclipse of English authority. The devaluation of 1948 announced the economic decline of the empire; Suez the military poverty of Britain. Kingsley Amis's *Lucky Jim* mocked the academic establishment which nevertheless gave him preferment. The established authorities were everywhere losing their nerve. John Profumo behaved no worse than many cabinet ministers before him, but he lacked the Wellingtonian pride (and victories) to say 'publish and be damned': they published and he was damned. His embarrassment amused those whom Somerset Maugham had earlier, and not foolishly, called 'scum': the new class of those who took manners and morals to be as dated as grey flannel. The 'satirists' who rejoiced at Profumo's humiliation were, of course, to behave much worse than he did, but they had dismantled the machinery of judgement and thus enjoyed themselves without having to lie to the House which their huff and puff had helped to blow down.

In the arts, aesthetics were blown away as ethics were in society. Why not? Who needed Charles Morgan or Dodie Smith, Sir Alfred Munnings or Somerset Maugham? Away with all that obsolete dust! H. Carleton Greene (one of whose desert island discs was, naughtily, the *Horst Wessel Lied*) put paid to Lord Reith. The new aesthetics contrived to render laughable not only the well-constructed play or novel but also a certain cosmopolitanism which both Morgan and Maugham exemplified. 'I like it here', Amis declared, and insisted that others agree: abroad and foreign literature were for shags.

Let me go straight to a point which I cannot prove, but may have some sharpness. From the 1960s onwards, English artists have lost any keen sense of allegiance to a common culture, even in the style of their attacks on it. The notion of innovation as an *end* in art is not without sense, but one of its malign consequences – and a central one – is the promotion of publicity as the measure and means of success. The fame of the creator is advanced by the scandal he creates, the rules he/she breaks. This is, in a way, like proving the sincerity of your religion by the ingenuity of your blasphemy. Blasphemy is, in truth, parasitic on a context of orthodox credulity; it must involve risk, one could say, if it is not to be mere bravado. (The Rushdie case makes my point, securing the importance of a book which no one, not even those who anathematised it, read from cover to cover.) D.H. Lawrence, like Byron, had been driven from an England which, as it showed in the Wilde case, was capable of breaking iconoclasts who had ceased to amuse it. When John Osborne, later parroted by Jonathan Miller, declared 'I hate you England', he was regarded as a merrily cheeky chappy and welcomed home without sanction. Rushdie was guarded night and day by the 'racist' government for which he showed steady contempt. Would I have it otherwise? Not I; but let us not, for that reason, lose the plot: the command post of English culture is now, like Gertrude Stein's Oakland, a place that has 'no there there'.

Once all is scandal, what is scandalous? When one need not be grammatical, in the largest sense (capable of saying the new thing in the old language, as Wittgenstein put it), what is left but the making of the loudest, most attractive noise, and reputation? *A Serious Man* is a lament for the passing of an England which was, perhaps, beyond saving: one in which the National Union of Mineworkers actually sponsored libraries and where deprived parents dreamed of educating their children. The best way of bettering oneself in today's middle England is to win the lottery on which all of our fortunes more or less depend: for the layman, no lottery win, no new Jag; for artists, no lottery grant, no art. Storey sees that the energy of the unions and of the Old Left was largely and futilely conservative. Arthur Scargill was only the loudest case of those who wanted to keep everything as it was. Why should he have his block-vote eroded by having the miners move on to healthy activities which did not fill their lungs with black death?

For all his resignation, Storey cannot quite accept, for sentimental rather than political reasons, that there was nothing intrinsically beautiful in the mining communities. The grimness of the miners' lives was redeemed, in part and without benefit to them, by the descriptions of them by novelists, such as Lawrence and Storey himself, who recognised the beastliness of the places they had fled (prettily 'compelled' by the vocation of art) and who deplored the philistinism in which they had been raised. Yet they remained convinced, despite themselves, that in their brave solidarity, their muscular manliness, the miners had been real men in a way which effete Londoners could not be (Rich Cohen's nostalgia for 'Tough Jews', in his book of that title, is of the same order).

What is sadly remarkable in David Storey, as it is in Arnold Wesker, is the devitalising effect, artistically, of removal from the sources of their young and enthusiastic revulsion. They have left what has not, and almost certainly could not have, survived: the loci of solidarity, Jewish or working-class, which gave their fathers a toughness and a sense of identity. *But* – and this is the big but – but the writers of the 1960s succeeded in penetrating a London incapable of welcoming them by challenging them, as Edward Garnett's editorial intelligence challenged Lawrence or as Ford Madox Hueffer did his peers. The London of the 1960s, and beyond, could contribute little or nothing to the provincial genii who stormed it. After forty years as a professional writer, Storey still thinks, as does Neil Kinnock, that 'between you and I' is English. Does it matter? No; if nothing matters, nothing matters, does it?

What does it matter then? It matters because, as we see in the work itself, it betokens the fact that there now is no central culture; there are no Edward Garnetts; there is, to put it simply, no sign that modern England wants its writers – or anyone else – to be educated. (I'm sorry, but what I think *I* am has very little to do with the case.) What we see in *A Serious Man* is a juvenile senility, in which a supposed genius has nothing to be serious about except his own reception as son, lover and artist. He may have given away half a million, but Richard Fenchurch is hung up about *success* (oh and mortality, a bit). The world which Storey challenged has yielded to him, as it did to Wesker: it asked them for nothing better than what they felt like doing, and that is what they did. It did not *nourish* their ambitions; it filled their pockets. It had no charge of wit or education with which to meet and inspire them. It had, as it has, prizes and celebrity events; it had no seriousness for Fenchurch to be seriously serious about.

The death of the old East End (now – what else? – the setting for a sitcom which substitutes itself for reality) and the deadness of middle England remind us that something substantial has gone: at the least, something which could spawn kids who believed it noble to get away and be artists. Instead we have 'people's' culture in which everyone and everything is as good as everyone and everything else. Artists are distinguished only by the fact that some get handouts and some do not (lobbyism is the only growing art today).

Storey and Wesker, in their different ways, hoped to be the prophets of regeneration, not least in the communities they had quit, but they have proved to be only their obituarists. Once they had written, and rewritten, the dolorous eulogies of what no longer existed, they had nowhere to move on to. They supposed that they themselves were at the centre of a new world which they had the means to transform. They lacked the wit to see that, without any malicious purpose, they – and many like them – were being promoted into sterility. D.H. Lawrence had sensed the danger of being crushed by the England of Joynson Hicks, but he was wise enough to cut and run: *that* England, albeit diminished after 1918, was still dangerous, still worth assault, still deserving of a certain respect and hence of the belligerently tubercular Lawrence's distant art/illery (good old Derrida again!). The generation of the 1960s and their epigoni (I have no wish, I swear, to cudgel Storey alone) found the ruling culture as elusive as the castle which Kafka's K. sought so frustratedly to locate and penetrate. The comedy of disappointment in which both Storey and Wesker feature so glumly was the tragedy of D.H.L. repeated on a stage bereft of tragic machinery. Lawrence, it would be nice to think (in view of the faith which we, like Dr Leavis, once had in him), just might have been a source of enlightenment to the England that burnt his pictures, banned his books and preferred to honour him in New Mexico. The writers of the 1960s came to a mirage which they took for a citadel, even though its lack of defenders should have warned them of its illusory character. The supposedly revolutionary artists of our time took for a vital programme the antique 'Socialism' (closed shop bossism) of the TUC and the opportunist 'aesthetics' of Ken Tynan and Lindsay Anderson, which just happened to make both of them the pivotal figures they so ached to be. (Anderson wrote an article entitled 'Get Out and Push', calling for social energy, but his real urge was to get out and push himself.)

The writers of the generation which Storey is said to lead uprooted themselves from dying cultures and planted their foundations in sand. The centre could not hold; it was not even central. The long British vanity concerning London theatre was, one could argue, typical of a minor culture to which an unimportant territory is ceded (cf. Napoleon on Elba). Conceit licensed London theatrical Poo Bahs to believe they were at the heart of some kind of social revolution. Laurence Olivier's patronising attitude to the movies – see Vincent del Brutto's account of his conduct on the set of *Spartacus* – was a symptom of its parochial smugness. In truth, pop and rock music were revolutionising England, and mimicking America, in a way which made the theatre what it always had been, and still pretends not to be, a means – after the opening night – of attracting suburban and tourist audiences which enjoyed the West End in the same dutiful way that they admired thatched cottages or King's College Chapel.

The amputation of high culture from Number 10's agenda is not, as Peter Hall and the Lord Puttnam affect to believe, an instance of the cruel trimming of vital shoots, but of the excision of moribund wood. In this sense, the government's 'arts' policy is doing little violence to society; rather it is doing what seems 'natural' and popular. Its conflation of Marxist and market logics (never *that* different, in their common cult of inevitability and the replacement of moral absolutes by economic necessity) leads it to the conclusion that the only art deserving of public cash is, as 'the people' confirm, not art. That they speak in the same breath of the vital need for education is, of course, the joke at which we dare not smile. Hall is crafty enough to base his appeal for funds on what the theatre does to make money from tourists. So much for the Berliner Ensemble.

If the 'revolution' sponsored (journalistically, of course) by Ken Tynan involved the defenestration of the Lord Chamberlain, followed by the enactment of theatrical cruelty, enlivening sexuality and brilliant *lèse-majesté* (in so far as these were compatible with bums on seats), the notion of Socialisto-Surrealist innovation, in which Ken starred as André Breton, especially for those who had never heard of André Breton, was always more camp than truly revolutionary. It was the 1960s habit to make the Americans the villains of most pieces (Peter Brook's *US* and David Lodge's *Changing Places* were offshoots of the same logic) as well as the solicited audience for them. By attacking America, the arbiters of the new inelegance chose a providentially benign antagonist (how many of them attacked, or even *imagined*, the mass murders in the Soviet Union and good old Mao's China?). The Americans replaced the British establishment in the days of its paternalist potency: the Yanks could absord and even be amused by the feisty playfulness of those who dared to thumb their noses at them (*and* ask for candy). Swinging London was a place in which the children set their own bedtimes and did not wait for lights out to do what would have horrified that old Puritan D.H.L. and is now a commonplace on TV. Age was the real enemy, of course: no one was ever to be over thirty again. Peter Pan was a militant for whom maturity was never, as they say, an option.

The abolition of anything except opinions, in art as in politics, and of any ambition but that of being successful and *known*, though never for one's knowledge of anything, was not the *direct* consequence of anything, but rather of *everything*. (This essay is, I confess freely, an irresponsible – not closely argued or documented – amalgam, very much in the style of the journalism it denounces, but I will excuse its provisional arguments behind a convenient title.)

To be a little more specific, in an area which concerns me, I think it fair to say that *A Serious Man* is conclusive evidence that some culturally fertilising elements, let us say, have been missing in our England: ingredients – intellectual *demand*, imaginative *development* – which might have enabled the writers of the 1960s, and after, to compose works of (God help us, but they do exist) *maturity*. Such prospects have been wantonly eliminated by a combination of public policy and private posturing. For simple instance, the New Jerusalem ethic with which the New Left (Old Left) attempted, so successfully, to infect neophytes, especially 'working-class', artists had, in truth, no fruitful season. (Wesker's decline is in exact proportion to his sense of overt purpose.) In claiming to speak for the unspeaking, and affecting to denounce the unspeakable, too many writers have excused themselves from developing their art on the old Wellsian grounds that they had better things to do than excellent, *worked* work. Let us dare to say: there is no better thing to do, because the world can be improved, so far as artists are concerned, only by their *teaching* it better, by being better artists. (Oh yes, of *course*, I was tainted by the same blight, or how should I deplore it so fiercely?)

When Richard Fenchurch seeks to give a personal account of himself – what else is an autobiographical novel? – he has nothing specifically personal to tell us, except his juvenile sexual and social misadventures. He is, in truth, a big baby. There is no implied lesson in his story, no thread which we can catch in order to be led to the centre of an intriguing labyrinth where a dangerous demon waits. No, Richard Fenchurch is a silly old fart, whose genius has not even matured enough for him to write passable English or sustain a plausible narrative. He is simply a quiver of unrealised pretensions and boastful lamentations. Yet he, like his author, has won all the prizes, the fame, the fortune, to warrant him to consider himself a genius. That he remains marooned in nostalgia for adolescence is typical of all our race. Like Charlie Chaplin, he has bruised himself by diving into shallow water. For want of deeper waters, he has again and again and, now, again melodramatised his youth. Working-class origins supply a cross which has made the yellow-brick road into a *via dolorosa* which (a new element, I must admit) he dares now to compare to the train to Buchenwald. At the end of more than thirty years, Storey has, it seems, digested my old jibe, not by taking a wider view of the world, and its horrors, but by appropriating them to his own condition.

The (waning?) English class system now does little for its privileged layers, but continues to blight the lower, while denying them access to what our betters promise those not in their circle of cronies is not better at all. The House of Lords is rendered ridiculous not by satire but by the promotion to it of artists of the quality of Archer and Bragg. Can no one find it a little bit funny that the government with one breath deplored the street theatre of football hooligans who did not know how to behave and lack manners or decency and, in the next, gave a knighthood (now a peerage) to John Birt, whose mandate – unchanged since the despicable Tories endowed him with it – was to reduce the BBC to a parody of Fascisto-Stalinist philistinism and whose programmes supply instruction in mindlessness, vulgarity and abuse?

The want of a demanding élite, sure of itself and its values (expressed, for easy instance, in the use of literate English, rather than ungrammatical vulgarity tricked out with absurd Latinate coinages such as Storey's 'transcendity' and 'robosity'), means that an ambitious provincial genius now renounces one identity in favour of, he finds, none at all. At, or towards, the end of famous careers, the artists to whom we might look for considered wisdom and mature achievement can offer us only splenetic regrets and incoherent resentment. Having been given every incentive anyone can think to give them, their gratitude takes the form of claiming 'We wuz robbed'. What then is to be done? Better work would be a start.

Fossils and Their Fate

Who needs another damn thick book about the Jews and their misfortunes? David Vital's 900 pages of densely argued and documented text is a fiercely dispassionate, perhaps definitive, analysis of what led, remorselessly, to the destruction of European Jewry. It takes us from the blissful dawn of 1789 – when the French Revolution promised Jewish emancipation – to 1939, when Hitler's Europe became first the prison and, very soon, the condemned cell from which there was neither reprieve nor exit.

Vital sees 1881 as an intermediate date of fatal augury: the Russian pogroms of that year proved how defenceless the Jews were and with what impunity (and pleasure) they could be killed, or raped and robbed by those whom the Tsar insisted on regarding as the honest peasants of Mother Russia. That the killers were also alcoholic and brutal was blamed on the extortionate Jews who sold them liquor (for the greater profit of the nobility who had the distilling monopoly). The corruption of the Autocracy was matched only by its determination to find plausible scapegoats for the degraded state of the people. 'What goes on in Russia?' a conservative historian once asked himself, and answered: 'Thieving.'

The Jewish authorities received neither respect nor protection from the Russian Autocracy, not even in return for the delivery of quotas of their male children, at the age of twelve and sometimes younger, for military service, under vicious conditions, often for a period of twenty-five years.

In Poland, poor Jews were bullied by the Jewish bailiffs whose business it was to extract labour from them and rent from Polish farmers who detested them far more than the landlords to whom the revenues were delivered. These bailiffs had something painfully in common with the *Kapos* – the Jewish 'policemen' in the concentration camps – who were so often to treat their co-religionists with vindictive harshness.

Professor Vital is a British-born Zionist historian whose work declares his conviction that Theodor Herzl was the man who, in

Review of David Vital, *A People Apart*, in the *Sunday Times*, 1999.

Churchill's phrase, 'made the weather'. Herzl's 1895 Zionist manifesto, *Der Judenstaat*, was published, supposedly, in the sour light of
the Dreyfus affair. However, anti-Semitism had already become fashionable in Vienna, whose mayor Karl Lueger (curiously ignored in the
text) set an example of populist rabble-rousing which Hitler was to
follow. Herzl – who had been a keen 'Alemannist' until 'bounced' by
his anti-Semitic German student fraternity – breathed life into a
dream which was to come true, long after his early death, in the
restoration of the State of Israel. Kenya was mooted, at one point, as
a plausible destination for unwanted Jewry, but 'Next Year in Nairobi'
did not have a rallying ring.

In view of what we now know, all non-Zionist 'solutions' to the
so-called Jewish Question have an air of futility or folly. Bourgeois
Jews who argued for assimilation seem like naïve trimmers;
Orthodoxy resigned the *hasidim* to stagnation and sitting-duckery.
Those who hoped to recommend themselves to Gentile compatriots
by bravery, by intelligence or – like Bismarck's banker Bleichroder –
by becoming plutocratic grey eminences prove to have been either
self-seeking or self-deluding.

Revolutionaries such as Trotsky or Martov predicted the withering
away of Judaism (and other superstitions) in the wake of October
1917. They lived – for as long as they avoided Stalin's executioners –
in an ideological dream whose waking reality was a nightmare of
endemic prejudice. What could be more savagely ironic than the
hapless dependence of the Jews on the men and nations with whom,
supposedly, they shared a God? Their own Talmud offered little
prospect of relief: 'Until the coming of the Messiah, enslavement to
alien kingdoms will continually mark the lives of the Jews.'

This was the good news. The bad news was that the terms of Jewish
servitude varied, from bad to worse, according to the caprices of
those to whose ruinous taxes and officially sanctioned violence they
were obliged to submit. Divisions among the Jews, though often deep
and implacable, did not affect the Gentile perception of 'the Jews' as
one devious hydra with a plethora of greedy heads. Mass eviction, if
not murder, was advocated by respectable academics and Protestant
pastors and Roman Catholics such as Cardinal Hondl in Poland as
late as 1936.

Anti-Semites could never be satisfied: they both urged Jews to
abandon their hermetic insularity and despised them for seeking to
pass as fellow-citizens. Abuse and thuggery were routine; the blood
libel – the myth that Jews abducted and sacrificed Christians, often

children, for their abominable rituals – was repeated as often as it was denounced as absurd. Jews were not only the providential enemies of Christianity, they were infuriatingly persistent in honouring what Arnold Toynbee was to call their 'fossil religion'.

If Jews wondered, with increasing regularity, what they could do to be saved from the eternal return of persecution, few European nation-states had a much more polite answer than '*Juden raus*': Jews out. Those, like the great poet Heinrich Heine, who got out by being baptised, rarely escaped either the taint of their origins or the shame of their apostasy. 'We no longer have the strength,' Heine wrote, 'to wear a beard, to fast, to hate and to put up with hatred; that is what is at the bottom of our Reformation.' Heinrich von Treitschke still called the Jews 'our misfortune'. He was only one of theirs.

Among the few pleasures of an unsmiling story whose ending, the Holocaust, comes as a tragic postscript, is that the British, if not unfailingly benign, were the first to dignify a Jew (Solomon de Medina, a Dutch/Portuguese military supplier, knighted early in the eighteenth century) and to admit Jews both to full citizenship, and then to Parliament. Benjamin Disraeli may have been baptised (after his father had a row with members of the Bevis Marks synagogue), but he remained an unapologetic Jew. At the Congress of Berlin, Bismarck called him 'The Man'. What continental Jew ever attained such dizzy heights?

Vital's determination to omit no detail of the long calvary which ended in the camps gives his book a solemnity unalleviated by its portentous style. He deals at length with Russia, Poland and Germany, but hardly touches on Italy, whose Jews were remarkably assimilated. Alexander Stille's *Benevolence and Betrayal* – an engrossing account of five examples of Italian Jewry (one of them a Fascist) – earns no mention. No more does the Greek community which so impressed Primo Levi by its unflinching, and sometimes predatory, solidarity at Auschwitz.

Even Vienna – that ferment of Jewish and anti-Semitic thinking – hardly comes into full focus. Freud, Karl Kraus, Otto Weininger, Arthur Schnitzler and Wittgenstein might as well not have existed. Freud and Einstein are cited only to be reproached for not having turned up to plead at Evian in 1938, when the Western powers held a hypocrites' sabbath which did nothing, and was meant to do nothing, to help the 'political refugees' who were to become ash in the next few years. After 1948, Israelis with guns won more respect than had been gained by Jews with genius.

What emerges, yet again, is the impossibility of saying precisely why Europe became a conspiracy of murderers. Anti-Semitism was a crusade without a plausible motive, apart from theft. Freud argued seriously that it derived from the Gentile dread of castration, which was symbolised by the aberrant ritual of circumcision. A likely story! Yet – as Kosovo proved – nothing is more futile than the attempt to find sensible reasons for stampedes of human bestiality. Anti-Semitism was compounded of religious enthusiasm, posturing nationalism, mountebank philosophy, calculating greed and bully-boy opportunism. Those of us who still receive the occasional death-threat from total strangers (usually on lined paper) are the lucky ones who had the English Channel, and English decency, between ourselves and the savage malice of ideological crackpots, Aryan zealots and God-fearing bigots.

A Career and Its Moves

Gore Vidal's life illustrates that, in order for a writer to be famous, it is not enough to make friends who will speak well, and audibly, about him. He also needs reliable enemies with whom he can pick regular, newsworthy fights. This fat but finally seductive biography bristles with names that Vidal has dropped, and picked up, and dusted down, during the more than half a century of industrious celebrity.

Friendships with Paul and Joanne Newman, Tennessee 'the Bird' Williams, Ken Tynan, Christopher Isherwood are matched by long-running feuds with Norman Mailer, Truman Capote and, most explosively of all, William Buckley Jr. Buckley's studiedly condescending posture is not unlike Gore's but his opinions – extremely right-wing and fundamentalist Catholic – are diametrically opposed. By calling Gore 'you queer' on primetime TV, Buckley was the first to lose his complacent cool.

Gore has been the kind of dangerous animal who, when attacked, knows very well how to defend himself. He is as sharp in criticism – notably in his many, frequently excellent and always readable essays – as he is resentful of dispraise. Although copiously ambitious, he has his limitations as a novelist, not so much in his reach – which stretches from the ancient world, in *Creation* and the notable *Julian* to the future in *Kalki* – as in emotional scope. He has written unremarkable films and a hit play (*The Best Man*). When pressed financially, he wrote live TV drama and – to avoid accusations of hack-like fertility – thrillers under a female pseudonym. He is the very model of a successful modern writer who has made his name, and a fortune, by his own disciplined effort and scintillating self-promotion.

Vidal matches stamina with courage. He never fails to do brave battle with bigots, prudes and power-freaks. Alarmingly incapable of humbug, he is a tribune who has little use for the plebs but no deference towards the patricians. All the smart names are in his index, but many have smarted from his jibes, not least the Kennedys, despite his tenuous family link with Jackie.

Gore Vidal was born in 1925, in circumstances that were always

Review of Fred Kaplan, *Gore Vidal*, in the *Sunday Times*, 1999.

quite comfortable. The Depression did not markedly depress the family's standard of living. Although his handsome father Gene, a West Point sporting hero, was never rich, he was soon famous. He was a fearless aviator and a briefly favoured figure in Franklin Roosevelt's New Deal. Gene Vidal came from South Dakota and some at least of his European ancestors were, probably, *conversos*: Jews who, under the pressure of the Inquisition, converted to Catholicism.

Vidal has been critical of Israel and of the United States' partiality for its right-wing policies, but his disdain for prejudice is unremitting as it is for sentiment or kitsch. He is a pagan who prefers pluralism to dogma and polytheism to the Great Religions to which, in his well-argued view, so much guilt, shame and vindictiveness are due. He is not immune to the last: I think it fair to say that this long life proves that he finds it easier to like than to love and, in many cases, to hate than to like.

Gore's mother's family was smart and waspish. Nina was an attractive woman with some of the qualities, and beauty, of Scarlett O'Hara. Unsurprisingly, her son was an early admirer of *Gone with the Wind*. The marriage of two strikingly handsome people resulted in a handsome son, but in no happy or durable family. Nina was boldly shameless (never afraid to flaunt her desirable body to casual visitors) and happy to slake her flaming sexual desires with the nearest stud, including – Fred Kaplan believes – a black Washington taxi driver.

Nina had many lovers and many, many more drinks. For a long time, alcohol did not damage her beauty, but hardly improved her temper. She took intermittent pride in her son, but spared him little time and less affection. In the end, when she had accused him of being a 'fag' living with a Jew (the irreplaceable Howard Austen), he wrote saying that he would never see her again as long as he lived. Nor did he.

The young Gore looked to his blind grandfather, the Democratic senator for Oklahoma, for personal warmth. Nominally of the same party as F.D.R., Senator Gore was eloquently hostile to a president whom his domestic enemies came to call 'that man in the White House'. The senator's belief that the gold standard should be observed and that Roosevelt was ruining the country came to cost him his seat, but never his honour.

Senator Gore had been almost totally blind since childhood (disease destroyed one eye, an accident the other). His grandson, who was to take the grandpaternal name as a *nom de plume*, became his surrogate eyes. By reading all kinds of books to the senator, Gore became precociously literate. Although he went to a fancy private school, he never went to college. He has, however, become the icon-oclastic scourge of academic historians. With impudent and accurate mischief, his novels have not only stampeded the Republic's sacred cows but also milked them for laughs.

Soon and always intrigued by the machinations of Washington DC, the pettiness of the grand world has amused, disgusted and stimu-lated him. The conversion of the United States into a Caesarian empire riles and affronts him. When F.D.R. died, Gore – then on secondment to the navy – had the smart gall to remark: 'The king is dead, long live the President.' In later years, however, when he began to have political ambitions, which were never realised, he became quite the favourite of Eleanor Roosevelt, who puffed his first novel, *Willawaw*, in her influential newspaper column.

Although an admirer of many women, and occasional lover of several, including Elaine Dundy, Ken Tynan's first wife, the majority of Gore's many lovers and the whole of his legion of quick tricks have been male. He has no compunction in paying for sexual favours. Payment dispenses him from allegations of affection and from any obligation to perform heroically. Like Oscar Wilde, he can resist anything except temptation. He has, however, had the loyal compan-ionship of Howard Austen for fifty years. No less than cruising, he has evidently relished domesticity, particularly in his present *palazzo* in Ravello.

Until now, Vidal has been reticent about his personal life. However, if he has disdained those who parade their homosexuality as a kind of achievement, he has never failed to mock those who seek to legislate morals. A keen anglophile, he wrote presciently to Tom Driberg MP in the early 1960s:

I am troubled by what seems to be a new puritanism rising in England, fully blessed by socialism which does like nothing better than to involve itself in private lives under the guise of 'morality'...

Today, the popular press has restyled the Nonconformist conscience; tabloid exposure is a more paying form of moralising. *Plus ça change?*

His ample biography, stuffed with jokes and anecdotes about the famous, as well as (more than) twice-told tales, leaves us much more aware of Gore's verve, and nerve, than of his defects or follies. A truly professional writer, he has stretched himself and embellished the novel whose death he has both lamented and postponed. He is a good citizen of the naughty world he so often, and often rightly, berates. And he is not through yet.

Sophia's Worlds

'Encyclopaedia' is defined in the *OED* as '1. The circle of learning. 2. A work containing information on all branches of knowledge, usually arranged alphabetically.' The latter definition dates from 1644, when it was still feasible to believe that *all* knowledge could be collated in a single conspectus. The last man who was reported to know everything died at the end of the eighteenth century. After that, encyclopaedias became irreversibly specialised. The scope of human knowledge having surpassed the binder's embrace, partiality will always be an irrevocable feature of expertise. We cannot now avoid eclecticism except through renunciation or regression.

In a subject at once so specialised and so diversified, what compendium could encompass all those with claims to being philosophers, or *philosophes*? The *New Routledge Encyclopaedia of Philosophy* meets a multiplicity of postulants with a generous admissions policy. Its voluminous verbosity runs to some six million words (every one of which I have *not* read) compiled by a competent – 'striving together in company' – international panel of exegetes under the general editorship of Edward Craig. The latter has exacted a high standard of clarity in exposition and has, in most cases, judged nicely how much space to allot to doctrines, ideas and individuals (see 'Particulars'). The writing is never wilfully technical; solecisms and misprints are few: 'there would be little point of doing social science' is an untypical inelegance in Russell Hardin's helpful article on Rational Choice Theory.

It would be miraculous if one agreed with the choices and conclusions in all ten volumes, but – before offering qualifying quibbles – it is right to salute a monumental labour rarely laborious to use, always informative to read and diverting to browse. What is missing, inevitably, is the shaping spirit and single-handed genius to be found, for example, in Louis Jacobs's *Companion to the Jewish Religion*. The Routledge encyclopaedia has been compiled by a committee without either the premeditated scheme of the pious or the abbreviating icon-

Review of the *New Routledge Encyclopaedia of Philosophy*, in the *Times Literary Supplement*, 1998.

oclasm of, say, the Vienna Circle (q.v.). The good news is that no axes are ground, the bad that there is not much edge. As in the Nile delta, what is gained in spread is lost, to some degree, in profundity.

It would be surprising, not to say reckless, for so vast an enterprise to have been undertaken without measured appreciation of its likely customers. Zeal for global reach sometimes involves arid stretches: several of the more general articles – for instance on Mexican and on Latin American philosophy – overlap without thickening our knowledge. Others are either diffuse (Charles B. Guignon on existentialism does not find occasion, in nine pages, to mention A.J. Ayer's puncturing point that the whole enterprise is based on a misunderstanding of the verb 'to be', which led Sartre to observe 'Ayer est un con') or too specialised: is this the place for prolonged instruction in the pronunciation of Sanskrit and Tibetan words? In view of some unfortunate truncations and omissions, such digressions smack too loudly of marketing considerations.

If Professor C.E.M. Joad – a famous wartime Brains Truster, along with Bertrand Russell (who when invited to review one of Joad's books declined, saying 'Modesty forbids') – has gone deservedly into the out-tray, John Anderson is unduly promoted, perhaps to lend persuasive force to reps doing the rounds of Australian university librarians. The absence of Kenneth Burke (except in the often sweetly opinionated bibliographies) is a mistake: his *Grammar of Motives*, especially where he analyses 'scene' and 'substance', deserves fuller recognition. The omission of Raymond Aron is ignobly matched by undue deference to Jean-Paul Sartre. Is a post-1989 encyclopaedia the place for implicit endorsement of the dated *soixante-huitard* notion that it is better to be wrong with Sartre than right with Aron? If Hannah Arendt's lucubrations on totalitarianism merit her inclusion, do we really need to hear again, at length, that Eichmann was 'not an evil man… whose evil deeds, although not done inadvertently [!!], had no deeper meaning for him and were incidental [!!!] to his murderous job'? B. Parekh lacks the nerve to assert, or the wit to hint, that Arendt's 'understanding' of Eichmann might have been a function of her unspoken desire to exempt her Nazi lover, Martin Heidegger, from the damnation he deserved, not for his opinions but for his cowardice. At the same time that metaphysical elaborations continue to be venerated, their critics are ignored. Marxism cannot, of course, be omitted, but why are we denied mention of *L'Opium des Intellectuels*? Aron – who outshone Sartre as a student – wrote his anti-Communist Manifesto knowing that it would lead to his ostracism by those who preferred not to disillusion Billancourt rather than to respect the truth. Aron embarrassed post-war *Gauchistes* just as *La Trahison des Clercs* by Julien Benda (also uncited) challenged ideological opportunists of the *entre deux guerres* (André Malraux would be furious to discover that he is not even vilified here, although his aesthetics were, at one time, taken very seriously, not least by him). If it is said that neither Aron nor Benda was a proper philosopher, why should we accept the mystagogue Lacan and the modish Julia Kristeva (whose best work, *Le Temps Sensible*, a study of Proust, is not mentioned in her bibliography)?

As far as English philosophy is concerned, it is a pleasure to see Charlie Dunbar Broad accorded respect. His cuttingly tolerant thought is well conveyed, but those who attended his lectures will notice how much of the *flavour* of a teacher cannot be discovered in any A to Z (*a posteriori* – a great place to start – to Zytkow J.). The charm of philosophy is not merely in published texts or theories; personality graces reason with seduction (what else made Socrates *beautiful* to Alcibiades, as Sartre was to Giacometti?). Broad, like A.C. Ewing (uncited), did not go with the Wittgensteinian flow; his meticulous scepticism was that of a man who took smiling pride in being discreetly exceptional. His lectures were notable both for their articulate preparation ('I shall now list seventeen objections to Berkeley's theory') and for the fact that he repeated everything he said, he repeated everything he said. As a result, I still have an almost complete rescription of his objections to Berkeley, and to other philosophers, though I cannot say that I *remember* any of them. His indices – for instance that in *Five Types of Ethical Theory* – were the wittiest I know (e.g. 'England, Church of, The Author's respect for'). If Broad's breadth was remarkable, so was his narrowness: like one of his own category of 'clever-sillies', he affected abiding admiration for the racial theories of the late Adolf Hitler. This did not prevent him asking me (and the Aryan Tony, now Professor, Becher) to dine with him in Trinity. Having written all his life on probability and physics, he confessed to us that, in old age, the sole remaining scientific experiment which it interested him to conduct was making yoghurt. 'You see, boys, even under *identical* conditions, of temperature and so on, sometimes it works and sometimes it doesn't!' What print also does not reveal is that Broad agreed with Wittgenstein at least in one department: he too was a regular visitor to Scandinavia, where (I suspect) he found male company as amenable as Housman's in Venice.

No doubt, none of this *should* be in an encyclopaedia, but it indicates how much remains undescribed when philosophers are taken to be no more than marmoreal fountains of ideas. Even A.J. Ayer, the cocksman and Tottenham supporter, whose stylishness made the derivative *Language, Truth and Logic* seem original, committed this mistake in his dismissive study of Wittgenstein. Having discounted a philosopher's aura, it is often difficult to convey the reasons for his influence. Even Plato's literary genius could not 'deliver' Socrates: to write of *eironeia* is not to catch its accents, still less its hesitations and pauses. What encyclopaedia can *teach* as a great teacher does? I may have Broad's notes in my files, but in John Wisdom's case – although I have no written record of a word he said – I have the voice, the anguish, the irony, in my head and, at argumentative times, in my hands (oh those Wittgensteinian manual brackets!). 'Say it if you like, but be careful', is no bad slogan for philosophers.

The great stylists bring a flair to the game which no catalogue can capture. There was something so decidedly *English* about Wisdom's whimsical urgency that I cannot take him to have been merely a deutero-, still less a pseudo-, Wittgenstein. His hushed humour was *almost* indistinguishable from shyness, or slyness; the unpreparedness of his lectures seemed irresponsible until you realised that he was inviting you to think along with him, to feel the elusiveness of the matter, the *oddness* of philosophy. He had a wincing distaste for definition as a prelude to discussion. Required by an insistently crass 'tourist' to define 'good', he was unusually nettled: 'Suppose I said that "good" was anything that added up to an even number, would that resolve anything?'

Wisdom's literary excursions led him to use David Garnett's *Lady Into Fox* to illustrate the way in which definition rarely worked when you needed it: 'At what point are we likely to say "By Jove, look at that pointy nose, with the slightly russet bloom on it, she's *definitely* a fox now, isn't she?"' Wisdom did not captivate all of his audience. Piers Paul Read records his disgust at the memory of the request for an example of a metaphysical question. The young Read proposed 'Does God exist?', to which Wisdom responded, 'Oh! Oh! I was thinking of something more along the lines of... "Is this a table?"' Wisdom did not subscribe to the modern view, 'I publish, therefore I am important', but his influential *Other Minds* set the agenda for Ryle (properly valued here by William Lyons), while his series of articles on logical constructions is an essential part of the philosophy of his time. His essay/parable about the invisible gardener whose attentions may, or may not, account for the appearance of order in an overgrown park (or paradise) is a very English didactic myth about the existence, or non-existence, of God and, in particular, the argument from design. If the human mind is indeed immortal, and philosophy is what we shall do throughout disembodied eternity ('Very long,' said Woody Allen, 'especially towards the end'), I should be sorry to sit in on a celestial colloquium from which Wisdom had been edited out. He made the subject *fun*, which was less true of unsmiling analysts who asked deterrent questions such as, 'Are facts irrevocably wedded to that-clauses?'.

I stumbled on some *ben trovato* surprises: for instance, the Ghanaian-born Anton Wilhelm Amo (c.1703–56) who learnt Dutch, Hebrew, Greek, Latin, French and German and both argued bravely against slavery and lectured on Leibniz at German universities. After eventual 'racial rebuff' in Europe, he returned to Ghana where, reverting to Ashanti tradition, he became a goldsmith and seer. Among mavericks who might have been expected to figure alongside him is the Triestine Carlo Michelstaedter, the precociously 'Wittgensteinian' author of *Persuasion and Rhetoric* who committed suicide at the age of twenty-three, supposedly on the day he finished his remarkable 'tractatus' ('Apesbeetheen' was his last word). Otto Weininger, who killed himself at the same age, also fails to make the cut, a more serious lapse, in view of his influence: he was the only Jewish philosopher cited approvingly by Nazi thinkers, on account of his self-hating dichotomies. T.E. Hulme's maverick *Speculations* (intelligent *and* proto-Fascistic) might have earned him a mention too.

In the lavish mass of what remains, we are reminded that philosophy is a subject of unnerving and inexhaustible perplexity. The curious tourist may also wonder why, or whether, it is still of urgent significance. Is it a lubricant or a motor? Over forty years ago, Jean-François Revel (also not cited) asked the militantly impatient question 'Pourquoi des philosophes?' In that long essay, the recently graduated *normalien* ironised on the smug way in which philosophers 'discovered' conclusive evidence for conclusions to which they had already come. Is it not still odd that they so seldom *surprise* themselves? Even more rarely are they Popperian enough to go in search of reasons or evidence why they might be wrong. Plato, like Berkeley, used the dialogue form to give the *appearance* of taking objections seriously, but the chat was as rigged as a French presidential press conference. By actually refuting his own early self, Wittgenstein was as unusual as Frege was noble when confronting – not to say *applauding* – Russell's objections to what had been his life's work. Russell himself was never the same again after Wittgenstein worked the same trick with him, though he paid him back by omitting him from his *History of Western Philosophy*. (Russell included Byron – whom Edward Craig's severity does not – perhaps less because they were both wicked lords than because Byron too was a moralising amoralist who dreaded madness.)

Whether or not Revel's juvenile polemic (like Gellner's *Words and Things*, which Gilbert Ryle notoriously disdained to review in *Mind*) was more than a clamorous claim to early fame, the programmatic circularity of an encyclopaedia is appropriate to a discipline which Wittgenstein famously asserted neither possessed specific subject matter nor changed anything (!). One might philosophise, he suggested, but one could not pin philosophy strictly in its proper territory. Like the pronoun 'I', the heart of the matter was systematically elusive.

Back in the 1950s, it seemed lean and mean and aggressively moribund. Whole departments were gleefully threatened with ignominious closure by those who might have staffed them. Metaphysicians were held to be either spurious or fraudulent ('misplaced poets' was the best that could be said for them). The exclamatory nature of ethics and aesthetics, the pointlessness of asking 'why?', the futility of arguments about God or the Ultimate Nature of the Real, the comic vanity of intuitive (ha!) pretensions to 'knowledge' when only science *knew*, the absurdity of bypassing ordinary language (the repository of sound sense) in favour of a 'truer' vocabulary, all of these aberrations proved that there had to be better things to do – grinding the lenses of Science – than to re-chop old logics.

Therapeutic positivism, we happy few believed, would massage away all the remaining cramps and cricks. Man would stand truer, if not taller, once he had jumped down from the shoulders of the giants who had given him a stilted conception of the world. In the event, the dog it was that died. Metaphysics (as Popper had warned, or promised) were more enduring, perhaps more useful, than *Language, Truth and Logic*. *Ta meteora* are still being considered: 'Possible Worlds' (q.v.) may be, well, possible. New departments are opening: Women (see 'Feminist Ethics, Gender and Language', etc.) have a floor to themselves. The movies – did not Wittgenstein have a famous *faible* for the flicks? – provide texts more easily read than Aristotle's Metaphysics Lambda (about which I still dream in recurrent Tripos nightmares). Renascent philosophy spreads into 'Politics' (Anthony

O'Hear is excellent on 'Conservatism'); Medicine (Noam J. Zohar on 'Bioethics, Jewish', encapsulates the now generally inextricable inter-penetration of religious and clinical proprieties); 'History', including 'Chinese Theories of,' elucidated by Philip J. Ivanhoe and 'Philosophy of', in which the deplorable return of Hegel to respectability, if never readability, is symptomised by Gordon Graham's haymaking swipe at *The Open Society and its Enemies*; and 'Linguistics', where his specific eminence licenses, perhaps, Chomsky's wide-ranging, *and* -raging, opinions. This relentless, if not accelerating, torrent of doubt and certainty suggests that philosophy, whatever it may be (or not be), has never had such a boom.

René Girard (improperly uncited, when Mircea Eliade is included) would be unsurprised to note that religion and philosophy are still *frères-ennemis*. Has he not reminded us that everything that man – the mimetic animal – thinks about is instinct with duplicity? The Catholic Church's recent 'apology' to the Jews again displays the *viavai continuo* of buck-passing, by accusing the Enlightenment of furnishing the warrant for genocide on which, in their turn, the enlightened read the signature of Christianity and hear the silence of the Pope. Must the same phenomena always admit different logics? Does the world keep changing, as Heracleitus declared, or does it never change, as Parmenides did, or both, as Plato proposed? The garrulous hell of the philosopher will surely be that of Jean-Paul Sartre, in whose *Huis Clos* the concluding imperative is 'Recommençons' and the only available company is other solipsists.

Can the way forward ever avoid also leading us back? Philosophers such as Heidegger have often sought to purge themselves of cant, or abort the nightmares which they have not scrupled to furnish, by seeking to retreat to the fork in the path where We All Went Wrong (in a similar regression, Alistair MacIntyre's *After Virtue* sees the Enlightenment's incoherent ethics as the fallout from the kind of exploded community which he, like his fellow neo-Thomists, imag-ines Aristotle to have commended). Was there ever, in fact, a time when societies lived by a single logic? Even the Spartans – Plato's ideal statesmen – had their nocturnal council, which does not argue a want of dissidence among the Equals. How clean of outside influ-ence were Heidegger's pre-Socratics? Did not the Ionians' alarming neighbours, the Persians – with their aristocratic cult of truth-telling – have more influence on early Greek 'science' than Germano-Hellenising chauvinism cared to acknowledge, or honour?

Syncretism is endemic in human thought. Retrieval and innovation beat a circular path: as Heracleitus said, mischievously (or would he have said it?), 'the road up and the road down are the same road'. Can any *retour aux sources* retrieve the unalloyed truth about Being, if there is any? Can even an encyclopaedia avoid *arrière-pensée*, and should it? The antiquity of language means that, as was said by Althusser (too gently handled by Alex Callinicos) and as Paul de Man (down the drain) agreed, there can no longer be any such thing as an innocent reading, or an innocent (as against a naïve) text. Blandness may be more proper to a work of reference than *parti pris*, but the price of uncritical tabulation is the re-gilding of tarnished reputations. I am not competent to judge the value of Teilhard de Chardin's scientifico-religious amalgam, but to omit reference to Peter Medawar's informed demolition is a serious flaw, as is the failure to mention Richard Webster (and Karen Horney) on Freud.

Is it significant that Leo Strauss is one of the few teachers seriously to exasperate his exegete here? Strauss 'outed', so to say, the usually hidden agenda of philosophers and gleefully revealed (*and* endorsed) their systematic tendency to encode their dangerously true thoughts so that only the initiated can share them. This 'élitism' elicits the usual boos from Shadia B. Drury, but how different is it from Berkeley's 'we ought to *think with the learned and speak with the vulgar*'?

An indelible aspect of the ambiguity of language is the duplicitous ambition of those who use it. Power as well as wisdom has been the regular target of philosophers. In its pursuit, they can be graded along a scale which runs up, or down, from Diogenes, Kierkegaard and Wittgenstein at one end to, say, Plato, Russell, Hegel and Heidegger at the other. The integrity of the former set was fortified by an *ascesis* which involved the renunciation of worldly power and comfort: the coin-clipping Diogenes in his vat, like Wittgenstein in his indoor deckchair, disdained fortune, though neither was indifferent to fame. However, when offered favours by Aristotle's most famous pupil, Diogenes asked only that Alexander the Great move out of his light. This anecdote, like the one which promises that he masturbated in public in order to draw cynical attention to the hypocrisy of others, is not mentioned in his decorous entry. There is less squeamishness in telling the story of Hypatia (AD 370–415) who combined 'exceptional' beauty with enough nerve to 'temper a love-sick student' by removing her bloody sanitary towel and throwing it at him with the words 'This is what you really want, young man, and it is no good'. This, we are told, rather surprisingly, 'agrees with other descriptions of her as "solemn" [!] and "virgin/unmarried" to the end'. Film

Studies (and *Eternal Return*) buffs will recall that Judy Holliday did something similarly philosophical when she threw her falsies at Darryl Zanuck, as she got out of his car, saying 'Take the damn things, you've been trying to get your hands on them all evening.'

If Wittgenstein agonised over supposed 'sins' which Diogenes might have flaunted, he renounced a fortune and wore even professorial robes with the air of someone who would have preferred sackcloth and ashes. For all their paraded humility, those in the ascetic tradition do not necessarily lack desire to impress, and reform, the world: the gnomic, aphoristic style to be found all the way from Heracleitus to the early Wittgenstein both intimidates and seduces, beckons and repudiates uninitiated tourists. The article on 'Ambiguity' here is dryly instructive on sentences of the order 'The girl hit the boy with a book', but it neglects, in an excess of caution, to speculate on the *usefulness*, as well as the logic, of ambiguity: the Delphic oracle contrived always to be right (at least until the Persians led the priestess to lose her balance) by, for famous instance, telling Croesus that if he attacked Cyrus he would 'destroy a great empire'. The riddle lies at the source of both poetry and philosophy (and its elucidation funds criticism); the obscurity of the oracle makes the journey to it, and the conclusions we draw, as enchanting as they are hazardous. The Sphinx warned of the dangers of insufficient wit, just as Plato did of the scandal of unduly loud laughter. How sweet, in the light of Ryle's view of him, in *Plato's Progress*, as a frustrated crowd-pleasing dramatist, that the latter was 'shadowed', as it were, by a comic poet of the same name whose stock in trade was elegant eroticism!

The element of *play* embedded in deep thought, the addiction to paradox and scandal, is not sufficiently remarked here. Leo Strauss did have a point when he alleged that Socrates/Plato had no convincing refutation of Thrasymachus and that the whole of *The Republic* can be read as a concealment of that fact. Rudiger Safranski is no less bold, in his new biography, in suggesting that Heidegger was (partly?) joking in his humourless accounts of *Dasein*, in which his stammering (and Nazi-mocking) brother, who was also his archivist, revealed the element of Dadaism.

Karl Marx accused earlier philosophers of describing the world which he proposed to change, but he knew very well that description *is* a way of changing it. Philosophers at the Plato/ Russell/Heidegger end of the axis have been less consistently loyal to disinterested speculation (a characteristic, D.H. Lawrence alleged, of Jews) than eager for literally leading parts in the world's game. Francis Bacon was not the first of them to discover, though one of the few to admit, that all ascent to power is by a winding stair, nor was he the last to take it. Paris was worth a mass to Henry IV, and philosophical autocracy a 'Sieg Heil' from Heidegger.

Disillusionment usually follows the tortuous climber's ambition: Plato did not find Dionysius II a satisfactory student and Heidegger, after his unbecoming (shall we say?) infatuation with Hitler was asked, quietly, by colleagues, 'Back from Syracuse?' By a nice coincidence, it was in Syracuse not only that Plato learned the difference between theory and *praxis*, but also where the dangers of combining abstract thought with practical politics led to the death of Archimedes. Like the Alexandrian (and Manhattan project) scientists, he willingly lent his genius to military matters. Having supposedly concentrated the sun's rays in order to set fire to the approaching Roman fleet, however, he affected to care more for triangles (a Roman sergeant felled him all the same). The link between other-worldly theories and their mundane application seems almost fortuitous (unless God is a mathematician, as Stephen Hawking seems to believe, or a dialectician, as Hegel did), but there appears to be no impermeable division between the sublime and the mundane.

Applied philosophers may first win their spurs by undertaking arduous and abstract work – *Principia Mathematica* is an egregious instance – but this can be used to certify a genius which is then held to be authoritative in fields where its logical warrant does not necessarily run. Hence Wittgenstein advised that certain of Russell's works should be bound in blue, and be obligatory reading, while others (on morals, politics, etc.) should be bound in red and put on the *Index Librorum Prohibitorum*. Plato was not the first philosopher to seek access to worldly power (Anaxagoras was to Pericles what Lindemann was to Churchill), but he was the first to propose a blueprint for government. (Pythagoras' communities were more modest and his ideas more homespun than normative). Affecting to despise Peitho, Plato introduced into philosophy a strand of tendentious duplicity which has bedevilled it ever since. The *gennaion pseudos* (however emolliently translated by his fans as 'the genealogical fiction') was a trick modified and appropriated by millennarian philosophers down the ages. Philosophy has regularly flirted with and sought to influence the princes who govern the world. How curious that the names of three of the most renowned pre-Socratics all began with Anax-, the Greek for 'king'!

The charisma of Plato and Aristotle, in whom all ancient wisdom seemed to be incorporated, meant that Athens became the other pole to Jerusalem in the evolution of Christianity: syncretism *and* affectations of doctrinal purity have been typical of Western thought. The want of innocence to which Althusser drew flashy attention has been both the virtue and the bane of the civilisation which has, it seems, now more or less conquered – or subverted – the world. From time to time, Savanarolan attempts have been made to purge society of its impurities but the genius of Europe is happily hybrid: it lacks one fundamental principle. Duplicity has been its natural style ever since it helped itself, with both hands, to the religious and philosophical language and practice of the eastern Mediterranean. What has seemed a flaw (to both Popes and positivists) has licensed a diversity as fruitful as it has, at times, been murderous. The Wars of Religion might have been avoided if there had been no Reformation, but who will claim that a single intellectual currency would not have impoverished thought? 'And', 'or', 'but', 'if' are the small words that sap all mental monoliths.

The comedy of philosophy is that its fire goes out unless certainty sparks scepticism. Its tragedy is that, again and again, philosophers – Plato, Hegel and Marx above all – have imagined that ultimate truths were available to them and that their keys could turn the lock of history. By consequence, what Auden (without irony at the time of its composition) called 'the necessary murder' became a genocidal duty. Man seeks both rigour, in order not to be misled, and liberty in order not to *be* led. Philosophers, once they leave the hermetically abstract redoubts of logic and mathematics (or the self-validating schemes of religion), are to be judged by the honesty with which they confront their limitations as well as by the ingenuity of their revisions of the human condition. Men (and an increasing number of women) go round and round in hermeneutic circles. This Encyclopaedia, grandiose but never definitive, testifies to both their nobility and their folly. Luckily, however, it can never offer the last word. *Recommençons!*

Puff and Its Pastry

The sweet difference between literary criticism and other critical texts is that the former can be made of the same stuff as its subject. Who will deny that Sainte-Beuve and Roland Barthes, Edmund Wilson and even Frank Leavis belonged to the medium on which they passed judgement? A painting or a film or a play may, explicitly or implicitly, criticise or pay homage to another painting, or play or film, but neither art nor film critics typically create art or make movies. Dramatic criticism may be a soliloquy; it is not theatre.

Literary criticism and its practice, on the other hand, actually converge in culminating works like *Ulysses* or in monumental pastiches such as *Possession*. Film critics, in particular, make little contribution to the cinema, even if they can intimidate or flatter filmmakers or, albeit rarely, recruit audiences. The original *Cahiers du Cinéma* pals progressed from affectations of theoretical detachment to a frank *politique des copains* (in which they advanced each other's directorial ambitions, in a sort of Young Boy Net), but the medium of film criticism, *per se*, is not film-making. If Pauline Kael had a brief, fruitless, experience as a studio executive, Ken Tynan, though he played to many galleries, never – it seems – wrote 'that play' or authored, as they say, a film.

What then is the purpose or achievement of film criticism? More specifically, why do we need or want to read Gilberto Perez's *critique-fleuve* of the cinema? Professor (of course) Perez began as an engineering student, but eventually, seduced by the 'taste of fame' and the fact that 'everyone on campus knew who [he] was' when he reviewed movies, adopted film buffdom as a career. He now conducts Film Studies at Sarah Lawrence and doubles as film critic of the *Yale Review*. Credentials, right?

His enduring love affair with cinema and *cine-crit.* is manifest as he drifts, paddles and punts down the long river of his own and others' opinions. Jean Renoir's *The River* is a confessed favourite of his and the languid, plotless progress of that masterpiece (it has always bored

Review of Gilberto Perez, *The Material Ghost* and Adrian Turner, *Robert Bolt*, in the *Times Literary Supplement*, 1998.

me as much as the rest of Renoir's acclaimed stuff) is echoed in an unhurried cruise down the stream of film history, from Murnau's silent classic, *Nosferatu*, to Antonioni's so-called trilogy.

There is something mildly perverse about spending much more time on *La Notte* and, especially, *The Eclipse* than on the peerless *L'Avventura*, but teases will be teases and an old trick in gaining fame as a critic is to play Canute to the tide. Perez, for controversial instance, tells us that Godard's *La Chinoise* was 'splendidly attentive', when in fact it was – as my favourite (Italian) producer used to say – 'of a tedium beyond'. To what it was 'attentive', the discursive Perez leaves us, for once, to imagine.

Didactic obligations require the author to drop many names, if few anchors. It is hard to distinguish the line – though intermittently informative to go with the drift – of his text. *Almost* honouring Jean-Luc Godard, Perez's discourse has a beginning, a muddle and an end. The muddle is in a clotted sediment of authorities and references, enthusiasms and pieties. It is clear that a course is being, or has been, *taught*; less certain that it is being purposefully steered. The intrusion of (once?) fashionable names – Lacan, Althusser, Heidegger, Kracauer, etc. – suggests that the professorial intent may have been to kindle his class's interest in deeper and more difficult subjects than Film Studies, by a process of inveigling allusion, but as *arguments* in print, these thick paragraphs amount to less than the sum of their parts; there are too many premises without conclusions and tautologies posing as insights. The most searching way, therefore, to remark on the best and the worst of what we have here is to look more closely at some not untypical fragments.

Early on, Perez cites André Bazin (*encore lui!*) when he claimed that 'photography affects us like a phenomenon in nature, like a flower or a snowflake'. Bazin, we are promised, thus laid himself open to

> the charge of 'naturalization' – taking as natural what is in fact cultural, a human construction – though he didn't say photography *was* a phenomenon in nature, only that it affects us that way. Precisely because it affects us that way photography is a prime instrument of naturalization.

The word 'precisely' here serves as the prelude to imprecision, if only because I cannot imagine being affected by a photograph, even *of* a flower or a snowflake, as if it *were* a flower or a snowflake. And even if this were to happen with visual phenomena, is it something remarkably new? Did not the fabled bird mistake the grapes that

Polygnotus had painted for real grapes? Do we not see a *trompe-l'oeil* Paolo Veronese coming in from the chase at the end of a corridor in the Villa Maser? The trouble with criticism which adopts the free associational method and turns citation and repetition into a form of validation is that only a hair's breadth divides the intelligent *aperçu* from a hank of *n'importe quoi*.

'If the city was natural to Aristotle,' we are next told, 'photography is natural to our civilization.' What does the conditional imply and how does the protasis relate to what follows? Aristotle's now trite point was that man was, by his nature, a city-dweller (a 'political animal', as we were taught). Does that mean the same thing as that cities are 'natural'? And, even if it does, how is the photographic image somehow in the same basket? If man were – truly? – said now to be a *televisual* animal, that would be another matter, since TV is of its nature fugitive; 'framing' is not its typical style. So TV is now 'natural' or 'naturalised' and what was the point of all this again?

Further on, as we glide between the banks of often impenetrable verbiage, our guide tells that, ever since 1933 at least, 'whether faked with back projection or shot on location, the place (in films) in most cases counts for little... Reality is as commonly attenuated, and as rarely confronted, in films now as it was then.' But in fact, surely, there are significant moments in film history (not forgetting the advancing 'real' train which sowed panic among the first credulous audiences) that were linked with the use of genuine locations: for that very reason, among others, *Open City* (Rossellini), *On The Town* (Kelly and Donen), *Naked City* (Dassin) and *On the Waterfront* (Kazan) were innovatory in their different categories. The care taken today over computer-generated images indicates that audiences are (presumed to be) demanding about the 'reality' even of what is faked or simulated.

Perez's enthusiasm for theory soon leads him into generalised aesthetic pronouncements. 'A narrative can go on and on' – much like a film critic – 'coming to an end at some point but even then potentially continuable; a painting is all there before us.' This is either banal or false; one can very well imagine a 'potential continuation' of, for example, Goya's firing squad; and his *Naked Maja is* a kind of continuation of the *Dressed Maja*, and vice versa if it comes to that. In *Los Desastres* we see a body being flung into a pit and find the image almost literally moving because we seem to hear the dead slap of the corpse hitting the bottom, even though it is not yet there. As against Perez's next generalisation, a literary narrative *can* be contained, for instance in a sonnet, which by definition cannot exceed its allotted lineage. None of this may be very important, but what is said recklessly, and with an air of erudition, requires challenge before its author certifies it by repetition, as Perez does again and again (how else?).

Among the cited sources is David Bordwell, who is said to promise that 'no purpose is served by assigning every film to a *deus absconditis* [*sic*]'. The pundit may be right about the necessity, or not, of an at least implied storyteller's point of view; it remains a shame that he learnt Latin at the same school as Gore Vidal. In larding the text with classical gravity, Perez offers us Auerbach on Homer: 'never is there a form left fragmentary or half-illuminated... never a glimpse of unplumbed depths' (trust a grandiose critic not to spare us the dreariest clichés). Is this true? It seems to me that the effect, if not the purpose, of Homeric similes is – *precisely*, as Perez would say – to relate the present war to the absent peace: it is often to aspects of bucolic rural life that the fighting is compared. The world back home is allusively but sharply depicted, though I cannot, I confess, recall an umplumbed depth.

Later on, Karl Marx is alleged to have been superficial in his appreciation of the 'eternal charm' of Greek art:

> Marx seems to have missed the way Greek art, as the revered ancestor of European civilization at a time of colonial expansion, served in its perceived supremacy the interests of European world supremacy. It was, as Marxists like to say, no accident that the Elgin marbles ended up in the British museum.

How do you like it? Marx missed little, in fact, and he was adverting to the unceasing, eternal *value* of Greek art, even in a world which had moved on from antiquity. When Perez speaks of 'perceived supremacy', does he imply that Greek art doesn't add up to much or that its value was exaggerated by capitalists and colonialists for some dark purpose which does not immediately present itself? And, of course, it *was* an accident, and quite a happy one, that the vilified Lord Elgin finally lost his marbles to the BM, since they might otherwise have found their way into a Turkish limekiln, as William St Clair indicates in his biography of his well-meaning lordship.

Much of what Perez would have us believe is close reading of the matter in hand is, in fact, a reading *into*, and a grotesquely far-fetched one at that. Take this (*please*, as the comedian said of his wife) concerning Renoir's *Partie de Campagne*:

From an imaginary plenitude, a Lacanian might say, we retreat here to the recognition of loss – loss of what was lost already, always already lost, the trees and the river that were never there on the screen... the Lacanian reading assumes that there was nothing there to begin with, that there can be nothing there. Taken literally, this is merely obvious: we never thought the river and the trees were actually there on the screen. Taken in its implications, it tells us that we can make no real connection with the material world around us, only an imaginary connection. Henriette (incarnated, as it happens, by a woman Lacan married) was deluded from the start... We are all deluded from the start if we seek freedom and tenderness in the world. Alienation in this view becomes something inalterable, all but metaphysical, not a social condition but a given of the human condition.

Etcetera, and plenty of it. Ignoble as it may be to say so, this passage and many, many more recall to me the despicable joke of the St John's Wood lady who answered the telephone with a genteel 'Hello' and to whom the anonymous obscene caller then spelt out what she really wanted him to come round and do to her. He did this in specific detail for half an hour, after which the lady said, 'All this you could tell from "Hello"?' The academic overloading of cinematic narratives with significances which never remotely occurred even to the most pretentious film-maker has become an 'artform' as implausible as the attempt of the ivy to grow taller than the tree.

The usefulness of Perez is more evident when he admires less known film-makers such as Jean-Marie Straub and Danièle Huillet, whose *History Lessons* sounds very interesting, though one may hope it will not prove as witlessly jejune as Sally Potter's much-praised *Tango Lessons*. Perez is also quite good on the Western, though he fails to follow up a hint from Henry James, of all people, who seems to have perceived the novel on which *The Virginian* is based as a veiled myth of homophilia. Isn't the final duel in Westerns a kind of erotic rendezvous in which at least one of the two men dies more than a little? More generally, it is only as one of them dies that manly men are licensed to embrace or express tenderness.

Where I warm, finally, to Perez is in his accurate appreciation of Antonioni; he does at least finish *en beauté* with an encomium on that unmatched artist, though he fails to remark that the best tribute to him is, perhaps (ah perhaps!), the Steiner sequences in *La Dolce Vita*, where Fellini 'criticises' and almost impersonates his rival in

unmocking parody. The bewildered anguish – the *visione straniata* – of
Marcello tells us more, more entertainingly and more touchingly,
about cinema than any curricular verbiage.

Adrian Turner's biography of *Robert Bolt* is a well-documented
cautionary tale about a once modest Midlands schoolteacher who
became first a West End playwright and then a very highly paid
screenwriter and, in the process, lost his wife, his children and,
perhaps, his genius. Bolt's best scripts were written for David Lean,
who was nothing but a great craftsman posing as an artist. It is
tempting to suppose that Bolt would have done something more
worthy of his talents had he not got mixed up with 'Hollywood'.

Despite Turner's catalogue of Bolt's degrading ascendancy in the
movies, one still wonders whether he did not, in fact, make the best
of himself. His dialogue was good, but it was often dignified by the
dignitaries, such as Sir Thomas More, who graced it in his costume
pieces. His more 'personal' work was rarely impressive: *Flowering
Cherry* was an enviable success, but was it a good play?

Self-revelation or self-criticism was never Bolt's style. When he had
a chance to direct his own film, *Lady Caroline Lamb*, he chose to
pastiche Lean and, in the process, proved only that, with the right
budget and backup, almost anyone can direct stodgy and uninventive
'classic' films with good parts for the usual British stalwarts. His
Byron, however, was Richard Chamberlain, who did not limp.

Turner catches the mood of, in particular, 1960s London with
uninfatuated percipience (the only manifest error, or misprint, is
when he calls Michael Bakewell 'Michael Blakewell'). Bolt was always
more John Braine's Joe Lampton, translated to showbiz, than he was
John Fowles's faustian Daniel Martin. A man of some wit, high
competence, and large ambition he received a good price for his soul;
when one looks at how scurvily he treated the majority of his wives,
his children and his old friends, it is not certain that he would have
had much other use for it.

There'll Always Be an English

Katharevousa is defined, in the *New Oxford Dictionary of English*, as 'a heavily archaized form of modern Greek used in traditional literary writing, as opposed to the form which is spoken and used in everyday writing (called demotic)'. If there is nothing wrong with this definition, it fails to emphasise (or should that now be emphasi*z*e?) that *Katharevousa* was deliberately confected, as Chambers does say, from ancient sources. Inaugurated in the wake of the liberation from the Turks, it was intended to dignify Greeks by their common use of a language purged of servile slackness.

This wilful recovery of antique Greek may have inspired the Israelis' unifying resurrection of Hebrew. *Katharevousa* was less successful, however, in homogenising Greece: having failed to supplant demotic, it created a schism between the official class of neo-Phanariots (whose documents had to be expressed in it) and those who lacked the competence, or opportunity, to learn its convoluted formalities. When the Colonels took power in 1967, they sought to disadvantage the Left by once again denying official places to anyone unversed in the artificial language.

The Jacobins' largely successful attempt to centralise power and to suppress regionalism by standardising French was probably the model for both Greece and Italy, where Sicilian remained a separate, often separatist idiom. As Theodore Zeldin has pointed out, even of those living in France little over a century ago, only 50 per cent had French as their first language. In the days of their insular hegemony, the English/British were able to smile at the more or (often) less successful attempts of European states to grace themselves with a single linguistic currency within their own borders. By contrast, Scots and Welsh and Irish were condemned to idiolectic parochialism if they did not subscribe to the dominant English style (and accent). Local obstinacy might be poetic (Hugh MacDiarmid is the emblematic instance), but it could not lead to the prosaic dividends of emulation (not to mention epulation, which Cassell, Collins and the

Review of *Collins English Dictionary*, the *New Oxford Dictionary of English*, the *Chambers Dictionary* and the *Cassell Concise Dictionary*, in the *Times Literary Supplement*, 1998.

ODE do not, but Chambers does). Other nations might have 'language problems' but the British came to see themselves as free speakers of a 'naturally' coherent tongue, which the *OED* collated but did not formally codify.

The King's English has changed a good deal since Osbern Bokenham first spoke in its favour in the mid-fifteenth century. However, the way the monarch presumably wished to express things, or to hear them expressed, set a steady theoretical standard for rectitude, even when the sovereign's own practical command of English was modified by alien provenance. An ability to use language subtly was the mark of the courtier; allusive artificiality tested the claims of the ambitious to mount the *cursus honorum* (not cited anywhere, though cursus, *tout court*, is there in Chambers). Although the English never had an official *Katharevousa*, those who spoke, and wrote, correctly could exclude the clumsy, in diction and in grammar, by the exercise of a discrimination which – *almost* by chance – fortified the ruling class and humiliated the unaspirated aspirant (those who dropped aitches were themselves apt to be dropped).

The English thus contrived a mandarin *argot*, which defined the well-spoken, without being vulnerable to precise definition. While social and political barriers were tricked out with unflagged pitfalls involving spelling and accent, women were, to some degree, exempt from their rigour, as they were from office and from access to bad – masculine – language. Byron's one-time mistress, Lady Oxford (whose children were known as the Harleian miscellany on account of their eclectic paternity), spelt with an insolent eccentricity which her aristocratic style alone distinguished from illiteracy.

If G.B. Shaw's desire to license her style of phonetic spelling can be construed as an addled attack on the ruling class's proprietorship of language, it could be argued that only with the rise of the bourgeoisie, and of the Arnoldian public schools designed to pump out the fathers of gentlemen by the imperial gallon, did English become standardised both in spelling and in pronunciation. By the time the empire was in its evening, grammars were among the first indoctrinating texts which schoolboys such as my eight-year-old self were handed. My little green book included, in an early chapter, instructions on the correct forms of deference when speaking to Ambassadors, Earls and Dukes (and their sons and daughters), Bishops, Archbishops, Judges, Mayors (Lord and common) and Members of the Royal Family. Diligence in verbal niceties was essential for those desiring preferment: good form was essential to content.

Until the 1960s, accuracy continued to be more impressive than originality. In the days when classicists still composed verses and proses, teachers of Latin and Greek did not expect us to coin phrases, but rather to retrieve and collate pertinent ones from respectably golden sources. T.S. Eliot's compositional piracies and his normative suspicion of 'the individual talent' were a metic's tribute to the self-effacing stylistic arrogance which he had so decidedly adopted. To be educated was to be less one's unbridled self; sincerity, like outspokenness, was not an art form.

Well, things change, innit? Having said that, we can hopefully achieve a blend of what's good and what's – I didn't say bad – *new* and... how about we agree on cool? Both the self-vaunting publicity and the editorial policy of the *New Oxford Dictionary of English* – which belongs, we are promised, to 'The World's Most Trusted Dictionaries' – struttingly endorse the classless demotic of post-hegemonic Brito-American chat, if you get me. Collins' 'Millennium Edition' of what has, it is claimed, been 'voted the world's best dictionary' takes the same low road. 'Usage' is, in both cases, determined by the voters' habits and not decreed by their betters.

The notion of rectitude is programmatically abandoned: so much for *Katharevousa*. Those who balk at 'very unique', for instance, are slightly rebuked in both Collins and *ODE* ('go with the flow' is their common advice), though Chambers' definition 'without a like' disdains debasement. Like some sighing, equivocal Jeeves (cited in *ODE*, but – unlike Jeez – not *chez* Cassell or Collins or Chambers), the *ODE* comments:

> Words like **unique** have a core sense but they often also have a secondary, less precise sense: in this case, the meaning 'very remarkable or unusual', as in a *really unique opportunity*. In its secondary sense, **unique** does not relate to an absolute concept, and so the use of submodifying adverbs is grammatically acceptable.

This dodges the vexed issue, since it appears to, but does not *quite*, license 'very unique': 'really – i.e. genuinely – unique' is not of a piece with 'very unique', is it?

In the same spirit, *ODE* promises that 'decimate' can (even should) now mean 'kill or destroy (a large proportion of)'. Although the root meaning is acknowledged afterwards, Collins' *first* definition is 'To destroy or kill a large proportion of'. Chambers is more correct, while Cassell offers a classic fudge, citing both 'meanings' as alternatives.

In other words, No Rules Rule, OK?

Happy? The Old Oligarch isn't; the O.O., with his obsolete pedantry, is putting it about – in one sense of that phrase – that the *New Oxford Mathematics*, when it comes out, is probably going to state that twice two doesn't *have* to be four, more four*ish*, because, well, it depends who's counting, and on whose fingers (and how about people who don't run to four digits, how are *they* going to feel? Fink about it!). The O.O. would like to know what the adverb 'grammatically' is doing in qualifying 'acceptable' when it comes to warranting what makes the language less precise, less geared to truthful declaration, less honest, less grammatical. Well, he would, wouldn't he? (Yes, Keeler, Christine, is *ODE* listed, but Rice-Davies, Mandy, is not; call that democratic?)

The O.O. – yeah, yeah, still wittering on – wonders how soon 'perjury' will be acceptably defined as 'a subjective way of telling the truth'. The suppression of irony (effective only by virtue of a common awareness of sources and nuances) and hence of all allusive accuracy will soon follow, he complains. Can literature survive the wilful evacuation of all meaning? OK, look, sorry to intrupt, but who says we – the people – need litricher? Bang on about it and there may well have to be a democratic referendum, innit? Meanwhile, George Orwell's 'Some Animals are more Equal than Others' is ceasing to be a joke, since 'more equal' too gets the Oxford/Collins nod. Orwell's contradictory slogan thus becomes an unparadoxical (you what?) explanation of, for instance, why transport policy does not envisage ministers legging it to the Commons and why some People (not necessarily better than the rest of us, but equaller) now find their names alphabetically ordered in reference books.

Byron wrote to Douglas Kinnaird from Venice wanting to know the latest gossip – who's in, who's out – in the London rogues' gallery. Today, he would hear that, for Oxford purposes, Jeeves is among the (small) fictional in-group, but Sam Weller ain't. As for *glitterati*, Amis *père et fils*, the sisters Drabble (as Dame Edna, not cited, might say 'Hands up anyone who *finished* reading *The Virgin in the Garden*') and the brothers Attenborough are among the chosen (by Collins too). The Lord A. is lauded for the movie of *Oh! What a Lovely War*, an anodyne travesty of Joan Littlewood's 1963 production and for *Shadowlands*, a clumping revision of a much better TV 'play'. Ms Littlewood is, in her turn, ambered for posterity, though defined by her early left-wing allegiance rather than by her mature devotion to the Baron Rothschild. The late Lindsay Anderson is included (though

If... was followed only by buts), but he is unaccompanied by his Oscar-winning chum from Free Cinema days, Tony Richardson. Cary Grant is there, but of the two credits cited, one is a forgettable movie called *Holiday* (1938). Gene Kelly is acknowledged to be a director and actor by Collins, but not by Oxford.

Neither Ken Tynan – the first man to deliver 'fuck' to our living rooms – nor Bernard Levin (whose pseudonym, Taper, was arguably – which is hopefully OK – the Junius *de nos jours*) makes the cut. Junius himself – one of the great polemicists in our language – is mentioned by Collins, but not Oxford, unlike Ms Brookner and David Lodge and Malcolm Bradbury (one good taxonomist clearly deserves another). When Jeffrey, Lord Archer is sanctified as a novelist, who shall complain at lacking a halo?

As for playwrights, there is room in the *ODE* for Stoppard, Pinter, Osborne and Wesker. 'Pinteresque' is defined by Collins, but not Oxford, though neither mentions the playwright's radio or screenplay work. Neither of the latter forms rates much attention; though Dennis Potter is in, Paddy Chayevsky, a much more important TV writer, is unmentioned in both volumes containing proper names.

As for those who share a surname, James, P.D. is in the *ODE*, but not Clive; Steiner, Rudolph, but not George; Hall, Radclyffe, but not Peter; Collins, Michael *and* Joan(!!), Burgess, A. and Burgess, Guy (wrongly stated to have been 'charged' with espionage). However, J.R. (Ewing) – the iconic TV anti-hero – is in the oubliette. Both Giscard d'Estaing and François Mitterrand *sont là*, perhaps more because they are difficult to spell than on account of their immortal deeds. Oxford's inclusion of Madonna, at the expense of Lady Antonia Fraser, is bound to cause widespread indignation.

There is a certain snobbism in the *ODE*'s sporting choices: Sir Stanley Matthews and Sir Tom Finney (shorn of his nickname, the Preston plumber) are on the wings, but Tommy Lawton is missing in the middle. Shilton is in goal, but his abbreviation to Shilts is omitted. As for Gazza, the lad will be understandably disappointed (he has, so to say, been 'gazundered'). In cricket, Hutton and Compton make it, but Edrich (with whom Denis will always be associated by those who watched them from the Large Mound Stand) does not. 'Wicket, sticky' gets a Collins but not an Oxonian explanation; 'dog, sticky' is not there, though Oz iz.

In malis partibus, there is little flinching. The F-word gets all the coverage its celebrity deserves, though some squeamishness can be detected in the *ODE*. 'Reaming' and 'rimming' are bravely defined, but 'butt-fucking' is left in the dark, as is 'fist-fucking'. The latter term may well be a pleonasm, since 'fuck' itself is possibly derived from 'an Indo-European root meaning "strike", shared by Latin *pugnus*, "fist".' Thus the Andrea Dworkinian view of male sexuality as essentially an assault gets radical backing. The *ODE* accurately defines 'Short-arm' as '... a blow or throw executed with the arm not fully extended', but – although American usage includes 'pooper scooper' – no account is offered of 'short-arms inspection', a US army term for a genital examination for VD. The black provenance of 'mother-fucker' is tactfully ignored everywhere; 'pizza' is said generally to be 'of Italian origin', where Neapolitan is more accurate. (Some scholars say that Aeneas and his companions ate pizza, thus fulfilling the prophecy that they would one day 'eat the tables at which they fed'.) Its etymology is said, by Cassell, to be the feminine of *pinceus*, by Collins to be *piceus*.

Is the pursuit of the American language, and market, necessary to Oxford's trusty activities? The minting of catchy neologisms is so industrious in the US that tabulation seems impossible, especially when coinage and obsolescence can be almost simultaneous (how long will 'Monicagate' be current?). What logic omits 'squaresville' – a 1956 term for a boring place – and retains 'dullsville', which is questionably said to be adjectival? The *locus classicus* is *The Facts of Life* (1960), a movie in which Bob Hope falls illicitly in love with Lucille Ball, while on a weekend trip. Later a friend asks him (I quote from memory): 'What was it like up there all alone with her? Dullsville?' As for 'technopaegnia', surely an everyday term in literary theory, it is not to be found in any of the volumes under review. Diabolical, right?

In literary (as opposed to fashionable) matters, the Oxford touch is uneasy. Vladimir Nabokov is duly cited, and 'Lolita n.' is attributed to him, but 'nymphet', although dated from the 1950s, has no source reference in Lolita ('nympha(e)', incidentally, is omitted by *ODE* but accessible in the three C's). The *ODE*/Collins definition of 'Lolita', as 'sexually precocious' and of nymphet as 'sexually mature young girl' are both surely wide of the mark. It was Lolita's pre-pubescent immaturity which excited the unmentionable Humbert Humbert.

In the prevailing all-shall-have-prizes climate of English literary life, it is fair to say that all these dictionaries have their merits: Chambers and Cassells are both compendious and, as promised, concise as well as clear for crosswords and Scrabble; Collins is plumply thorough without *quite* being overweight. As for the *ODE*, it is, no doubt, a very modern volume, but I did sometimes see its editor as Ludovico Manin, the last sad, impotent Doge of Venice, who signified his enforced resignation from authority by throwing his ducal hat into the Adriatic. A dictionary of noble provenance which defers systematically to admass, journalistic usage, even when it unhinges the logic of the language, and disdains the humane refinement which derives from nuance, may still have its guide-book charm, as Venice does, but by sorta endorsing whatever might, in another time, have discountenanced the lazy or rebuked the vulgar, the *ODE* risks betraying the tradition to which it affects to belong. In a recent novel, Ian McEwan (absent here) quotes Stendhal: 'Le mauvais goût mène aux crimes'. See what I'm getting at?

Perhaps each of these variously useful, programmatically po-faced volumes can best be attacked, and defended, in the light of Ambrose Bierce's (1906) definition of 'Dictionary', in his *The Enlarged Devil's Dictionary*:

A malevolent literary device for cramping the growth of a language and making it hard and inelastic. The present dictionary, however, is one of the most useful... ever produced. It is designed to be a compendium of everything that is known up to date of its completion, and will drive a screw, repair a red wagon or apply for divorce. It is a good substitute for measles, and will make rats come out of their holes to die. It is a dead shot for worms, and children cry for it.

Better Even than the Book?

The novelist and the screenwriter run on parallel lines which sometimes meet at the bank. Even when they inhabit a single body, the novelist's persona has the better-things-to-do air; the screenwriter's usually gets a bigger smile from the manager. If 'Literature good; movies bad' is a Manichean distinction few critics have challenged, the cinema has influenced the Century's Classics more than is routinely acknowledged: Eliot's *The Waste Land* is a montage, owing as much to Eisenstein as to the Upanishads. Dos Passos' *Manhattan Transfer* and his *USA* trilogy, like his admirer Sartre's *The Reprieve*, are full of stylish *clins d'oeil* at Hollywood. In Our Time, the movies have done as much for fiction as fiction has for the movies. Discuss.

What about those awful people though? Doesn't the callous treatment of Scott Fitzgerald, in his last, Californian years, prove that the moguls are heartless cigar-smoking carnivores? Well, they endured and pampered Scott more lastingly than the magazine editors who fawned on and then dumped him. *The Last Tycoon* is as much a tribute to Irving Thalberg as the Pat Hobey stories are the *Tristia* of the hack whom their author chose to become. It remains true, however, that it is advisable, very, to have a world (or at least a roof) elsewhere before delivering oneself into the honey/money trap of The Coast.

Even if screenwriting is a degenerate activity, it requires a certain skill. Thirty-something years ago, when Penelope Mortimer was reviewing films for *The Observer*, she alleged that my script for Schlesinger's *Far From the Madding Crowd* was nothing but a copy-out from Hardy. Had it been, the movie would have run for at least fifteen hours. In fact, I had, I thought, done quite an artful (certainly arduous) job of editing, abridging and supplementing, but there we are: critics are pricks against whom we must never kick.

A few weeks after Penelope had publicly put me down, she phoned to say that she had been asked to write a movie, based on her own novel, by 'dear Kenny Hyman', one of the legion of American producers then winging into swinging London. She had no idea what to do, so – if I wasn't too busy – could she come round and have me

Review of John Irving, *My Movie Business*, in *The Spectator*, 1998.

give her a few pointers? I told her to save herself the taxi fare: didn't she remember that all she had to do was copy out her prose as stage directions and her dialogue in the standard dramatic format and then stand back and wait for the golden rain? 'Oh Freddie!' she said.

One of the oldest of Hollywood's chestnuts is about the Polish actress who thought she could advance her career by – as the workplace jargon puts it – fucking the writer. Why is this a joke? Because the director alone is the pantocrator from whom all blessings, and castings, flow. Control rests more with him than with the once powerful producer, whose decline from commanding authority began with the fracture of the studio system.

Although there is no evidence that John Irving entertained any actresses during the making of *The Cider House Rules*, the pronominal adjective in his title, *My Movie Business*, indicates how much clout he managed to retain, including approval of cast and director (Lasse Hallstrom). Even for a best-selling writer, however, there was no unlaborious road from conception to delivery. This brief memoir is a tale of prolonged frustration before eventual fulfilment. It took thirteen years to get his picture made. Such persistence proves that the lure of the movies is more than financial.

Irving's *violon d'Ingres* is wrestling. What better preparation for the gouging and arm-twisting which goes under the name of show-business? I was prepared for a no-holds-barred account of studio interference and directorial two-facedness by an author totally prepared to go to the mat, even with Harvey Weinstein. Alas, and congratulations, everything seems to have gone so nicely that there were no villains; the world according to Irving is as cosy with charmers as Garp's.

Before scripting *Cider House*, Irving served a quite protracted novitiate under a number of famous tutors, including the great George Roy Hill and (in 1969) Irving Kershner, later to be the director of *The Empire Strikes Back*, with whom our author worked on an unfilmed version of his first novel, *Setting the Bears Free* (I can wait, I can wait). Irving's account of Kersh as 'a wild man with a nonstop imagination and boundless energy' is, like most of his prose, more platitudinous than the case deserves.

In 1967, Kersh and Stanley Donen and I were conscripted, by 20th Century Fox, to a PR exercise in which the 'college editors' of America were invited to meet the company's current film-makers. Although they preceded the now common studio policy of favouring 'no-brainers', the late 1960s saw the height (identical with the nadir) of corporate America's panicky deference to the Next Generation. One of the juvenile editorial upstarts, flown in at Fox's expense, yelled that 20th Century Fox should build a 'bridge' between the company and 'us, the youth of America'. Darryl Zanuck indicated to Kersh to field this non-negotiable demand. Kersh stood up and said, 'You don't get no fuckin' bridge. We swam. You swim.'

The movies are always a business, often a sport, and only occasionally an art, though you might never guess it from the just-back-from-Parnassus affectations of ranking *auteurs* or from the all-kneel commandments of their executive entourages. John Irving's privileged standing during the production of his movie was due more to the belief that, as a best-selling novelist, he had the secret of What People Want, and could deliver it, than to any deference to literature.

How suitable Irving's best-sellers are for screen adaptation remains uncertain. He recalls Tony Richardson, who directed *The Hotel New Hampshire*, with obituary admiration for the madcap eccentricities of a Limey on the lam, but he is too polite (or too misty-eyed) to admit that the result was catastrophic. The want of a clear narrative thrust (vital for movies) is inherent in Irving's winsome fiction. His novels tend to be sprawlingly Dickensian, lavish with lovable roguishnesss and plausible improbabilities. *David Copperfield/Augie March* marches on, and on, exhaustively life-loving and on the side of the angels, as long as their faces are dirty enough.

My Movie Business is a marshmallow easily consumed. It also sticks to teeth which would relish something more substantial. The text is roguishly plumped out with a preambling family memoir, featuring Irving's Most Unforgettable Character, a philanthropic gynaecologist grandfather. This legendary New England medico aborted unfortunate pregnant girls, at a time when such activities were as illegal as they were, in his case, charitable. In the movie of *The Cider House Rules*, Michael Caine plays this New England maverick who was not above writing raunchy (lovably anti-Semitic) verses. Among the medical fraternity, these acquired the canonic standing enjoyed by ''Twas on the Good Ship Venus' among rugger players.

Unfortunately, the star names – Paul Newman and others – who drift through Irving's narrative, *always* conduct themselves with numbing decorum; no friction, no sparks. Irving writes and rewrites, in compliance with the rules of the movie game, but he never proves that he is aware of how film dialogue differs from the novelist's. He supplies long instances of his versions and revisions, but the indented chat is always (supposedly) *dramatic* and cute, never startling or emblematic. Has he mastered the technique well enough to be instructive? Irving seems to think that it was enough to 'track' and compress his novel. He says early on, 'The passage of time, which is so important in all my novels, is not easily captured in a film.' But isn't it an essential aspect of the screenwriter's skill to manage time, preferably without those wearisomely frequent 'cards' which read 'Six months later'? *Citizen Kane* and *Jules et Jim* prove that time present and time past presented can be fused in movies, without awkwardness (even the cumbrous *Doctor Zhivago* does it quite well). Was Irving doing the movies too much of a favour by hanging in there? His memoir's sucrose blandness cannot quite mask a smug conceit which takes it for granted that we love his work as uncritically as the author does himself.

Being Himself

One of the classic post-war jokes concerns variety agent Harry Jacobs telling theatre-owner Abie Cohen about this fantastic new act: he walks the tightrope, juggles eighteen plates, twelve flaming brands and a set of bowling-pins and at the same time sings 'Yankee Doodle Dandy'. Abie is fired up to book him. 'What's his name?' 'Adolf Hitler.' 'Adolf Hitler? Not the *same* Adolf Hitler?' 'So?' Abie goes crazy: how can Harry Jacobs of all people represent Adolf Hitler? 'Abie, Abie,' Harry says, 'so he made one mistake.'

Heidegger is the philosopher who, his defenders maintain, also made one mistake. In 1933 he joined the Nazi party and gave a fervently Hitlerian inaugural speech when appointed rector of Freiberg University. He also introduced the Führer-principle into academic life ('Sieg Heil' became his greeting) and abandoned his Jewish friends, including his mentor Edmund Husserl, to whom he had dedicated his great work *Time and Being*. The dedication was subsequently and ignobly effaced and he did not attend Husserl's funeral in 1938, unlike the very few members of 'the faculty of the decent', colleagues who had retained a sense of honour and independence.

Heidegger would claim, after the war, that he had been ashamed of the infatuation with Nazism which had led him to greet Hitler as the man of destiny, just as Hegel had greeted Napoleon. Hitler, he drooled, had 'beautiful hands'; he never noticed, still less deplored, the blood on them. He would always deny that he had been an anti-Semite (though he referred to previously esteemed colleagues as, for instance, 'the Jew Fraenkel') and it was true that Hannah Arendt had been, and probably remained, the (illicit) love of his life. His wife, Elfride, was a thorough-going Nazi to the very end, though she later became reconciled, after a fashion, with Hannah. As Hugo Ott reported, and Rudiger Safranski does not, there was more than a hint of anti-Semitism in the Heideggers asking Arendt to help sell his manuscripts in the America he had always denounced. Jews got good prices for things, they said. Nice people.

If he did indeed withdraw into the aloof study of early Greek

Review of Rudiger Safranski, *Martin Heidegger*, trans. Ewald Osers, in the *Sunday Times*, 1998.

philosophy, as Hitler's war became a disaster, Heidegger never resigned from the Party. His indignation against the Nazis seems to have been greatest when, at the very end of the war, in his late fifties, he was conscripted to defend the régime for which he had been so militant.

He may have been embarrassed after 1945; he was never apologetic. However, so mesmerising was his verbose jugglery, and so insolent his self-pity, that – after a brief period of disgrace, during which he suffered the hell of *almost* having his library confiscated – he emerged into mature academic eminence as the leading 'existential' philosopher in renascent Europe: he became Jean-Paul Sartre's atheistic godfather and the sorcerer from whom apprentices of the Left acquired their cult of 'authenticity'.

Heidegger was born into lower-middle-class Catholicism in 1889 and, as a clever scholar, seemed bound for an academic career within the Church. By 1914, however, his doubts (and a failure to achieve quick promotion) led him to the atheism which was to be typical of his philosophy of 'Being', from which Sartrean existentialism derived. He was briefly and reluctantly in the army at the end of the Great War and, like Hitler, rose to be a corporal. The latter was a decorated front-line soldier, however, and Heidegger an unendangered meteorologist. He was always to be very alert to the way the wind was blowing.

It is not necessarily relevant to the merits of a man's abilities whether or not he is nice. We do not ask of a brilliant brain surgeon whether he cheats at cards (unless we are to play cards with him). In Heidegger's case, however, it is hard to distinguish the man himself from his skills; what he was good at was mystification and the cult of his own ideas. His 'philosophy' is inseparable from his incantatory method of advancing it. The inspirational guru and the enthusiast for tyranny co-exist in the same being.

The most plausible defence of Heidegger argues for his genius in the critical reading of other philosophers, of poets (Hölderlin, in particular) and of 'the Greeks'. There may be justice in these claims, although I suspect that he misread the nature, origins and significance of what he called 'Greek theatre', which was, of course, an invention of the Athenians and played a crucial part in the evolution of the kind of open society which Heidegger scorned and feared.

As a 'moralist', Heidegger preached against all systematic and objective thought; he said of science that, because of its objectivity, it 'cannot think'. With him, the great truths (his own) were incapable of verification; they were spun out of solipsistic intuitional verbosity (he once wrote 150 pages on the subject of boredom and the way that it alerted one to the Being of Nothing). His morality involved our recognising man's need consciously to re-invent himself and his values. By being aware of our individual destiny of living-towards-death, we must learn to jettison conventional morality and do *our* right thing even if this cannot be defined or identified.

Authenticity (a key term) involved rejecting the 'They' in human society. 'They' were the crass majority, in which 'Everyone is the other, and no one is himself'. The free man liberated himself into genuine Being. The term 'Being' recurs constantly, almost neurotically, in Heidegger. Sometimes it implies what existed before God: 'Being is the trembling of Godding'. Sometimes Being is a force that resembles God, but without moral qualities or any capacity for love or forgiveness. Success proves that the force was with you; hence Hitler's failing was failure. Then again 'Being has nothing about it… Being is nothing one can hold onto.' Got it? Then you haven't.

Under Hitler, Heidegger altered the solipsistic message of his masterpiece, *Time and Being*, and asserted that 'What is important is the We-ourselves… the authentic We is the nation that asserts itself as one man… a National whole, therefore, is a man on the large scale.' How do you like it?

Rudiger Safranski's huge biography lacks the aggressive vigour of Hugo Ott's studies of Heidegger's conceited opportunism and moral slipperiness, but it is a generally noble attempt at an overview of German philosophy and, as far as that is possible, combines rigour with readability. One of its rare wild speculations is that Heidegger's whole philosophical edifice based on *Dasein* (Being) was a kind of straight-faced joke, deriving from the larky nihilistic Dadaism. Heidegger's overtly anti-Nazi brother stammered and referred – revealingly? – to '*Da-da-dasein*'.

The only mistake (misprint?) I spotted was in dating the Eichmann trial to 1951, when it took place in 1961. As for Heidegger's 'logic', one either accepts it on its own terms or is at a loss to understand what its appeal or value can possibly be. Safranski gives us everything we need to know, except for what might interest us most: an account of the psychic constitution of a thinker with the mental equipment of a genius and the moral grandeur of a rat.

Bliss, Was It?

For the Emperor Hadrian, all roads led from Rome. He was as compulsively centrifugal as Pope John-Paul II. Publius Aelius Hadrianus was, in many respects, an exemplary *princeps*: between AD 117 and 138, he established stability in the empire, both internally and on the fractious frontiers. His famous wall, confirming Scottish independence, was one of a series of thus-far-and-no-further statements of Roman intentions. He instituted professional magistrates, which partly emancipated Roman justice from politics. He created a scrupulous network of paid civil servants. It was not his fault that it could be no more efficient than the available communications system (fax machines might have made all the difference) and eventually degenerated into sclerotically centralised bureaucracy.

Himself of Spanish birth, Hadrian introduced non-Italians to the consulship and to the senate. If he imposed strict discipline on an army which, thanks to his policies, enjoyed long periods of peace, he also demanded quality control for weapons-manufacturers, promoted rankers and showed paternal concern for veterans. Yet his renunciation of many of Trajan's juiciest conquests – they were too risky and expensive to police – was not as popular as it was prudent; it limited the legions' opportunities for booty and perks. His preference for negotiation with barbarian kings, rather than whacking them, gave him the reputation for wimpishness rather than for being a second Augustus, which was his not unwarranted ambition.

Hadrian loved Greek culture. Soon unaffectionately nicknamed 'Graeculus' (the little Greek) by *la toute Rome*, he founded or embellished many cities in the eastern provinces (Pliny credited him with the *nitor*, glitter, of his epoch). His amateur passion for architecture led him, despite a sceptical temper, to complete the enormous temple of Zeus in Athens and to sponsor the innovative Pantheon in Rome. Having commissioned what is now the Castel San' Angelo as his tomb, he composed an epitaph for himself which begins 'animula vagula blandula...' (Little soul, little wanderer, little charmer), which

Review of Anthony R. Birley, *Hadrian* and Elizabeth Speller, *Following Hadrian*, in the *Sunday Times*, 1997, 2002.

may have been more than a little too self-pityingly whimsical for Roman tastes.

Edward Gibbon famously remarked 'If a man were to fix the period in the history of the world, during which the human race was most happy and prosperous, he would, without hesitation, name that which elapsed from the death of Domitian to the accession of Commodus.' Hadrian's principate lay squarely within that blissful bracket (from AD 98 to 180) and laid the foundations for what followed. Yet the historian Cassius Dio declared that Hadrian was 'hated by the people, in spite of his generally excellent rule, on account of the murders he committed at the beginning and at the end of his reign, for they were unjust and impious'.

Hadrian was also hated by the Jews ('May his bones rot', the Talmud repeatedly requests). He both provoked the Judaean rebellion under Bar-Kokhba, by banning the barbarous practice of circumcision, and put it down with draconian ruthlessness. After slaughtering half a million Jews, the Romans eradicated Jerusalem from the imperial map and called it, in celebration of the emperor's middle name, Aelia Capitolina, which did not catch on. This ruinous spasm of nationalism on the part of the Jews was crucial, if not providential, when it came to the triumph of Christianity. Although the emperor was not tender with Christians, their *attentiste* meekness exempted them from anathema and allowed them, in due course, to inherit the Roman world.

Hadrian's wife, Sabina, detested him and he her, though she often travelled with him. She was not above suspicions of having found erotic, probably lesbian, consolation *en route*. However, it was hardly her fault that she failed to supply her husband with an heir; he preferred boys. Antinous, a Bithynian of rare beauty, was the love of his life. If the Romans did not regard pederasty with the same tolerance, let alone enthusiasm, as sophisticated Greeks, they were even more embarrassed by the unmanly lamentation in which Hadrian indulged when Antinous was drowned in the Nile after one of their many hunting expeditions.

Those 'early murders' had been of four consulars, men of distinction. They included Avidius Nigrinus, who had hoped to succeed Trajan. The newly empurpled emperor was still abroad when the Roman senate fawningly and shamelessly condemned the four 'conspirators' to death. Hadrian claimed, on his return, that the executions had not had his approval.

Although previous emperors had not been reluctant to proscribe those whose vices, or virtues, were too manifest for comfort, Hadrian's now blood-stained *arrivisme* laid him open to sustained obloquy, despite prompt measures to secure popularity. These included a massive remission of taxes which (intentionally or not) reflated the Roman economy and hence created the standard of life for which Gibbon gave the emperor more credit than his contemporaries, who included the sarcastic and feline historian Cornelius Tacitus.

Anthony R. Birley's scholarly, if unTacitean, biography is the first full-length study for over seventy years, though he acknowledges that Marguerite Yourcenar's novel *The Memoirs of Hadrian*, was a brilliantly fanciful reconstruction of his inner life. Yourcenar dwelt on Antinous's drowning, which Birley also analyses with sourced thoroughness. It happened in 130, when Hadrian was already tubercular and suffered from dropsy. Some Egyptian guru may well have suggested that the superstitious emperor could be rejuvenated by the voluntary sacrifice of a young man. The myth of the resurrection of the dying god Osiris, who was also drowned in the Nile, warranted that the trick could work and may have impelled Antinous to offer himself.

Hadrian's favourite was now twenty years old. What had been acceptable, at least to Greeks, when he was a youth would become scandalous, for both parties, if it continued into the beloved's manhood. Since the lovers had come to the end of the road, what would cap their passion more handsomely than such a sacrifice? Antinous' prompt deification was intended to prove than he was not guilty of the sacrilege of suicide. But if the pliant Greeks accepted their new god, grudging Romans merely repeated the old rumours. Hadrian shaved off his beard, as if to prove that he had indeed grown younger, but his illness persisted and his unpopularity grew.

On returning to Rome, he became morbidly paranoid, like so many tyrants. 'Unjustly and impiously', he now obliged Servianus, a venerable man nearing ninety, to commit suicide for supposedly plotting against him. The latter prayed to the gods 'May Hadrian long for death but be unable to die'. Within quite a short time, his prayer was answered. In terminal agony, Hadrian asked his adopted son and designated successor to stab him to death. The piously callous Antoninus refused to be a parricide. Hadrian's suspicious nature, no less than his sense of duty, left him utterly alone. The most impermeable of his walls was the one he built around himself.

Elizabeth Speller has the nerve to tread in distinguished footprints.

Birley's biography is scholarly and thoroughly sourced; Yourcenar's *Memoirs of Hadrian* – which ghosts the emperor's own lost autobiography – is a masterpiece. Speller challenges both by interleaving her somewhat academic account of Hadrian's peregrinations with the fictitious journal of Julia Balbilla, the companion and solace of Hadrian's increasingly bitter, childless empress Sabina.

Known as the Roman Sappho, a few of Julia's verses – in Aeolic Greek – do survive; her prose, however, is unmistakably Speller's. *Following Hadrian* is in part a nice travel book, nicely achieved. Abridging political and diplomatic history, Speller concentrates on Hadrian's very grand touring – there were sometimes eight thousand people in his suite – and on his infatuation with Antinous.

The ancient attitude to homosexuality was never one of unmitigated tolerance. Romans took their pleasures without apology, but they made no mystique of 'spiritual' bonding, as Plato did. Even Athenian orators jeered at anyone suspected of taking the passive, penetrated role, especially once their beards began to grow. Antinous is said to have soaked his face in milk to keep it soft and, he hoped, beardless.

Though she tells us that he was the first emperor to wear a beard, in the Greek style, Speller does not mention that, after Antinous' death, Hadrian shaved his face, perhaps in the hope that he had acquired the youth of his lost love.

Hadrian's grief was as genuine as it may have been guilty. He even persuaded himself that he had observed a new star in the sky, which proved Antinous' ascent into heaven. The same star (a nova?) may well have led Bar-Kokhba to unleash the insurrection which resulted in Hadrian's near-extermination of the Jews. Speller sees the emperor's untypical ruthlessness as evidence both of his desolation and of his Greek 'anti-Semitism'. In fact, the Greeks were commonly anti anyone who was not Greek; they certainly had less love for the Romans than Hadrian had for them. When did ancient conquerors need 'prejudices' to sharpen their swords?

Speller is at her best in describing Hadrian's restless progress through the Fertile Crescent and into Egypt where, emulating Alexander the Great, he sought confirmation of the divinity which the Athenians had already wished on him. However, she dwells with more intuition than substance on the possibly sado-masochistic relationship between emperor and favourite. Anyone with old-fashioned chalk on his sleeve would point out that the Greek god was called Dionysus, not 'Dionysius', and that Alexander the Great's lost love was Hephaestion, not Hephaeston.

Nor would my Fifth Form master allow Speller to get away with telling us that Julius Caesar was 'emperor'. And why does she fail to explain that his alleged homosexuality was a diplomatic (and youthful) concession to the king of Bythinia, not a matter of appetite? His soldiers may have mocked him, affectionately, as 'the Queen of Bythinia' (where Antinous came from), but that was in the course of a Triumph, when insults could be thrown like bouquets. Julius was more deservedly celebrated as 'the bald-headed adulterer'. Hence the straight-faced gall of his demand that his wife be 'above suspicion'.

Speller is informative, but eclectic in describing Hadrian's travels. She never mentions his contributions to the (still extant) city of Aphrodisias, or the Vale of Tempe, which – like Canopus in Egypt – he reproduced in the 'villa' (more like a small town) which he built, outside Rome, for his retirement. Its delightful ruins prove that Tivoli was a sort of Hadrianic theme park. It reminded the ailing, woebegone emperor of the gorgeous east he had abandoned. Its underground passages enabled slaves to service, without intruding on, the emperor's lonely, and eventually agonised, nostalgia.

A Story and Its Ghost

When Demetrios the Besieger marched into Athens, the citizens offered him divine honours, on the grounds that he could do them more good than any conventional god. The published praise now gushed over famous men, and infamous women, is our acknowledgment that Epicurus was right: while of the gods we know nothing (and if they are lucky they know less of us), there remain those here below who can supply better Edens than the Lord, and with more varied refreshment and entertainment. Walt Disney's own Anaheim Disneyland was the first of such paradisaical spreads. Now, all over the globe, there are similar, but extended, welcomes for every Adam and every Eve, accompanied by all their little Cains and Abels (still the best of pals, but watch your brother's eye with the end of that flagpole, junior).

Michael Eisner is now incontestably *primus inter pares* of the world according to Walt. He declares himself a collegial man, always amazed by malice, embarrassed by in-fighting, genuinely saddened by non-team players. He likes to hear another man's point of view; and always hears him out, sometimes right out. Those who demand equal parity too loudly can find themselves falling from morn till dewy eve. Unlike the Miltonic Lucifer, however, Jeffrey Katzenberg and Mike Ovitz, both one-time angels, had soft landings on cushions of cash, though only the former subsequently made profitable use of it. The mirror on his wall still tells Eisner that he is a good guy, *and* god.

More, he is *such* a team man that he has not even written his own autobiography. If he whistles while he works, Tony Schwartz is one of those who come running. Today the liveliest of living men can have ghosts *before* they die. Now an invaluable friend, experienced wordsmith Schwartz has, I suspect, intruded toney words like 'ameliorator' (to describe young Michael's kiss-it-better mother). One of Eisner's most valued associates, Howard Ashman (Oscar winner for the song in *The Little Mermaid*), constituted himself the chief of Disney's 'simplicity police'. It's a shame he did not survive Aids to truncheon the verbiage which keeps the subject of this book Samuel Smilesing

Review of Michael Eisner, with Tony Schwartz, *Work in Progress*, in *The Spectator*, 1999.

through (or did Ashman's successor, Simpler Simon, break the door down to *improve* it with a bunch of new clichés?).

Aside from the hope of finding an overlooked nugget of mordant detail or a slightly uncensored confession, the only reason for reading this kind of stuff is, I suppose, the chance that it contains a formula for effortless ascent to the gilded company of those who get to play golf with Bill Gates or have the clout to ask George Bush, when president, to get François Mitterrand to visit Euro-Disney (emended to Disneyland Paris when the Euro-bait did not hook the punters).

Sulky old *littérateur* Mitterrand had refused all earlier invitations ('It is not my cup of tea,' he supposedly said, a simplicity-police translation – one must guess – of 'Ce n'est pas mon potage de Cresson'). President Bush got him to change his mind and even, it is alleged, told him 'Smile, François,' when the cameras were clicking. He did. So much for the great days of Yanks Go Home, not to mention *au revoir* to the cultural autonomy of France (Britain, being smart, doesn't even *pretend* to be disgusted by cultural pollution from torrents of tosh). In a charming example of *ignoratio elenchi*, Eisner refers to all this garbage as 'intellectual property', though he has to concede that it can contain its measure of 'pablum' (didn't feature on the spellcheck, Tony? So what? Nor does curriclum. Whack it in!).

The story of the near-catastrophe of Disneyland Paris is the most interesting section here. Eisner does not *quite* confess that he made, still less licensed, grievous miscalculations, but he clearly kept his head when revenues plummeted and banks threatened bankruptcy. Would he still be wearing it otherwise?

At the height of that crisis – it can now be told – I happened to be lunching with Stanley Donen at a terrace table at the Locanda Veneta in Los Angeles (inside is for customers who had to spell their names when they called for reservations). Jeffrey Katzenberg – then still very much Eisner's indispensable legate – was working the room and came to salute Stanley, who was just back from visiting Tokyo with mega-Michael Jackson (this was before Certain Allegations minified him). Jackson, Donen told us, so loved Disneyland Tokyo that he arranged to visit it at night after it closed: the only way to avoid being mobbed by grockles. All the rides and shops were kept fully manned and womanned during his and Stanley's dual solo excursion. When I said, 'Might have been easier for them just to fly to Paris. There's nobody there even when it's open to the public', Katzenberg showed me some expensive teeth, but I couldn't call it a smile. Lesson of the day: not every executive riding on a loser enjoys a joke.

Gods may or may not exist. Like big Demetrios, Eisner does. Proof? Loss soon became success (profit). The Disney Organisation proved to be a *Titanic* that can hit icebergs and sail on, stronger, more confident, with scarcely a lurch violent enough to spill a fun-lover's malted. Eisner had enough leverage to make European banks think thrice (they were going to lose more of their own money than Disney's). He also had the savvy both to lower prices at the hotels and to play down the evangelical Americanism. No kind of alcohol was ever previously on sale in Disneylands (from Orlando to Anaheim to Tokyo, you either overdose on sugar or you go hungry), but the French appetite was said to be incorrigible, so the edict went forth that the taboo could be broken.

In fact, fewer frogs than *prévus* went to Marne-la-Vallée in order to have a *verre*, or even a *demi*, but flexibility was established. How long before the 'Venus Villas' brochured so lasciviously by Vladimir Nabokov in *Ada*, are part of the adult landscape of a global village in which infantilisation and – so far neglected in Walt's world – eroticism are the growth industries? If you don't do it, Michael, somebody else will. And what a great third act it will make for the company history! Or is that going to be the Loony Tombs project, where Mickey warbles the last rites and you get waved on your milky way by big-mittened staff-members in Goofy and Donald masks? Hey, and how about Robin Williams does the voice-over eulogy, Patch Adams-style? People will go up chuckling for their slice of Pie in the Sky.

Work in Progress is an (alas) unmitigated tale of a nicely brought up, not *over*bright student who learns at summer camp – the great Doc Arnoldian influence in our hero's life – to be a good scout and family man. When this guy ties a knot, as he does with his wife Jane, it *holds*, baby, and good for him. Sane Jane is right there behind him as he climbs to fame and fortune. He learns (of *course* he does) that, as Francis Bacon might have said, not all ascent to a great place is by the fast elevator, yet 'hard but fair' remains the motto.

The apprentice Eisner is well enough placed socially and has enough get-in-there nerve to scramble to important attention doing horrible daytime TV shows horribly well for East Coast networks. With typical modesty, he makes light of juvenile acts of – yes, I'll say it if he won't – genius. For small instance, as a tiro he seems to have had a hunch that *Hollywood Squares* would be a top-selling, all-time hit game-show, when Fred Silverman, TV's *quondam* Mr Can-Do-No-Wrong, gave scheduling thumbs up to *The Face is Familiar*, which proved a clinker. Now Eisner is lion-king of the *Hollywood Squares* (he has seen the stage show of *Beauty and the Beast* over a dozen times). He is one of the few top guys who prefer the line of duty to a line of coke. Is mere awe underdoing it here?

The most remarkable – and probably genuine – aspect of the story is our hero's unblinking certainty that he has, in almost all instances, kept the faith. If you could make a fortune only by helping old ladies cross the street or showing underprivileged kids how to rub two sticks together at a camp fire, he would have done those things and *still* been one of the richest and most successful men in the world. Like so many 'intellectual properties' on which huge advances are paid, this book tells us absolutely *nothing* we could want to find out in order to become a fearsome corporate raider or one of the hundred richest shits in the world, because what can Sunshine possibly know about those dark, dark secrets?

With incorrigible tact, *Work in Progress* omits quite the most interesting fact concerning M. Eisner's and J. Katzenberg's recruitment by Disney from their earlier posts at the top of Paramount Pictures. It is, however, scarcely a secret that 'Walt' – that eternally venerated unMosaic guide to so many promised, and profitable, lands – was no admirer of Jews. None featured on the board until corporate decline led brother Roy (after Walt's death) to revise priorities. Eisner is, of course, a very *nice* Jew, and a very American one. All he wants, like *crazy*, is for the world to be one happy family, worshipping at nonsectarian shrines, with ecumenical tills, devised by truly top architects and imagineers (*sic*), staffed by 'casts' who, from top to bottom, think Disney and its profits. Looking back, might God not agree that what was wrong with the original Eden was that it had no shareholders? Of course, our modern Edens *have* no trees of knowledge, just a mythology of mindless animals wearing diapers. That way we can all stay ignorant bone-heads who grow up to be big babies and never have to use fig leaves.

When was hard ball played by a man with a softer heart than our part-author? He is donating his royalties to the education of Disney employees. Will it become their Authorized Version? Its hagiography is impeccable and its grammar is predominately (*sic*) reliable, but why no pictures (why no *pop-up* pictures?)? I would have warmed warmly to pictorial tributes to lovely Scandinavian-style wife Jane and the boys, Anders, Breck and Eric. Plus, how come no arms-around-each other shots of Jeffrey and Mike and Barry in happier times? And what kind of golf swing does Bill Gates have? These damn writers, they leave out so *much* we still ache to know. Do I hear someone murmuring 'Volume II'?

Good Old Athens, Bad Old Rome?

To advocates of 'relevance' in education, Peter Jones is a fire-breathing dinosaur who regularly goes over the top in defence of Latin and Greek. In this opinionated compendium, his tactics are Napoleonic: the whiff of grapeshot hangs over modern philistinism as he bangs on, to good effect, about the charms of antiquity.

Jones knows little of the moderation recommended by the Greeks. 'No Egyptian ever produced anything even remotely resembling the Parthenon', he asserts. But aren't the great temples of Luxor in some ways more magnificent, in size and elegance (and colour), than the Acropolis? The crucial difference is that Athens stands for something central in Western civilisation. The Parthenon was partly a place of worship, but also a calculated advertisement for Athens' imperial, and imperious, fifth-century superiority.

The political genius of the Greeks is properly vaunted, not to say thrust down our throats. 'Cleisthenes', we are told, 'instituted the world's first and last democracy' and so put an end to aristocratic rule. Up to a point, Dr Jones. After all, as Charles Freeman remarks, Athens continued to be dominated by toffs throughout its most glorious years. However, at the battle of Marathon, in 490 BC, the Athenian (middle-class) heavy infantry had played the decisive part, and afterwards could not be denied their measure of political clout.

At Salamis, ten years later, the mass of the rowers who helped the Greek navies to outmanoeuvre Xerxes was supplied by the (urgently trained) urban rabble, after which their votes too had to be counted. 'War,' said that sour Ephesian aristocrat Heracleitus, 'is the father of all things.' Including democracy (which he would have hated). The slaves, though essential to the economy, never managed to count politically, any more than the British working class did until the nineteenth century, or women until the twentieth.

Jones's claim that the Greeks 'invented... radical democracy' suggests some generous act of consciously conceived idealism. In fact, what happened was more like an ingenious compromise, a 'peace

Review of Peter Jones, *An Intelligent Person's Guide to the Classics* and Charles Freeman, *The Greek Achievement*, in *The Spectator*, 2000.

process' between the classes. In any case, the majority vote did not procure a 'People's Athens'. It led to the elected autocracy of Pericles. Under his leadership – he was so godlike that his nickname was 'the Olympian' – democracy was sustained by an empire whose books were cooked to Athenian recipes. Almost all Athens' one-time 'allies' were reduced to heavily taxed colonies. Radical imperialism is a better description of the city in its greatest days.

Dr Jones contrasts Athenian democracy with what he regards as the despicable 'elective oligarchies' of our present system. In fact, neither the wisdom of their decisions nor the durability of their *polis* promises that ancient Athens was the ideal state (the democracy of Rhodes, which neither writer mentions, was more modest in its ambitions and lasted a lot longer). When the whole citizen body (the *demos*) did decide what was to be done, the Athenians voted for gambles such as the disastrous Sicilian expedition. It was advocated by the flashy, opportunistic aristocrat Alcibiades. The people then nominated a trio of commanders, representing all shades of tactical opinion. The eventual commander-in-chief, the priggish (but rich) Nikias, had been a fervent opponent of the whole enterprise and, left in sole effective charge, after the defection of Alcibiades, finally did for them all with his plan of retreat.

As grouchy Plato later insisted, democracy and wisdom are not synonyms. In the near future, electronic e-voting may once again allow all the voters to take instant, press-button decisions about war, taxation and morals. Should we undoubtedly do everything we can to hasten the day?

As for the Romans, Jones is less starry-eyed. He says that 'Rome never solved the problem of ethnic disunity', which seems questionable. In contrast with the Greeks, who always regarded 'Barbarians' (i.e. the rest of the world) with distrust and distaste, the Romans co-opted or coerced first the rest of Italy and then most of the empire to more or less equal citizenship, at least among the educated. Did not the Jew St Paul say, famously, 'civis Romanus sum' although Tarsus is hundreds of miles from Rome? Emperors, generals and poets (Martial, not least) came from all over the Mediterranean.

The Roman populace was never fully enfranchised, on the Greek model, but even under the empire it could cheer or howl to demanding effect. Bread and circuses are mentioned here, but Rome's main drainage at least mitigated the kind of epidemics which ravaged Athens under Pericles and, perhaps as much as any military catastrophe, contributed to her eclipse. The Greeks did (or at least thought of) many innovative things, but never invented the arch or concrete, which enabled the Romans to build their aqueducts and other massive (and beautiful?) works of engineering.

Charles Freeman's *The Greek Achievement* is a more measured, and monumental, effort. It contains much useful information, and several dubious opinions. Although he underestimates the place and significance of drama in ancient Athens and is, I think, unduly simplistic about the uses of myth, Freeman is a diligent and generous scholar. However, is he right when he says that the traditional classical education 'cannot be disentangled from... determination to maintain the British class system'? The classics may have set hurdles too high for the free-range student, but clever boys like Dr-to-be Johnson in Lichfield, and less clever, like Shakespeare W., in Stratford, scarcely had Latin and Greek beaten into them because they belonged to the upper crust. The classics were as much a way of achieving access to high(ish) places as of barring it.

Freeman maintains that the public school emphasis on sport was the fault of the Greeks. But the Greeks played no team sports, unless you include warfare. The Olympic Games were won by individuals, never by teams (except of horses) and – as anthropologists have shown – they were not simply 'a way for nobles to show off'. It has been argued that the winner of the foot race was originally destined for sacrifice, and later officiated at the killing of a surrogate bull on the altar to Zeus. There were dark shadows among those colourful temples.

As for the present, Dr Jones may be right in arguing for the utility of Latin and Greek, but the rewards to be found among the dust are not measurable in careers or kudos. What is most durable and worthwhile in the Classics is the practically pointless solidarity of those who love them. However rancorous their quarrels, classicists share an extra-territorial culture that transcends social, religious or ethnic divisions. A supposedly narrow range of texts, and commentaries, furnishes a wide base on which every conceivable topic can be discussed with disinterested shamelessness and (in theory) accurate enthusiasm.

The classical world is not dead, but sweetly underpopulated. Its distant past is another country unvisited by charter flights. The Roman poet Horace wrote, with unguarded snobbery, 'Odi profanum vulgus et arceo': I hate the loud-mouthed crowd and keep them at a distance. Marcus Aurelius was more tactful, but no less trenchant: 'The noblest way to avenge yourself is not to become as others are.' These 'others' are the ones who write 'between you and I' and – like the BBC weathermen – 'there's been outbreaks of rain'. They also claim credit where it isn't due and think that keeping your word is bad business.

Pace Dr Jones, the Classics *are* the province of élitists and Pharisees and those who crave a world elsewhere. They *can* be both dull and demanding. That's the price of admission. In return, the classicist travels all his life in an undying (but not unchanging) landscape, uncrowded by six-packed louts, publicists, investment bankers, commissioning editors who know-what-the-People-want, management consultants or estate agents. Tempting?

Any Relation of Alan?

Colin Clark's memoir of a sumptuously louche life is illustrated with snaps of varying degrees of artlessness, including one of him and his twin sister, Colette: they are sitting in infantile innocence under a huge Old Master, too blitzed with light to be accurately ascribed, which the caption tells us was later sold to the Tate Gallery by their brother, Alan. Thus two weighty shadows fall, invisibly, over the twins: that of Kenneth, later Sir and even later Lord, Clark and that of Mrs Thatcher's junior minister whose memoirs, morals, and *morgue* (not to mention his money, though he often does) rendered him indispensable to the Kensington Conservatives. They dumped an MP who was too drunk to drive, and fell down somewhat, but they could not wait to have one who, on his own boastful admission, was pissed at the despatch box and was, as he put it, on another occasion 'economical with the *actualité*'. Petronius, thou shouldst be living at this hour.

The *frères* Clark's early life could have been illustrated best by the photographs which Bill Brandt took of London upper-class life in the 1930s. Starched maids waited on starchy toffs whose children were frigidly segregated, beyond a green baize door, with their own cook and domestic staff. The Kenneth Clarks' lordly and metropolitan disdain for the bourgeoisie was funded by the fortune compiled by K.'s provincial bourgeois family in the cotton-reel trade. Kenneth went to Winchester (about which he wrote an entertainingly dry memoir) and bettered himself, and them, by sending his sons to Eton, where Alan was too squeamish to watch his younger brother being educated with the usual cane.

All the same, Colin was not entirely sorry to go away to school. The war had cut down the family establishment in Portland Place and he had had to spend nights during the blitz sharing a Morrison shelter with, among others, his father, who grew testy when constricted. Kenneth Clark is depicted with more wryness than affection by the neglected younger son whom, later in life, he failed to recognise when he returned to Saltwood Castle after a plump spell in America.

Lady Clark (Jane) had been a beauty in her youth. K., as his wife

Review of Colin Clark, *Younger Brother, Younger Son*, in *The Spectator*, 1997.

called him, drew a comely portrait of her on their honeymoon (which he later thought too good to be able to attribute it correctly), but her charms did not satisfy her husband's appetites. He was an incorrigible philanderer, although his wife did her loud best to correct him. Lady Clark spilled her affections, and her lavish tips, and her drinks, on all manner of casual acquaintances, but she seems not to have much cared for Colin. He regards her across the years with magnanimous compassion. Despite small spasms of brotherly animosity, he refrains from remarking on the irony that Alan's tolerant wife is also called Jane. Clark major inherited Saltwood and its riches, which derived not only from cotton-reels but also from his patrician father's mercantile eye for paintings with growth potential. He did not have to buy his own furniture.

K.'s attentions to his sons seem to have consisted largely of rehearsing the matter and style of his famous television series, *Civilisation*, in the many galleries to which he conducted them on foreign tours. Overdoing the principle of primogeniture, the great man ceded priority to Alan even before he died and became a pensioner in a dower-house in what had been his own castle grounds. Alan's idea of a joke was to set the dog on him if the old man strayed back, like some scholarly Lear, towards his bookshelves. Good old A.C., nothing like mobbing papa!

When Colin was bequeathed Edith Wharton's library (she was his godmother) he was not allowed to come into his inheritance until years later. Those who have read *The Prince, the Showgirl and Me* will know that Colin Clark endured his privileged privations with remarkably good humour. Why not? Eton gave him an enviable education in effrontery and Oxford allowed him time to tool around in faster and faster cars.

Sharing the Clarkly zeal for female company, Colin was sexually frustrated, like most of our generation, by the moral climate of the 1950s. However, he has since recouped in a style which could, one suspects, boost his index with as many girls' names as his immodest brother's. For someone who had not lost his virginity by the time he was an RAF officer (he was nabbed by the military police in an oriental brothel before he could complete the formalities), he certainly made up for lost time. When finally he married happily (he had married a couple of times before, without the adverb), it was to a Chinese woman for whom he advertises his uxorious devotion in a typically wholehearted and unambiguous fashion.

Clark has spent most of his life in and around the arts. Always disposed to see the best in people, he does not mince his epithets when it comes to 'monsters', of whom John Le Carré's father is the most spectacular and Bob Boothby clearly the most disliked. There is also the usual band of word-breaking TV executives and perfidious cinemagnates without whom no celluloid life can ring true. Colin's fairy godparents, Vivien Leigh and Laurence Olivier figure once again. Larry is declared roundly to have been a great man, though Vivien commanded more of Colin's affection: for him, she was as intelligent as she was beautiful, as brave as she was inexhaustible.

Having blundered from smart society into the film world, Clark's acquired professionalism is manifest in the shrewd pages distinguishing the talent of Marilyn Monroe, who understood cinema instinctively and performed for it magically, from that of Olivier, whose staginess rendered him incapable of making a camera (or a movie audience) love him. Clark is very polite about another totemic figure, Alistair Cooke, whom he calls 'incomparable', though I have heard him compared to several things, not all of them complimentary.

Cooke's vanity impelled him to think, like everyone else in the world, that he could direct films. His clout secured him the opportunity, twice. It fell to Clark, as the producer, to tell Cooke that his lavishly funded work was unscreenable. To show where and how the Great Man went wrong, Clark supplies a shot-list for how a seemingly simple sequence should have been filmed in order to be cinematically grammatical. It is to be recommended to all those who imagine that making movies is a doddle.

The author is unremittingly fresh, amusing, and understated. He does not so much drop Names as allow them to drop him. Were it not for the apparently inadvertent evidence of his warmth, loyalty and lack of malice, it would be difficult to understand how he has managed to befriend so many amusing people and enjoy so many delightful women. This is quite the *nicest* memoir of room-serviced Bohemia since David Niven's *The Moon is a Balloon*. Making light both of his parents' indifference and of his brother's superbious eminence, Clark succeeds in seeming to have had many more ha'pence than kicks. His style is chatty but, in the notable cases of Princess Margaret and Prince Charles, he does not lack mordancy when bite is merited. Although well-travelled, unlike big bro he flashes no foreign tongues, perhaps in mute tribute to the many solecisms to be found in Clark Major's impeccable French as paraded, *tambour battant*, in his *néanmoins* delicious diaries.

Ancient and Modern

Byron's friend, the banker-poet Samuel Rogers, used to say that whenever he heard of a good new book, he rushed out and bought an old one. Since Jacob Burkhardt's study of ancient Greek society derives from lectures given at the University of Basle over a century ago, it is certainly, in one sense, an old book. Oswyn Murray's brilliant introduction and Sheila Stern's fresh translation also make it new. By delivering the essence of Burkhardt's great work, they supply a fat and vivid reminder of the splendour (and miseries) of Hellenism. Rogers would rush out and buy it, and rightly.

The ancient Greek philosophers discovered, and exploited, all the uses of contradiction. Socrates was accused of making the worse appear the better cause. If he did, he was only doing what Greek politicians, legislators and citizens habitually did. Ancient Greece was a living ferment of antitheses. The Greeks invented democracy and also tyranny. They craved money and hated the wealthy. They despised barbarians (anyone who did not speak their language), but distrusted each other. Every city-state was riven by factions which willingly exiled or murdered their opponents whenever they could, even if it meant enrolling the aid of their enemies. Homer's *Iliad* celebrated the united Greeks' defeat of Troy, but it anatomised their internal quarrels, their spite, their treachery (Odysseus first promised Dolon his life and then collaborated in his murder) and their merciless sacrilege, for which the gods punished them by giving nearly all of them a miserably victorious journey home.

The ancient Hellenes admired virtue and relished vice; they advised moderation and practised excess (gluttony in particular). They demanded loyalty, but ambition often trumped it. If their most powerful and feared deities were goddesses, they treated women as chattels and objects (anyone, male or female, who was penetrated sexually was, by that token, despicable). They claimed freedom for themselves but their best minds rarely questioned slavery. Although

Review of Jacob Burkhardt, *The Greeks and Greek Civilisation*, edited with an introduction by Oswyn Murray, trans. Sheila Stern, in the *Sunday Times*, 1998.

two-faced Janus was a Roman god, he would have settled in very comfortably in Athens.

Alcibiades – Socrates' friend and the great Pericles' ward – was a flagrant example of duplicity. When he was dumped as a general by the Athenians, after the military catastrophe in Sicily (largely somebody else's fault), he turned his coat and gave the Spartans shrewd – perhaps decisively successful – strategic advice. When he tired of laconic company and (so rumour hinted) of the bed of his mistress, the wife of one of the Spartan kings, he turned his coat again. Because he was a pretty and talented aristocrat, with a glib tongue and a long purse, he was reinstated as an Athenian general and won a great victory at Cyzicus. He might have returned in triumph (and perhaps won the Peloponnesian war for Athens in extra time), but reactionary politicians at home and the angry Spartan general Lysander contrived, in the end, to have him murdered in Persia before he could do anybody else any good, or harm.

Greek art has always been a subject for veneration, but the Greeks had no word for art except *techne*, which suggested craft (and craftiness) more than any sublime activity. Phidias was paid the same wages for his Parthenon frieze as any day-labourer. He was chased out of Athens (unlike Lord Elgin, who loaded Phidias' work for transportation to England under indifferent Greek eyes and with the aid of suitably greased Turkish palms) and went to work in Olympia. There he contrived the greatest tourist attraction in all Greece – a gigantic seated statue of Zeus – and was then murdered by the Eleans, who had invited him to come.

The Greeks had a long reputation for turning spitefully on those whom they earlier blessed with fame. Even Themistocles (a dodgy character before he became the hero of Salamis) ended his life working as a civil servant for the Persians whom he had defeated. Few good deeds went unpunished in a society riven by envy, toadyism, malice and libellous recklessness on the part, for durable example, of Aristophanes, who mocked and vilified the democracy which gave him (and others) the freedom to do so.

Greece invented competition, and made a fetish of it: art, politics, sport, all were arenas in which dog ate dog whenever the chance arose. Greeks loved money, but they disdained to work for it, least of all with tools (hence, perhaps, their poor record as inventors). What were labelled 'banausic' activities – anything you did with your hands – were socially unacceptable. Sculptors like Phidias were rated lower than painters (who didn't have to chip and polish), but art remained a province for the disadvantaged, like the lame god Hephaestus, who actually had a *forge*, and the dirty hands that went with it.

The glory that was Greece was extremely gory. The great pan-Hellenic oracular centre at Delphi was beautified by the booty which Greeks had taken from other Greeks. The magnificent site of the Olympic games reeked with the blood of sacrificial victims. The place was so stinking and overcrowded that the sophist Aelian threatened to take one of his slaves to the games if he didn't behave himself.

The games themselves – as every schoolboy used to know – were conducted every four years from 776 BC until the emperor Theodosius the First put a Christian stop to them over a millennium later. A sacred truce enabled athletes from the eternally warring Greek world (which extended into Asia Minor) to take part without getting their throats cut on the way. But the famous Olympic spirit, sentimentalised by the founder of the modern games, did not inhibit bribery, cheating and rigging races. All that mattered to Hellenes was winning, no matter how (one of their gods, Hermes, was a thief). There were no second prizes, for anything; nice guys finished nowhere.

Olympic victors were supposedly rewarded only with a laurel wreath, but in fact they often received pensions for life. Sometimes a new gate was cut in the city walls to welcome them home. But philosophers (of course) disapproved of mere physical prowess. Plato was said to have been bought out of slavery (after messing with practical politics in Sicily) by one Anniceris, who loved chariot racing. The benefactor showed off his skill with a faultless tour of Plato's Academy. The students applauded, but their master said that 'a man so much in earnest about such trivial matters could not be serious about anything worthwhile'. Jacob Burkhardt cites the story as true, though it is now officially regarded as apocryphal.

So what? Burkhardt thought it impossible for us ever to know precisely what did or didn't happen in the past, which sources were truthful and which tainted. This did not encourage him to a lack of scruple, but he maintained that even tall stories and forged documents had their interest (Plato's letters, for instance) since they showed what their ancient authors thought would serve as a plausible fake. There are manifest dangers in such an accommodating attitude, as Paul de Man and similar post-modernist mystagogues have proved, but Burkhardt neither ground axes nor came to reckless or slick conclusions. Unlike Hegel, whose balefully pretentious influence was paramount in the Germanic world, he preferred to observe, not schematise; to describe, not prescribe. His view of the Greeks has, inevitably, aged in the light of recent research and discoveries. It remains enlightened and enlightening, a joy to read, delicious with anecdotes and a manifest labour of love, candour and open-mindedness. The Greeks would either have made him rich (as they did the first historian, Herodotus, for telling them what they wanted to hear) or given him hemlock to drink (for being insufficiently flattering). Or possibly both.

The Art of the Deal

Dorothy Parker once said that the two most welcome words in the English language were 'Cheque enclosed', but to some of us 'Table Up!' run them close. There are already many bridge books, of a more or less specialised nature – from 'Skid' Simon's immortal *Why You Lose at Bridge*, through *Reese on Play* to whatever temporary bible today's hot-shots swear by – but *Tales from the Bridge Table*, a causerie of legends, scandals and myths '1925 to 1995', is an appetising rarity for which little expertise is needed.

Having renounced 'serious' (duplicate) bridge at the end of the 1960s, like all addicts I dare not claim to be cured. How well, even now, could I resist three competent players craving a fourth? Never in the first flight, I had the good fortune to play with, or against, many of the heroes and sacred monsters whom John Clay recalls here. Reese and Schapiro, Flint and 'Konnie' Konstam, Rixi Markus and Fritzi Gordon, Iain Macleod and Harrison Gray, gentle Jack Marx and my old friend Guy Ramsey (whose *Aces All* is a properly honoured source for many good stories) return from the dear dead days when Crockford's and the Hamilton, Lederer's and Mrs Mac's were our rendezvous and Acol and Baron and Vienna, Blackwood and Culbertson and Stayman were our systems, long before the Little Major galloped into brief, elaborate prominence or transfer bids worked their dodgy trick.

Boris Schapiro has no need, of course, to come back from the dead; he is still so much among the living that he and his team won the Gold Cup only last year. Longevity is more common among bridge players than geniality: Pat Cotter (whom my father once described as '*almost* the nicest man in the world') continued to write columns for three publications well into his nineties. The illusion that one will always have time to squeeze in one more rubber makes bridge a recipe for eternal middle age.

Bridge is not a glamorous game. Dozens of films and stories have been written about poker, and its lone sharks; chess is an allegory of blood and domination, sombre with symbolism even for those who

Review of John Clay, *Tales from the Bridge Table*, in *The Spectator*, 1999.

have never mastered the Sicilian opening. Yet Willie Maugham's *Three Fat Women of Antibes* is one of the few stories in which bridge is featured. I played bridge a few times with Maugham; his game was steady and without frills, as he imagined his prose to be. Edmund Wilson once said that his short stories served to 'turn the weekly trick', but he liked to do it more often than that.

Bridge remains irredeemably bourgeois. Its partnerships have something of the mundanely conjugal about them: the Culbertsons and the Simses were in at the creation of Contract. Mrs Bennett, a very unJaneite character, committed one of the few literal murders in bridge history, in Kansas City in 1929, when she shot her husband for failing (unluckily perhaps) to make four spades, after opening without the requisite honor tricks.

Bridge regularly excites animosity between partners more venomous than that between opponents. However, one of its great dramas was what Clay calls 'The Buenos Aires Incident'. During the World Championships in 1965, Reese and Schapiro, the crack England pair, were accused of cheating by the Americans, with whom they had never been popular. The 'system' they were alleged to have employed was so witless – it involved signalling how many hearts were in their hands by displaying the fingers holding their cards in a variety of telltale ways – that it was hard to believe that two such shrewd professional gamblers could not have devised something more subtle than going digital.

The argument that merely exchanging information about holdings in a single suit was not worth doing is not, however, convincing: at the highest level, *any* advantage had to be considerable. Rather than amazement or aggressive indignation, Reese and Schapiro affected contempt for their bad-losing accusers. Terence – scholar of New College and First in Greats – rarely abated his drawling disdain, while insolence had always been part of Boris's scandalous charm: at a dinner party, he once observed a lady with a very ample décolletage and, holding out his knife to her neighbour, called out 'Cut me a slice'.

The two Britons were found both guilty and innocent, by a succession of tribunals and courts martial, until they emerged neither tarnished nor whitewashed. Without the video tapes which, today, might resolve the matter, the question of whether or not they cheated remains metaphysical, though they persistently said 'it ain't so'.

Reese was undoubtedly one of the greatest analysts in the game (when once, just once, I found a manifest mistake in one of his daily hands in the *Evening Standard* and called him to point it out, he took it well) and his *bête noire*, Harrison-Gray, in *Country Life* ran him close, but 'Skid' Simon – of whom a German opponent in the 1930s once said, 'If only the Führer could meet *this* Jew!' – remains the king of bridge writers. If there is a hell for bridge-players, it is one in which each of us is doomed, throughout eternity, to cut either Mrs Guggenheim or Futile Willy or the Unlucky Expert (Skid's immortal and instructive creations) and watch each of them, in his or her way, make a mess of the lovely dummy we have put down or ruin the glorious defence we have schemed. And where shall we be when we execute that perfect submarine squeeze against 'Skid' and Lederer, under the admiring eyes of partner Terence and are written up, in the celestial gazette, by Guy Ramsey? Heaven indeed.

Berlin Revisited

In my edition of the *Encyclopaedia Britannica*, Isaiah Berlin figures between Berlin, Irving (b. 1888) and Berlin, Isaiah ben Judah Loeb (b. 1725). The songwriter needs no new fanfare; ben Judah was a Talmudic scholar whose critical comments have been canonical since 1800. The accident of Isaiah Berlin's alphabetical placement is pretty enough to seem emblematic: as a philosopher, he was pitched between lively, if never jazzy, modernism and a scholarly precision with roots in Talmudic exegesis. Although born in Riga in 1909, he became so markedly English, or at least Oxonian, that there was, eventually, something almost Quixotic in his loyalty to the Jewishness whose uneasy nature he dissected, with pitiless tact, in the 1953 essay entitled 'Jewish Slavery and Emancipation', which I intend to revisit here.

By the time he died, in late 1997, Berlin was so accepted a member of the English establishment (the award of the OM was his apotheosis) that he enjoyed immunity from the problems of identity and allegiance which he analysed so keenly. His foreignness had become such an unlikely part of him that he often seemed more English than he pretended to be; his correct dress (the striped trousers, the flowered buttonhole) and his haughty diffidence might be *dated*, but they were scarcely alien. He was a very English philosopher: unlike Karl Popper, he was not aggressive; unlike Wittgenstein, he was not anguished. He had the knack of being both trenchant and likeable, shrewd and unthreatening. However you looked at him, he was manifestly at home in English high society. At the British Embassy in Washington during the war, he was valued as a perceptive and witty observer of the world's game. His brains made him many friends and few enemies; he used his intelligence intelligently.

Berlin had been clever enough to be a philosopher in the exclusive 1930s circle which included such cardinal figures as A.J. Ayer, Gilbert Ryle, J.L. Austin and Stuart Hampshire. Individually, none of them was as important as Wittgenstein, but 'Oxford Philosophy' was paramount even in the Cambridge of the 1950s, when I was reading Moral Sciences. By that time, Berlin had decided, with calculated modesty, that it was wiser to be a critical historian of other people's ideas rather than to advance one's own. However, he continued to practise the caustic dandyism of his Oxford colleagues. While the England of the 1950s seemed, in its impoverished pride, to be seeking to conserve its pre-war aloofness from Europe and to distance itself from its recent aberrations, political and intellectual (Heideggerian existentialism, for instance), Berlin was not able so easily to ignore the horror, whether practical or theoretical. His investigation of, in particular, German romanticism can properly be seen as a quiet way of seeking to extricate, if not extirpate, the intellectual roots of Fascism. It was typical of his fastidiousness that he never disparaged (and often saw significant merit in) ideas which had, in Herder and Hegel for example, contributed to Europe's moral delinquency. His even-handedness was more implacable than any denunciation, though some saw a certain Jeevesian obsequiousness in his lofty moderation.

Can anyone doubt that Berlin made a good decision when he renounced the analytic philosophy which his eminent contemporaries practised? Their notion of the subject has been largely superseded and their certainties have become questionable, as always happens in philosophy (were this not so, the subject might by now have come to decisive conclusions). Berlin's discursive style has yielded more durable results, by dealing with specific cases; his studies of European romanticism and liberal thought amount – not unlike Montaigne's essays – to rather more than the sum of their parts. They seem exemplary by virtue of their apparent lack of *parti pris*, although it has been argued (for instance by Ernest Gellner in *Prospect*, November 1995) that Berlin advanced a doctrine which turned tolerance into a kind of shrugging indifference in the face of competing and conflicting and finally incoherent notions of human liberty and values.

The charge of want of coherence would not, I think, embarrass Berlin. In 'From Hope and Fear Set Free', he wrote

the optimistic view – which seems to be at the heart of much metaphysical rationalism – that all good things must be compatible, and that therefore freedom, order, knowledge, happiness, a closed future (and an open one?) must be at least compatible, and perhaps even entail one another in a systematic fashion. But this proposition is not self-evidently true, if only on empirical grounds. Indeed, it is perhaps one of the least plausible beliefs ever entertained by profound and influential thinkers.

(*Concepts and Categories*, p.198)

It is not unwarranted to infer that Berlin regarded the notion of a homogeneous society, without internal contradictions and incompatibilities, geared to a smoothly articulated and universally applicable social and moral machinery, as not only unattainable but also undesirable, not to say repugnant. In this, I find him entirely congenial. What I have to say, in particular, about his 1953 essay on the 'problem' of Jewish assimilation should be read in the light of this confession. As Karl Popper pointed out, it is better to acknowledge one's partialities than to pretend to have risen above them; it is only through their candid avowal that they can then be discounted.

Perhaps in the same spirit, Berlin never affected to transcend his Jewishness, even if, in some sense, he rose above it. If, in the 1953 essay, he deals with the issues of whether assimilation is either a good or a possible thing and of whether Jews 'should' emigrate to Israel in order to resolve their contradictions, he does not seem personally involved in such a choice. He regards the issues as real, but not real *for him*: he asks 'What should *they* do?' rather than 'What should *I* do?'. In his habitual consultative mode, he seems professorially immune to the maladies which he diagnoses. Does this weaken his account of them or render it more likely to be correct?

The answer is *both*. We cannot seriously doubt that cool judgement, which attempts to look at all sides of the question, and at all the possible solutions, is desirable; the notion of being reasonable depends on not basing arguments on *feeling* or even on what A.J. Ayer called 'piety' (the belief that what was believed fervently by our fathers has some claim, merely by virtue of its venerable antiquity, on what we should believe). Who would want to come up in front of a judge who arrived at his conclusions on the strength of, for obvious recent example, his Masonic allegiance rather than as the result of an even-handed assessment of the merits of the case? (The question of whether the campaign against Freemasonry is a form of *religious* persecution, in which prejudice has a place, is a nice test of what we really mean, or *want* to mean, both by religion and by prejudice: how should we respond to a parliamentary requirement that synagogues publish their membership lists? And does the question 'What is the difference?' differ interestingly or importantly from the question '*Why* is there a difference?'? These are just the kind of morally and socially complex issues on which Berlin so often brought lucidity to bear. However, as so often, no clear answers clearly answer the questions.)

Since I had no personal acquaintance with Berlin, I cannot be sure that he was not, in private, a passionate advocate of some publicly unrevealed stance with regard to Jews, Israel or anything else. What is certain is that he did not care to regard his own emotions as relevant to the issues or appropriate to their evaluation. Berlin was more like Raymond Aron than he was like Jean-Paul Sartre, and just as well, I daresay, when it came to the history of philosophy. But is the 'Jewish Question', as it used to be called, a problem which can be treated both fully *and* dispassionately?

One is tempted to agree that, if one looks at Jewishness without being emotionally involved, there is no commanding reason to argue for its survival, *assuming one does not regard this as a 'metaphysical' obligation*. The comedy, if I can put it that way, of the Jewish condition is that one phrase which hardly fits the case is 'All things being equal'. Berlin wrote a long and elegant essay on equality in which, as one might expect, he took careful (slightly weary) pleasure in showing that the notion of equality, or at least of 'strict egalitarianism', is an impractical fetish:

> And of course there are many other goals or values which may deflect the course of strict egalitarianism, as, for instance, the desire to encourage the arts or sciences, or a predominant desire to increase the military or economic power of the state, or a passion for the preservation of ancient traditions, or a strong taste for change and variety and new forms of life.
>
> (*Concepts and Categories*, p.87)

These remarks about the impossibility of maintaining 'equality' as an end in itself apply, I suspect, no less forcefully to Zionism. The state which was created as a refuge for Jews, in which all were to feel equally secure and at home, has evolved in unforeseeable ways. The insurgent power of religious orthodoxy was probably one of the last of Ben-Gurion's concerns, but Israel is now a state with internal schisms of an order which highlight the naïveté of supposing that a Jewish state could be an answer to *all* the problems of being a diaspora Jew. Even in Israel there are now pressures to assimilate, with the added complication that there are several camps to which assimilation is possible, if not demanded.

Hence, although it remains interesting, the 1953 essay bears the marks of its age. It refers, at the outset, to an essay by Sir Lewis Namier (a figure to whom assimilation brought honour without quietening his irascible inner demons) in which he compared 'the effect of enlightenment upon the Jewish masses in the last century with that of the sun upon a glacier'. Three main consequences supposedly flowed from this: the outer crust disappeared entirely 'by evaporation'; the heart of the glacier remained stiff and frozen; but

> a great portion of the mass melted into a turbulent flood of water which inundated the valleys below, some of which flowed into rivers and streams, while the rest collected into stagnant pools; in either case, the landscape altered in a unique, and at times revolutionary, fashion. The image was not merely vivid [Berlin continues] but accurate, because such evaporation does, of course, occur, despite all denials; assimilation can sometimes be total.

One of Berlin's instances is, oddly enough, the Disraelis. They, like many Anglo-Jewish families (of which the Raphaels are a minor instance), may have 'entered the general texture of Gentile society and become divorced from their origins in the minds of both themselves and their neighbours' (my great-aunt Minnie believed that she did not become 'a lady' until she converted to Christianity), but it is still absurd to deny that Benjamin Disraeli was a Jew; he did not in any way deny it himself (indeed he added to the mythology of the Jews by harping, however mockingly, on their ancient and, in his case, royal lineage). 'Evaporation' often, if not always, left a marked residue which indicates that Namier's image was not as accurate as academic courtesy suggested. Berlin goes on to say that assimilation

> will be condemned by those who believe the Jewish religion alone to be the truth and, consequently, regard all forms of departure from it, particularly on the part of those who once believed in it, as being treasonable and, moreover wicked... and again by those who believe in the inner solidarity of races or communities as such, and view abandonment of them... as a species of disloyalty and desertion... Nevertheless... if it [sc. 'evaporation'] looked feasible on a mass scale, and not merely in the case of a minute percentage of the Jewish people, it would perhaps not be as easy to argue against it as in fact it is.
>
> ...the question of whether or not total assimilation is permissible or dignified or justifiable, or in any respect desirable, is, for good or ill, irrelevant to the Jewish problem... Nor is there any reason, if history and sociology have any lessons to teach, for thinking that it will ever succeed.

How unarguable is all this? Of course what Berlin claims has *some* truth in it, and by emphasising such words as 'total', it can be made unquestionable. But is it *now* true that Jews cannot belong, more or less completely, to civilised societies, such as Britain or the United States or France, without being pilloried or forked on an irresoluble and uncomfortable dilemma? The idea of a Jewish 'problem' is by no means unthinkable, but how problematic is today's Jewish situation? I am not showing Berlin to be wrong, in any logical sense; in fact, I am applying to his essay the method which he recommended, and on which the romantics insisted, which is of placing it in its historical (and local) context.

What Berlin took to be immutable has not, I think, entirely proved to be so. It may be that I am taking a neo-Panglossian view and that, as Woody Allen suggests *as a joke*, in *Deconstructing Henry*, the Holocaust has set a record which, in the nature of things, demands to be *broken*, but Allen would not say this if he 'really meant it', would he? Western societies are torn by contradictory impulses: they seek to advance, especially economically, by belonging to larger and larger organisations or political unions, but at the same time their inhabitants display a tendency to retrieve ancient allegiances and particularisms (whether religious or ethnic) and to cleave to them as a form of specificity. Jews are no longer the only 'Jews'.

Jews may have (or constitute) a unique 'problem', but their condition today is far more like that of other minorities (in states outside Israel) than it was when Berlin wrote his essay. To put it simply, it is now possible to be both assimilated (to a marked degree) and *un*like the dominant culture, precisely because modern Western societies now either pride themselves on or are reconciled to their diversity. The variety of restaurants and costumes (not to mention places of worship) in London now is colourfully banal evidence that the English no longer attach paramount significance to a single social standard, piety or style. This cannot be an argument against those who 'believe' in some imminent millennarian catastrophe, but it *is* an argument against accepting that there is, or need be – as Arthur Koestler maintained – an abrupt alternative: assimilation or Israel.

The notion of so stark a choice is now melodramatic. Many of us are perfectly content to be considered Jews, and to consider ourselves Jews, without feeling that we are either ignoble or evasive in not going to Israel or even to synagogue. It is possible that we are deluding ourselves by supposing, if we do, that we shall be exempt in the case of some future murderous spasm of anti-Semitism, but we do not suppose this, do we? Hence the idea of some inescapable pressure to decide to be what one is already said to be (and of the 'damage' this does to our authenticity) is exaggerated. Berlin is, of course, intelligent enough to see that assimilation is not an option often available to more than a few Jews (with the brains or talents to be acceptable immigrants into bourgeois society, just as 'the king's Jews' were accepted at court) and, as one might expect, he makes no peremptory recommendations. However, there is slightly doleful resignation in his view that Jews must remain exceptional, not to say incurable, in their misfortunes, unless they elect to go to Israel.

The 1953 essay is preserved in the amber of its period, when the 'success' of the Holocaust seemed to put Europe's surviving Jews in a perilously vulnerable position (the Labour government of 1945 imported clean Baltic SS men rather than smelly 'displaced persons' to work in Britain) and when Zionism seemed the providential answer to *all* the Jewish questions. The assumption that Israel would turn into a state like any other, in which Jewish policemen and burglars, whores and violinists, would be unremarkably at home was common to Berlin, Namier and Koestler. The present condition of Israel, both internally and internationally, fulfils few of these expectations. Who imagined that fundamentalist orthodoxy might determine the political balance of what was assumed to be a secular Jewish state, or foresaw that Israel itself might become, to put it plainly if crudely, the pariah of the Middle East? There is now small evidence that Jews can resolve their problems, still less their anxieties, by emigration to a state riven by irreconcilable views of what it is to be a Jew, or a loyal Israeli, and incapable of contriving even partial assimilation to the states around it.

Naturally enough, in view of his own origins, Berlin depicted the 'emancipation' of the Jews as emanating essentially from Eastern Europe, where they comprised communities within the (hostile) community of Russia and other states. Despite 'appalling poverty', their 'rich and independent inner life' is taken to be the source which gave birth to the tortured and insecure genius so typical, we like to think, of diaspora Jewry. Berlin does not aspire, in the 1953 essay, to a thorough psycho-history of European Jewry, but it is interesting that he ignores the experience, and disparate vitality, of Sephardic Jewry, whose eviction from Spain and Portugal did not give rise to the same kind of nervous brilliance to be found among, especially, German-speaking Jews. Berlin's generalisations, concerning the Jewish 'malaise', do not apply so neatly to Italian or Greek Jews (whose solidarity at Auschwitz was so remarkable) or, I daresay, to Moroccan Jews either. The 'suddenly liberated' Jews of the end of the eighteenth and beginning of the nineteenth century were not of a piece with those dispersed by Ferdinand and Isabella. Is it not a weakness of Berlin's analysis that he does not see what one might expect him to see, given his respect for Herder: the specific and various nature of the Jewish experience, and fate? It is not merely my own putative Sephardic blood which excites this comment; it is, I think, also the fact that, despite his show of mandarin detachment, Berlin grew more *agitated* about the condition of the survivors and descendants of *shtetl* Jewry than perhaps he quite realised.

As the 1953 essay develops, he introduces a new metaphor to illustrate the Jewish condition. Abandoning Namier's glacial image, he invites us to see the Jews as

> travellers who by some accident find themselves among a tribe with whose customs they are not familiar... The first thing [they] must do is to make themselves familiar with the habits and modes of behaviour of the tribe... They must not miscalculate, or their survival is in jeopardy... Consequently, if the travellers are at all gifted they presently become exceptionally knowledgeable about the life of the tribe. *They come to know far more about its habits that the members of the tribe themselves know or need to know...* The strangers become prime authorities on the natives... they interpret the native society to the outside world... their understanding is too sharp, their devotion too great, they are experts on the tribe, not members of it.

As my emphasis indicates, I think that Berlin is here drawing a portrait of his own attitude and sensibility. He displays his usual gravely impersonal mask, but the profile is unmistakable. The influence of Herder, and his plausibility, is later evident when he alludes to the Jew's *conscious* effort to be something which is natural to 'the natives' (a term which, in the 1950s, was still somewhat patronising, if not pejorative). Berlin seems to believe that Jews were conspicuous, if not unique, in needing to *learn* how to be like other people. In 1949, however, Simone de Beauvoir published *Le Deuxième Sexe*, which opened, famously, with the statement that women are not *born* women but *become* them. Since then, the place of mimesis in society, the urge and pressure to emulate, has been much more widely recognised (especially in the work of René Girard). Man is a much more artificial creature, much more unnatural, than Berlin seemed to allow in his gloomily flattering portrait of the burden of consciousness that weighs uniquely on diaspora Jews.

This is not meant to detract from the shrewdness of his analysis of the difference between Goethe and Heine, for instance, but his assessment of the 'fate' of the Jews in Europe and America has not been validated subsequently. It may be that American Jews are unduly confident, not to say reckless, in claiming parity with Gentiles, but their condition is certainly not marginal (the anti-Semitism of some black groups is the warrant of Jewish assimilation to the ruling élites) and the increasing social and linguistic diversity of American society means that 'the Jew' is not the only stranger, and is less strange than some. Berlin's later image of the diaspora Jew as a 'hunchback', obliged either to deny his hump, to declare it beautiful or to have it surgically excised, is of a brutality which, once again, suggests a greater agitation than is usually associated with him. An almost laughable instance of the 'hunchback' affecting normality is to be found in *The Thirteenth Tribe*, where Arthur Koestler attempts, with diagrams, to prove that the Jewish nose is not really hooked but fleshy and that it derives its (denied) racial characteristics from a southern Russian, not a Semitic, source.

Berlin stays calm and, in accordance with his principles (and predilections?), insists that Jews have a right to live their contradictions and that Koestler's demand that they assimilate or depart for Israel is entirely too dramatic. At the same time, and rightly, he emphasises that the creation of the State of Israel (only five years before the essay was written) is of absolutely capital importance. The very fact that Jews can now choose whether to persist in being wilful 'strangers' among the 'natives' or to go to Israel has been a liberation even for those who elected to stay. Which of us, who has no intention of leaving for Israel, or of living an exclusively Jewish life, will deny the accuracy of the claim that something changed forever when the Jewish state was created? If we now are faced with the problem of our attitude to this or that policy of the present Israeli government (and are we not?), even the most assimilated Jew knows that *that* problem would have been a luxury of incredible sweetness to the Jews amongst whom Berlin was born and for whom Zion remained only a hope, if not a fantasy.

Berlin's role in England was that of the privileged stranger who rendered the state some service and who enjoyed its respect without having too many illusions about his membership of the tribe. Because of his eminence, and his charm, he escaped the humiliations which other hunchbacks sometimes had to endure, but he did not sever his connection with them. He underestimated the degree to which the outside world was itself insecure, in flux, capable of change. The idea which he, and others, had of assimilation took for granted the homo-geneity and immutability of the societies to whose membership they aspired. He ignored the degree to which Jewish humour, for instance, or the humour of Jews, has become a universal part of the common language. This does not, of course, guarantee respect for Jews or the certainty that the world will continue to be amused by, for instance, Woody Allen's appalling franknesses, but then, as Berlin would concede, we cannot imagine what it would be for such things (or *anything*) to be guaranteed in the world we know. (Let us forego Benjamin Franklin's old joke about death and taxes.)

The nature of 'the Jewish problem' has changed, slowly but undoubtedly, since 1953 and so too have the circumstances in which we all live and the ways in which intellectuals and politicians assess and play the world's game. But then again, if we now dare to think that we know more than Berlin, it needs no T.S. Eliot to remind us that his work is one of the invaluable things we now know.

Introduction to *Dream Fantasia*

By the time Arthur Schnitzler was born in Vienna in 1862, Franz-Josef II had been already on the throne of Austria–Hungary for ten years. The emperor did not die until 1916. The dual kingdom survived only two more years before being dismantled by the Treaty of Versailles. Schnitzler outlived Franz-Josef by fifteen years (he died in 1931), but he never stepped clear of the shadow of the Hapsburgs whose myth continued to haunt Vienna at least until 1938. Hitler's *Anschluss* then brought about what the emperor had always dreaded: a pan-German Reich dominated by Berlin.

Almost the whole of Arthur Schnitzler's life was lived in the protracted twilight of an empire which ceased to be a major power when he was four years old, after Bismarck's Prussian military machine destroyed Austro-Hungary's bravely incompetent army at Sadowa. Karl Marx's dictum – that history repeats itself first as tragedy, then as farce – was reversed: a benign, aimlessly tolerant, comic-operatic autocracy was followed by a pitilessly purposeful dictatorship which evicted and often murdered the Jews who, more than any other of Franz-Josef's subjects, had given Vienna its unique flavour.

The effect of 1866 on the Viennese psyche cannot be exactly assessed. Austria had already suffered preliminary humiliation by the French, under Louis-Napoleon. After Solferino, in 1859, northern Italy was amputated from Franz-Josef's *imperium*; Sadowa confirmed that he would never again be a major player in the world's game. Yet conscious acceptance of Austria's vanished supremacy was repressed by the brilliance and brio of its social and artistic life. Who can be surprised that Adler's 'discovery' of the inferiority complex, and of compensating assertiveness, was made in a society traumatised by its dazzling decline? It was as if the city which spawned Arthur Schnitzler and Sigmund Freud feared to awake from beguiling dreams to glum reality. By a pretty, untranslatable pun, *traum* (the German for a dream) and trauma were almost indistinguishable in the Vienna which was at home to both.

Arthur Schnitzler's father (whose family name had been

Introduction to the Penguin edition of Schnitzler's *Dream Novella*, 2000.

Zimmermann) had come to Vienna from Hungary before the disasters which fostered Austro-Hungary's crisis of identity. Vienna became the forcing ground for a variety of diagnoses and putative cures: psychological for neurotic individuals and political or nationalistic for the fractious elements of a disintegrating empire. On the surface, however, it was business, and pleasure, as usual.

Medicine offered Schnitzler *père* a stable, respectable career. When he specialised, as a laryngologist, he became rich and comfortable. For a long while, assimilation to Christian society seemed a feasible destiny for the Jewish élite. In the first decade after Arthur's birth, professional and social life in Vienna showed few signs of the aggressive anti-Semitism which was to be marked – and politically rewarding – long before the end of the century. Only in the 1890s was the odiously affable Karl Lueger elected mayor of Vienna on an overtly anti-Semitic ticket, although individual Jews were indeed some of his best friends.

Unlike many successful families (the Wittgensteins were a prime example), the Schnitzlers did not renounce Judaism. Their observation of High Days and Holy Days was, however, no more than pious politeness. Respect for religion was a gesture to please the older generation; young Schnitzler enjoyed fasting not least because it sharpened his appetite for the delicacies which greeted its end. Hypocrisy could scarcely be distinguished from good manners.

Medical science was, in a sense, an ecumenical religion. The common anatomy of mankind assimilated Jews to Gentiles. What reason was there to feel inferior? As Shylock had pointed out, Jews and Christians bleed under identical circumstances. In the dissecting room, as Schnitzler recalls, students confronted the common humanity of the cadaver:

> like my colleagues, I tended to exaggerate... my indifference to the human creature become thing... I never went as far in my cynicism as those who considered it something to be proud of when they munched roasted chestnuts... at the dissecting table. At the head of the bed on which the dead man lies, even if the man who has just breathed his last is unknown to you, stands Death, still a grandiose ghostly apparition... He stalks like a pedantic schoolmaster whom the student thinks he can mock. And only in infrequent moments, when the corpse apes the living man he once was in some grotesque motion... does the composed, even the frivolous man experience a feeling of embarrassment or fear.

Despite early dismay at the realisation of his own mortality, Dr Schnitzler observed with clinical equanimity what was physiologically common to all men. Freud declared our psychological anatomy to be no less universal. Medicine and science, like the arts, convinced talented Jews that they could and should look to a more modern allegiance than Judaism; logically speaking, only atavistic prejudice stood between them and citizenship in the civilised world. At the same time, Freud and Schnitzler saw that what was reasonable was also unreliable. Who could depend on the fundamental decency of a society where, beneath the elegant surface, irrational motives made nonsense of constancy and a comedy of morals?

Schnitzler begins his fragment of autobiography – *My Youth in Vienna* – by telling us:

> I was born on the 15th of May 1862, in Vienna, on the Praterstrasse... on the third floor of a house adjacent to the Hotel de l'Europe. A few hours later, as my father liked to tell so often, I lay a while on his writing desk... the incident gave rise to many a facetious prophecy concerning my career as a writer, a prediction my father was to see fulfilled only in its modest beginnings and not with undivided joy.

The Oedipal theme which was to become central to Sigmund Freud's theory of human behaviour is noticeable at once. Schnitzler suggests both that his father told his story repeatedly and that he regarded his son's fame without enthusiasm. Despite his youthful zeal for scandalous themes and rakish behaviour, Arthur never wholly rebelled against his father: he too became a doctor, though he did not practise medicine regularly once his plays became fashionable. For a time, however, he did edit a medical journal which his father had founded. His 1912 play, *Professor Bernhardi*, shows thorough knowledge of the treacherous politics of the Viennese medical world. The success (and hence the menace) of Jewish doctors led to increasing, often devious, discrimination against them. The Roman Catholic tradition had fostered this animosity and the clergy did nothing to discourage it.

Freud's determination to make a name for himself, outside conventional medicine, testifies to apprehension of the impediments which Jews could expect if their careers took routine paths. At the same time as advertising his retreat to a solitary wilderness, Freud craved recognition by the very establishment whose ill-will he feared: by recruiting the Gentile Carl Gustav Jung to the psychoanalytic camp, he sought to establish the scientific and un-Semitic character of his challenging theories. He was not the only Jew to be torn between the desire for independence from the scornful majority and an appetite for its applause. Otto Weininger, Gustav Mahler, Hermann Broch, Karl Kraus, Stefan Zweig, no less than half- or crypto-Jews such as Hugo von Hoffmannstahl and Ludwig Wittgenstein, were but the most renowned of many who could not turn their backs on those who, at any moment, might turn their scorn on them.

Schnitzler neither denied his Jewishness nor asserted it. Denial was demeaning; assertion led to self-deluding vanity. The doubleness of their identity sometimes created inescapable (and not infrequently suicidal) strains in Austrian Jews, but Schnitzler's dexterity with dialogue, which served him well in the theatre, and his light touch can be seen as happy consequences of the painful obligation both to be and not to be as other men. All his writing life, he observed the Jewish condition with an involved aloofness which parallels the cold eye which Freud brought – or presumed that he brought – to his self-analysis. As Schnitzler observed:

> You (a Jew) had the choice of being counted as insensitive, shy and suffering from feelings from persecution. And even if you managed somehow to conduct yourself so that nothing showed, it was impossible to remain completely untouched; as for instance a person may not remain unconcerned whose skin has been anaesthetized but who has to watch, with his eyes open, how it is scratched by an unclean knife, even cut until the blood flows.

Schnitzler *responded* to the Jewish condition without affecting to provide a solution. His fame as a writer (he won the 'Oscar' of the Viennese theatre, the Grillparzer Prize in 1908) immunised him from artistic frustration, but did not spare him vicious critical attacks. He was accused of being a Hungarian upstart or, worse, a corrupting outsider (his famous *Reigen* – later filmed as *La Ronde* and 'improved' recently by David Hare in *The Blue Room* – was banned as immoral for twenty-five years).

Medical familiarity with syphilis as a source of dementia punctuated levity with horror. A keen, not to say addictive, pursuer of sexual quarry, Schintzler was not immune to squeamishness. Reluctance to take all his opportunities was a matter less of moral refinement than of clinical caution: his father had shown the adolescent Arthur lurid

pictures of the effects of syphilitic infection. He mocks his own juvenile attempts to redeem fallen women:

> While the pretty young tow-headed Venus reclined naked on the
> divan, I leaned against the window frame, still fully dressed in my
> boyishly cut suit, my straw hat and cane in my hands, and appealed
> to the conscience of my beauty who was bored and amused at the
> same time, and had certainly expected better entertainment from
> the sixteen-year-old customer who was urging her to find a more
> decent and promising profession... I tried to emphasise what I had
> to say by reading some appropriate passages from a book I had
> brought along for the purpose... I left her with two gulden for
> which I had my mother to thank. She had given them to me after
> I had declared that I simply had to have the Gindeley *Outline of
> World History*.

The hero of *Dream Fantasia* is no youth, but he is similarly affected
by the apparent innocence of a young prostitute. All his life,
Schnitzler's imagination relied on the imagery and typical inhabitants
of *fin de siècle* Vienna. His touch was light, and remorseless. He was
certainly no more indulgent to Jews than to anyone else. One of his
few full length novels, *Der Weg ins Freie*, or 'The Road to the Open',
was published in 1908 and dealt, with his usual scepticism, with the
various answers to what was called the Jewish question. It was typical
of his clinical egotism that he refused to be gulled by any panacea,
including Zionism.

Schnitzler's friend Theodor Herzl, two years his junior, failed to
achieve equal success as a writer, though he did become a fluent journalist. It is usually alleged that Herzl wrote his Zionist manifesto, *Der
Judenstaat*, as a result of the endemic, and epidemic, anti-Semitism
which he observed when he was in Paris, covering the Dreyfus trials
for his Viennese newspaper. In fact, reasons for proposing the
creation of a Jewish state were to be found, in abundance, at home.

Earlier, like many bright young Jews impatient of the ghetto mentality,
the student Herzl had seen his future identity as closely linked with
Germanism. He was a keen member of a *Verbindung* until the 'Alemannic'
Association decided to 'bounce' its Jewish members. Only then, as
Robert Wistrich remarks, in his *Jews of Vienna in the Age of Franz Joseph*,
was Herzl's 'allegiance to the semi-feudal values and German nationalism of the Austrian *Burschenschaften*... shaken to the roots'. He had
previously enjoyed 'the romantic ritual of the Teutonic student... the
sporting of glamorous swords, coloured caps, and ribbons'.

When, on the rebound, Herzl came to advocate a sort of Jewish Austria in Palestine and invited Schnitzler to imagine his plays being performed in Jerusalem, the reply was dismissively terse: 'But in what language?' Schnitzler belongs inextricably to *mittelEuropa*. He could not imagine himelf, or his work, without them. 'En Europe,' E.M. Cioran was to say, 'le bonheur finit à Vienne'. 'Happiness ends in Vienna'; Cioran offers a consciously two-edged tribute to a city where the dyarchy of love and death shadowed the dual monarchy of the aging Franz-Josef II.

The writer of fiction is free to invest himself in all his characters, and in no single one of them. Arthur Schnitzler accepted, and maybe somewhat gloried in, being doubly alienated: as a Jew and a doctor, he was resigned to being marked off from the society he amused and adorned. Why then should he try to be as other men were? If the Jew was an object of suspicion, he could return the sour compliment by regarding Vienna with an unblinking eye and an accurate ear. In this Schnitzler was not unique: the unveiling of unacknowledged (and often unsavoury) motives was typical of Austro-Marxism, of logical positivism, of psychoanalysis and of Schnitzler, whom Freud saluted as his 'alter ego', an artist who had come by instinct and narcissistic intuition to conclusions about the primacy of the erotic which Freud liked to believe he had discovered by the scientific observation of others.

The 'hero' of *Traumnovelle*, *Dream Fantasia*, is a doctor who, in obvious ways, resembles his author. He neither indulges nor spares himself in the trenchancy of the notes on his own case. Fridolin's adventure is not, we may assume, a transcription of his author's own adventures, or dreams (it is too shapely and too artful), but in his autobiography, Schnitzler wrote that his work was an intrinsic element of his existence: 'even if the story relating to some of them may not belong to literary history, it certainly does belong in the story of my life'.

The tone and attitudes to be found in *Dream Fantasia* are certainly true to the spirit both of Schnitzler's personal life and of decadent Vienna. Despite the fact that the story was not published till 1925 (though it may well have existed in Schnitzler's mind, or his files, before that), it shows no signs of taking place in a post-1918, post-Hapsburg world. Its characters and atmosphere are as dated as its traffic: there are no cars or buses, no hint of Austria's final reduction to a post-imperial republic.

When Fridolin is confronted by a band of rowdy students, one of

whom seems deliberately to insult him by bumping into him, the
smart louts are said to be members of just such an 'Alemannic' club
as bounced Theodor Herzl from membership back in the 1880s.
Fridolin is not declared to be a Jew, but his feelings of cowardice, for
failing to challenge his aggressor, echo the uneasiness of Austrian
Jews in the face of Gentile provocation; Freud, for famous instance,
never forgave his father for failing to stand up to a bully who knocked
his hat into the gutter. Jews were said to be natural cowards and not
worthy of Aryan steel. Robert Wistrich, however, suggests that the
reason for bouncing Jews from their clubs and for refusing to give
them 'satisfaction' when they were provoked was not, as the 'Aryan'
students maintained, their cowardice, but rather the fact that no few
Jews had become so expert at swordsmanship that they were embar-
rassingly likely to win in a duel.

Although no coward, Schnitzler disdained to duel. He satirised the
absurdity of the point of honour and the double standards of
Viennese 'morality' in a play (*Das Ferne Land*) in which a philandering
husband challenges and kills his wife's sole lover, thus extinguishing
a young life and bringing incurable bitterness to his marriage, simply
because vanity requires it.

The Jewish question is only lightly touched upon in *Dream Fantasia*.
The Bohemian wanderer, Nachtigall, is said to have had a quarrel with
a bank manager in whose house he played and sang a raucously inde-
cent song. His host 'though himself a Jew... hissed a Jewish
imprecation in his face', after which 'his career in the better houses
of the city seemed to close forever'. This Jewish anti-Semitism (by no
means the same as self-hatred) confirms Schnitzler's melancholy
observation of 'the eternal truth that no Jew has any real respect for
his fellow Jew, never'. He concedes that he sometimes says about Jews
more than may seem 'in good taste, or necessary or just'. He hoped
that when his work was read, it might no longer be possible to imagine
why the issue was so important to him. He died two years before
Hitler's access to power, and the events which followed proved that
even his pessimism was, like Freud's, unequal to the horrors in store.

Although Fridolin does not endure the same insult as Nachtigall,
there is, I suspect, cunning in Schnitzler's using it to 'trail' what
happens when his hero goes to the erotic house party to which
Nachtigall lures him. If he is not abused or revealed as a Jew, his
unmasking by the in-group and his summary eviction from the revels
surely resembles the kind of jeering ostracism of which any Jew might
at any moment be the victim. Fridolin's 'rescue' by the beautiful

woman is both romantic and degrading: when she takes upon herself the consequences of his transgression, she becomes, in a sense, more manly than he is allowed, or dares, to be. This, as well as desire, is one of the motives for his restless need to find her again.

It may be reading too much into a good tale to remark that Fridolin's monk's habit (though banal enough for a fancy dress occasion) means that, in disguise he has chosen to cross the line between Jews and Catholics and it is, in a sense, justice that he is discovered. The paedophiles disguised as 'Vehmic judges' whom he meets earlier in the costumier's shop presage the elegant company who, soon afterwards, will pass sentence on Fridolin. Vehmic judges sat on rather sinister nocturnal councils which, in the middle ages, supplied rough justice in areas where the central authority was too weak to assert itself. The ironic allusion to the waning powers of the Hapsburg emperor is both subtle and unmistakable.

Schnitzler's imaginary world neither outgrew nor spread beyond the empire which Franz-Josef II kept together as much by his longevity as by the exercise of power. What Claudio Magris calls 'the Hapsburg myth' was an unceasingly fertile source of revisions and fantasies, sentimental or cruel, or both. Franz-Josef was, in many ways, more bourgeois than imperial: the supreme bureaucrat in a state where official respect for forms was paramount. Like many Viennese males, the emperor went regularly to his office; like their emperor, many men had both wives and mistresses. Duplicity was a duty in a society where men were ashamed not to betray their partners and women were shameless if they did.

Schnitzler was a conformist rebel; he enjoyed the sweet wickednesses of which he was so accurate a chronicler. His affection for what he called 'das süsse Madel' (sweet young things) was matched by the alacrity with which he replaced one with another. *Anatol* – a series of sketches about a smart man-about-Vienna much like himself – brought Schnitzler fame by the time he was barely thirty and he never lost it. He wore success with elegant lack of surprise. He seemed to take himself no more seriously than his conquests. His reputation has perhaps suffered from his affectations of effortlessness.

The brevity and levity of Schnitzler's style, not least in *Dream Fantasia*, make it seem as if everything came easily to him. Because he was expert in the classic bourgeois genres – the boulevard play, the sophisticated magazine story – it is easy to miss the inventiveness and innovation he brought to them. He was one of the first novelists to use interior monologue; *Fräulein Else* is a neat instance (it too features a kind of delirious dream). Schnitzler's abiding sense of the disintegration both of Austrian society and of its individual citizens has no clearer expression than *Dream Fantasia*, in which a happy marriage is anatomised into the contrary impulses of murderous rage and reckless sensuality, of mutual desire and mutual revulsion, of tenderness and violence. Is it to become stronger as a result of what seems to fracture it or is it now fatally flawed? Schnitzler's irony is so deftly attuned to the ambiguity of conjugal love that his pessimism, when read in a cheerful light, seems not to bar an optimistic reading. 'Feelings and understanding,' Schnitzler once said, 'may sleep under the same roof, but they run completely separate households in the human soul.'

The calm, almost pompous, tone of his narrative enables Schnitzler to achieve what Wittgenstein tried to do in philosophy: say the new thing in the old language. *Dream Fantasia* is erotic without being pornographic. It unsettles as much as it excites; like a dream, it recurrently threatens to come to a climax which eludes the protagonist as it does the reader. It is both explicit and decorous, outspoken and reticent, believable and incredible. Albertine's dreams are what dreams *might be*, if they were more artistic and more explicit than usual.

Schnitzler does not scarify the surface of his text with literary experiment; he seems simply to track Fridolin in a world where dream and reality are no longer distinct. Do the events which so disconcert Fridolin 'really' take place? Or are the dreams which Albertine recounts in such cruel detail only part of a prolonged dream which is the story as a whole? The narrative avoids unreality and absurdity by virtue of its unexcited, matter-of-fact vocabulary. With its wealth of realistic detail, Fridolin's adventure seems to belong to the waking world, but does it? The reader must decide, though the use of 'Denmark' (as the password when Fridolin is seeking entry to the mysterious house where beautiful women are to be found) echoes, surely deliberately, the fact that Albertine's dream lover is a Dane. Perhaps there was such an oneiric quality to life in Vienna that, as Schnitzler's leading character says in *Paracelsus*:

> only those who look for a meaning will find it. Dreaming and waking, truth and lie mingle. Security exists nowhere. We know nothing of others, nothing of ourselves. We always play. Wise is the man who knows.

That knowing wisdom was at the centre of the solemn playfulness of Schnitzler's art, and life.

Author, *Auteur*

Just under thirty years ago I flew out to Los Angeles in order to kiss hands, as it were, on being given a major feature film to direct. Dick Zanuck and David Brown, who were running 20th Century Fox, thought sufficiently well of my script and of Faye Dunaway's commitment to it, to give me the nod. It was, and is, typical of American movie companies to back their hunches, especially with writers who, as Joe Manckiewicz pointed out, have always in some sense directed their scripts before a so-called *auteur* (who often can't write anything, except his name above everyone else's) gets his appropriating hands on them.

When I arrived on that first visit to LA, it was a ghost town. The slump in attendances, and in the East Coast bankers' confidence in movies as a source of profit, meant there was no cash for productions. Nevertheless, I was met by a studio limousine, which remained at my disposal twenty-four hours a day, quite as if there was somewhere to go in it. Dick and David received me with a show of unabated enthusiasm, but when I went to see the chief production executive, he listened glumly to my requirements and then said, 'I don't know about locations in Africa, but if you can use thirty Zero fighters anyplace, I can sure help you there.' The studio had recently made *Tora, Tora, Tora* about Pearl Harbor. The story of what *Private Eye* had called 'nasty Nips in the air' had not lubricated their cash flow. It looked as if TV was doing to the studios what Tojo did not quite achieve with the US fleet in December 1941.

By the time I had flown back to London, first class, Dick and David had had to cancel the picture. Not long afterwards, they were themselves cancelled. But if my career as a big-time director was over before it began, Dick and David went from being dead men to unprecedented resurrection: in 1975, they produced *Jaws*, after which things were never to be the same again, for them or anyone else in The Biz. That 1970s revolution might never have happened, if a rookie director called Steven Spielberg had stayed with a script I wrote for him, called *Roses, Roses*, and which he *liked*, but didn't finally *love*.

Review of Jon Lewis (ed.) *The New American Cinema*, in the *Sunday Times*, 1998.

When we parted, amicably, he was freed up to do *Jaws*. Typically, in their rare case, Dick and David had remained loyal to Steven after his first feature, *Sugarland Express,* was a failure (I admired it a lot). Rich, rich, rich was their reward.

The success of *Jaws*, and the method of its midsummer marketing, led to a revision of The Industry's strategy and totemology. It had always been assumed that Big Pictures had to come out in the late autumn; Christmas alone was blockbuster-time. *Jaws* took the people off the beach and into the movies.

In one of the most interesting of the chapters in *New American Cinema*, the volume's editor, Jon Lewis, details the changing logics of style, production and financing which enabled the Hollywood studios to emerge from quasi-terminal darkness of the late 1960s into today's boom, boom, boom in which The Biz contributes more to the American economy than anything except plane-making.

Alas, British producers are still too timid, too small-time and too unbusinesslike to learn the organisational lessons spelt out in the best chapters of this variously lively, informative and densely argued volume. David Puttnam's glorious bungling of his command of Columbia Pictures was an instance both of missionary megalomania and of ignorance of what it takes to be a player in the film world's biggest game. Puttnam's attempt to reduce salaries and budgets was bound to fail. Hollywood studios may be vulgar, wasteful factories, but it's not an accident: the 'over-payment' of talent also licenses top executives to give themselves immense bonuses.

More importantly misconceived, however, was Puttnam's idea that the future of the movies lay in modest productions of class scripts. The opposite (alas for 'art') has proved the case. Puttnam was like Coppola's *Tucker,* and like Coppola himself, in imagining that being small and beautiful could be an attribute of modern business. Having already made a mess of Goldcrest (oh yes he did, and so did Dickie), there was nothing left for Puttnam but ennoblement and his now chosen role as Euro-aesthete; in other – American – words, he blew it.

The 1970s shift in power from *auteur* directors to the once-despised executives is accurately and convincingly charted by Lewis. Once upon a time, the studios deferred to 'the talent', especially when it made big bucks (when else?). They still do, to a degree, but James Cameron and Arnold Schwarznegger are what they mean by talent. Where executives once waited humbly for *auteurs* and producers to bring them ideas, and endured the costs of their realisation with apprehensive impotence, today's hands-on hot-shots originate, and monitor, their own projects, which are very often 'no-brainers', otherwise known as High Concept. You got a problem with that? How about you go work someplace else?

As the philosophers of the Vienna circle might say, if they could be with us today, the meaning of a film is now the method of its selling. On another of my visits to LA, an independent producer (fired top executive) told me about his projected movie. He had as yet no script, no director, no stars, no start-date, but things were going great: he already had the poster. Bob was not kidding (he was using a lot of coke, but he was not kidding). Once the publicity is in place, everything which once preceded it now follows. Since advertising budgets are often double those of what they sell, movies are genetically engineered just like any other kind of consumable. First design the kind of fruit you want, then programme the seed.

Jon Lewis and Justin Wyatt supply the best essays (and excellent notes) in this collection. Wyatt is almost as good as his editor on mercantile mechanics, though he fails to remark that one of the reasons for the (relative) prosperity of smaller studios, like Roger Corman's outfit, in the late 1960s was that they were unencumbered by the feather-bedding union agreements which the studios – like the British newspaper proprietors before Wapping – had not challenged in prosperous times. In Hollywood, however, the smaller studios were often secretly funded by the large ones. Their product was thus marketed by the same organisations with whose studios they appeared to be competing 'unfairly'. When Reagan became president, it became easier to tear up the old agreements, or get round them. Most of the small outfits then got taken over or went to the wall.

After the double-whammy of *Jaws* and *Star Wars*, the big studios lost all interest in small budgets. Doubling their money on penny-ante bets was yesterday's kind of a gamble. George Lucas made *Star Wars* in England, but California got rich on it, as he did. I can remember a Fox executive (he happened to be English) saying that they wanted to cancel the picture: '$10,000,000 already on a movie with Alec Guinness in it! We have to be crazy.' They were too: they had so little foresight that the studio's lawyers made no provision for rights in the sequels, or the prequels. Who's surprised that contracts in dreamland are now fatter than screenplays and take longer to get finalised (do *they* get 'notes', or what?)?

Odd as it may seem, the readability of this compendium varies in proportion to its emphasis on financial structures. The least entertaining pieces are politically more or less correct analyses of paranoid film-makers such as Oliver Stone and Francis Coppola, whose *The Conversation* receives adulatory treatment from Timothy Corrigan. The latter seems unaware that the premiss of the movie – a verbal ambiguity – makes sense only when the script is *read*, but cannot survive its performance.

Tania Modieski's account of *Pacific Heights* is verbosely ingenious when she is seeking 'to explore my own investment in the figure of the female protagonist who, by way of her investigations into the performative psycho-male, achieved an empowered selfhood that feels real', but – are you still with me? – it is typical of her narcissistic feminism that she attaches no importance to the fact that the movie's director, John Schlesinger, had his own 'investment' and (why not?) psycho-male performativeness. Christopher Sharrett confesses himself much indebted, in his anatomy of Oliver Stone's *JFK* to the 'pioneering research and writing' of Ralph Schoenman, once Bertie Russell's *éminence rouge*, now a realtor-rich Californian. This may not reinforce everyone's faith in Sharrett's conclusions about the link between the CIA and Kennedy's assassination, but if the majority of readers go for it, it has to be true. That's democracy, isn't it? Oh yes it is too.

Language, Truth and Style

Sometimes the middle-aged man looks across a room, or a street, and catches sight of someone who was the object of his youthful ardour. Can this be the girl whose embrace he could never forget? It is not only girls who excite such passions. Consider this account of a young writer's first encounter with the object of his love:

> The first book which Thornton Ashworth recommended was *Language, Truth and Logic*. No sooner had Paul begun it than he felt he had found in it the solution not only to his problems but to all his difficulties as well. The book's icy articulation of language and the remorseless destructiveness of its arguments were alike agreeable to him… He felt the author to be his saviour from a world of tangled and ponderous pieties… Nothing in Paul's past was relevant to this new philosophy. It was a fresh, sterilized scalpel with which he might excise the scar tissue that still pained him with its adhesions. There was nothing he might not do. There was no reason on earth to be anything that he did not want to be. There was no reason why he should acknowledge his Jewishness. There was no reason to remain faithful to Julia. There was no reason to pay attention to the rumblings of his inner moral indigestion, it remained only to purge it, to ridicule it, to prune his own contradictory and nonsensical feelings till his personality had something of the cold and confident resolution which was so obvious in Thornton Ashworth…

All the symptoms of infatuation are there: the sense of being delivered from an adolescence of confused and futile sentiments as the result of a single encounter, exhilaration at the prospect of a fresh beginning, inability to see anything whatever wrong with the god-like object of one's admiration. We are listening to Paul, the hero of my first big novel, *The Limits of Love*, as he falls in love with philosophy.

Philosophers whom we admire in our youth are not always the best. Yet their hold can be tenacious. The reasons for such tenacity are

A paper delivered at a Philosophy Symposium at London University, 1999, and subsequently published in *PN Review*.

likely to be both intrinsic and extrinsic to the work in question. Oddly enough, in my first draft I wrote: 'the reasons… are likely to be both intrinsic and extrinsic to the *world* in question'. The misprint is a clue to one of the ways in which I want to reconsider A.J. Ayer and the contemporaries with whom he can be compared and contrasted. Their world is not today's; their ambitions in it, and for it, demand more than individual assessment. We need also to recover the kind of air they breathed and the political and social climate in which it circulated.

What I say here will be in good part what Cambridge philosophers used to disparage as 'mere autobiography': statements preceded by naïve fortifiers such as 'I strongly believe' or 'I am sincerely convinced'. I lack credentials to take other than a subjective view of the style, and content, of – in particular – the man who became both Professor Sir Alfred Jules Ayer, logical positivist and Freddie Ayer, man-about-town, *homme couvert de femmes* and Tottenham Hotspur supporter.

Language, Truth and Logic recruited me to philosophy, but it was not my first providential text. Somerset Maugham's *Of Human Bondage* took its title from Spinoza's account of the necessity to which, in his implacably determined world-view, we are all subject. Maugham's protracted gloss on it was the first adult novel I ever read. Ah Miss Wilkinson! Her shameless desires disgusted Philip Carey, but she sounded just the job to me. Admiration is a relation which always involves the admirer as well as the object admired. Styles, and arguments, need to be seductive.

Before going to medical school, Maugham was a philosophy student, at Heidelberg, under Kuno Fischer. In his notebooks, he observed that the metaphysician is like a man who climbs to the top of a high mountain and who, on getting there, finds it to be wreathed in impenetrable mist. It is not surprising if, when he comes to report to those who have waited for him in the valley, he tells them that the view from the peak was sublime. Heidegger was a keen mountaineer.

There is a certain cousinship between the ideas and the tone of Maugham and of Ayer. Curiously and perhaps significantly, both men owed something to a common, and unlikely, influence: Walter Pater. In *Of Human Bondage*, the sententious Cronshaw cites Pater's famous dictum that one should aspire to 'burn with a hard gem-like flame'. Maugham then sentences the aesthete to die of dysentery in South Africa, in conditions ignominiously at odds with his high-flown Oxonian aesthetic.

In Ben Rogers' sympathetic account of Ayer's life, Richard Wollheim is quoted as having

> detected a sadness... which he associated with (Ayer's) being an only child. Wollheim was reminded of an autobiographical story by... the Oxford aesthete, Walter Pater – 'The Child in the House' – in which Pater describes the development, in a book-loving, cosseted, philosophically minded little boy, of an enchanting awareness of the beauty of the world along with an aching recognition of the sorrow and suffering it contains.

There is a singular similarity to Bertrand Russell's idea of the young Bertrand Russell. It is not surprising that the adult Ayer should have constituted himself Russell's advocate, even though the relation was never reliably reciprocal. 'As a young man,' however, Rogers assures us 'Ayer identified with Pater', though there is no evidence that Freddie – as the modern style licenses us to call him – ever read 'The Child in the House'. 'Dickens,' Rogers says, 'offers firmer ground.' Ayer returned again and again to Dickens's novels, which are 'often a source of incidental reference in his philosophical writings'. David Copperfield is only one instance of children 'of excellent abilities with strong powers of observation, quick, eager, delicate, and soon hurt bodily or mentally', obliged to make their own way in an unfeeling world. Maugham's Philip Carey falls into the same category and so did the only child who read, and was enthralled by, both *Of Human Bondage* and *Language, Truth and Logic* within the span of a few postwar years.

Maugham and Ayer both had a sense of being somehow foreign. Maugham was born in the British embassy in Paris and, although his parents were English, his first language was French. He came to England for the first time only at the age of eight, as an orphan. He knew no better than to call out 'cabriolet' when attracting the attention of a cockney hansom-cab driver. He spent the remainder of his childhood under the joyless tutelage of his uncle, a vicar in Whitstable. Willie's revulsion from Anglican Christianity was primed by a sense of personal injustice: when he heard tales of divine mercy, he thought of his dying mother, though he spoke, more impersonally, of the children suffering from meningitis whose agony he could do nothing, as a young doctor, to alleviate. His model of English hypocrisy was the uncle, who once said, perhaps with more wit than his nephew cared to appreciate, 'Clergymen are paid to preach, not to practise.' How different are philosophers?

Ayer called his paternal grandmother 'Bonne maman'. She was of Swiss origin. His grandfather, Nicolas Louis Cyprien Ayer had been an 'important educationist, geographer and linguist', noted for vehement anti-clericalism. His textbooks, however, are said to 'make for very dry reading'. In other respects, he was 'un homme terrible'. In the late 1800s, *bonne maman* left him and brought her children to London, where she became a governess.

The maiden name of Freddie's mother, Reine, was Citroën, which now sounds French, on account of the cars which one of the family started to manufacture. The name is actually of Askenazi provenance; the Citroëns were originally Eastern European Jews. Reine's father, Dorus – 'a stern but loving patriarch' – was first a fruit trader in Antwerp, but went diamond prospecting in South Africa. He came back rich enough to help found Minerva, an engineering firm set up to produce the newly invented motorbike. Although avowedly agnostic and assimilationist, he married Sarah Rozelaar, the daughter of a Dutch-Jewish diamond dealer.

In the 1890s, the family moved to London, where Dorus, an Anglophile, 'deeply admiring of British tolerance and commercial spirit', set up a new branch of Minerva. During the First World War, his company produced shells and fuses. At the end of it Dorus was offered a knighthood. His wife persuaded him to decline, on the grounds that as foreigners, 'it would make them look ridiculous'. Perhaps Freddie Ayer was taking a satirical swipe at social pretensions when, as a lifelong supporter of the Labour Party, he embraced the knighthood which his adored grandfather had denied himself.

The introduction to *Language, Truth and Logic* acknowledges that its views derive from the doctrines of Bertrand Russell and of Wittgenstein, whose guilt-ridden asceticism was never his *quondam* disciple's style. Academic prefaces are often gorged with gratitude to those who can, by honeyed deference, be recruited to roll the author's log. It is not certain that either Russell or Wittgenstein recognised his 'doctrines' in Ayer's acerbic recension of them. The pugnacious text won its author fame in London; it struck many of his fellow Oxonians as vulgar and ungrateful. Rogers tells how two of them, Joseph and Prichard, were overheard in a bookshop by R.G. Collingwood, complaining to each other that *Language, Truth and Logic* should never have found a publisher. (They might have guessed it would be that dangerous pro-Communist Victor Gollancz.) Collingwood, although no friend of Ayer's thesis, turned to them and said, 'Gentlemen, this book will be read when your names are forgotten.' They are, and it is.

Keener to prevail than to persuade, Ayer made enemies who have, as recent attacks prove, waited till after the bell to hit him. Oliver Cromwell's body was dug up after his death and dragged through London on a hurdle. Metaphorically speaking, something not dissimilar has happened recently to Ayer and to his reputation. There are those who never forget first loves, and others – such as Colin McGinn – who also never forgive them.

It has been suggested that Ayer's pro-science posture was invalidated by ignorance of how scientists work and by his advocacy of 'linguistic philosophy', with its supposed faith in common sense. Lewis Wolpert has pointed out, no doubt correctly, that science is *not* in accord with common sense. This does not substantially damage Ayer's case, since he put no large bets on 'what we actually say'. Wolpert does, on the other hand, challenge the plausibility of Ayer's contemporary J.L. Austin's view that ordinary language must have the last word.

Austin's conviction that there could be no appeal from the common sense of the English people, as vested in their usage, could be read (though never by Austin) as a refinement of Rousseau's populism. Just as twelve good men and true were incapable of delivering a wrongful verdict, so what enough Englishmen had said was all that could or needed to be said about epistemology, ethics or most anything else. There was no appeal against the general will as codified in grammars and dictionaries.

How did Ayer come to write *Language, Truth and Logic* in the form he did? The essence of a style is that it is adopted. Wittgenstein remarked the difficulty, and the obligation, to say the new thing in the old language. Charles Darwin wrote *The Origin of Species* in the very tones of the society whose preconceptions it was to shatter. In the same way, during the first half of the twentieth century, the prose even of those like Shaw, Wells and George Orwell, who seemed to argue *against* British hegemony, gained world-wide currency because it belonged to the culture of a great power. Fabianism became current thanks to the Grand Fleet, the Bank of England and to the imperial redness of so much of the map which social revolutionaries wanted to change.

In much the same way, when the young Freddie Ayer returned from Vienna in 1933, at the age of twenty-three, eager to pass on the lessons of the logical positivism to whose source Gilbert Ryle had despatched him, he announced the gospel, in which the only divinity was science, with the confidence of what read like classic English cadences:

The traditional disputes of philosophy [he began] are, for the most part, as unwarranted as they are unfruitful. The surest way to end them is to establish beyond question what should be the purpose and method of a philosophical enquiry...

We may begin [he continued] by criticising the metaphysical thesis that philosophy affords us knowledge of a reality transcending the world of science and common sense.

Robert Skidelski wrote quite recently that Ayer's

absurd doctrine managed to be both trivialising and nihilistic... trivialising because it dismissed all the traditional problems of philosophy as 'pseudo-problems' arising from the misuse of language... Nihilistic because it consigned the whole of human thought outside the natural sciences to a limbo of personal opinion about which nothing true or false could be said.

Is this criticism wholly, or at all, justified? Does Skidelski believe that metaphysics *can* supply transcendental knowledge? Does anyone else? Will he tell us that there is no important difference, in kind and in logic, between scientific truths, backed by objective experiment, and the 'truths' of moralists and ayatollahs, politicians, priests and historians?

Ayer's opening volley reminds us of the vanished world of complacent English supremacy in which, and at which, it was fired. In 1933, Ayer returned from a continent rabid with ideologies to an Oxford both insular and inhibited. Its High Tables welcomed appeasers and toadies, snobs and nobs. Ayer was soon at the heart of a rather cautious philosophical revolution. Its self-elected central committee was composed of young men such as J.L. Austin, Stuart Hampshire, and Isaiah Berlin. Their caution was due partly to civilised habit (all wrote mandarin English) and partly to ambitious prudence. They might seem to be burning the kind of academic boats in which their seniors had long cruised so smugly, but they also wanted to be sure that at least some first-class accommodation escaped the flames.

Language, Truth and Logic contains deferential references to Carnap and Schlick, Russell and Moore, Wisdom and Mace, as well as a snappy (and abidingly valid) dismissal of Heidegger 'who bases his metaphysics on the assumption that "Nothing" is a name which is used to denote something peculiarly mysterious'.

There is something conspicuously well-spoken in the iconoclasm with which Ayer sought to naturalise, what was, for all its affinity with

Hume, Mill and Russell, a foreign philosophy. Whatever Skidelski and others may now say, logical positivism can be seen as an honourable (if mistaken) attempt to create a doctrine which, by its nature, and that of the science it promoted, would be both universal and modest. Like Communism, it offered escape from personal particularism. Identity was lost in collegiality; racial or national origins in a universal and systematically third-personal activity. In science's ecumenical commonwealth there were to be neither Jews nor Gentiles. Though matters of taste were not in the Viennese curriculum, a certain similarity can be seen in Dr Leavis's notion of literary criticism as a 'Common Pursuit'. In theory, scientists and Leavisites were selfless musketeers, though in comic practice critics and philosophers strove for individual eminence. Leavis believed that he was a friend, and equal, of Wittgenstein. The belief was not shared.

Does Ayer's immaculate prose conceal (and so declare) a certain dread of being taken for the Jewboy which, he later confessed, he always feared he was? If he is accused of drawing attention to himself – a standard charge against clever Jews by those who are being careful not to be anti-Semitic – the intellectual dandy dares to ask to whom attention can better be drawn. Ayer was a prodigy who never tired of being a naughty boy. However, if he was often socially impudent, his professional style was irreproachable, even conventional, especially when he became head of department at UCL. This less appeased than exasperated some of his enemies. Good behaviour was the last thing they wanted of him. The logical breach between ethical statements, which he held to be merely emotive, and those of natural science, which belonged to the realm of objective truth, was matched by the division of Ayer's own life between duty and pleasure. He may have been two-faced, but neither face was more, or less, genuine than the other. Stylishness was the narrow bridge between them.

In controversy, he had something in common with the fictional character who remarked 'I can be very grammatical if roused'. Ayer's chance confrontation with Mike Tyson, in which Colin McGinn (in his *TLS* review of Rogers) finds the essence of Freddie, and does not greatly admire it, was a pretty demonstration of how reason can be used – to employ a Platonic metaphor – to stabilise other men's wild horses. Tyson was in the process of forcing himself on 'a distraught Naomi Campbell'. Ayer chose to play the wise man who rushed in and recruited Tyson to philosophy with a one-two that countered 'Do you know who the fuck I am?' with 'I am the former Wykeham Professor of Logic. We are both pre-eminent in our field; I suggest we talk about this like rational men.' As a way of initiating, if not clinching, the peace process, this mandarin line seems to have been as effective as any.

In the domestic ring, Ayer boxed clever. He out-pointed Oxford, which he said always sickened him with dread, by sounding imperturbably Oxonian. Such stylishness, at once aggressive and concessive, can be the function of a response to threats, real or imagined, from the society in which its author seeks to make his name. *Style* was the title of one of Pater's most famous 1890 essays. He argued that the prime condition of good writing was *truth*. In scientific writing, the truth to reality of the facts stated is the thing of value. The writer's task, in such cases, is to find exact expression in words for a particular series of facts. The privileged place given to scientific propositions by logical positivists seems of a piece with Pater's idea that good writing is defined by its truth. What lacks clear meaning, both agreed, clearly lacks truth; and what has meaning must be true.

As Edmund Chandler points out, in his *Pater on Style* (Copenhagen 1958), Pater saw no *systematic* distinction between scientific and personal truth. Prose art begins, he says, when the author presents a subject *as seen by him*; and it is a fine art according to the degree of perception attained. Is there not an affinity between Ayer's persistent belief that sense-data are the primary stuff from which physical phenomena are constructed and the Old Aesthete's view that there is at least some truth in common between science and art? Pater claimed that 'the one beauty of all prose style' was to be found in the fusion of word and insight. As Chandler points out, he 'pushes the problem of style further back than words and makes it one of perception...' Was not perception one of A.J. Ayer's recurrent topics?

Anticipating Roland Barthes, Pater points out that anyone who uses words employs a material that is 'no more a creation of his own than the sculptor's marble'. While the subtlety of language is almost infinite, any individual's knowledge of it is bound to be 'relative'. Nobody thinks or writes *entirely* by himself. Language, Pater insisted, is the 'product of a myriad [of] various minds and contending tongues, compact of obscure and minute associations'. The writer must make it his perennial study; he must know the mechanisms and rules of language: 'the attention of the writer, in every minutest detail, being a pledge that it is worth the reader's while to be attentive too'. The recommended alertness to nuance, and to the accretions with which previous usage has informed the language, is of a piece with the theory and practice of J.L. Austin. The style in which Austin declared the virtues of common sense was a careful display, even parody, of donnish unaffectedness. Savour the menacing blandness of the opening of chapter 4 of *Sense and Sensibilia*:

> In due course we shall have to consider Ayer's own 'evaluation' of the argument from illusion, what in his opinion it establishes and why... Ayer makes pretty free use of the expression 'look', 'appear', and 'seem' – apparently, in the manner of most other philosophers, attaching no great importance to the question which expression is used where, and indeed implying by the speed of his philosophical flight that they could be used interchangeably... there are cases, as we shall see, in which they come down to much the same [*sic*]... But it would be a mistake to conclude that, because there are such cases, there isn't *any* particular difference in the uses of the words; there is, and there are plenty of contexts and constructions which show this.

Austin affects a neutrality which could hardly be more bristlingly hostile to Ayer. One seems to hear a tone not far from hatred even in so superficially inoffensive an expression as 'pretty free use'. The real kicker comes (appropriately enough) in a footnote. After, 'there are plenty of contexts and constructions which show this', Austin subjoins

> Compare the expressions 'right', 'ought', 'duty', 'obligation' – here too there are contexts in which *any* of these words can be used, but large and important differences all the same in the uses of each. And here too these differences have been generally neglected by philosophers.

Austin applies the stigmatic word 'neglect' to philosophers who fail to take account of moral nuances. Need we doubt that a certain grim smile made the general observation particularly performative? We are incited to conclude that delinquent linguistic sensibility leads to delinquent morality.

It may be a sign of Ayer's losing some of the cool he displayed with Mike Tyson that, in referring on one occasion to Austin's *Sense and Sensibilia*, he made a rare gaffe by asserting the singular of the Latin word *sensibilia* to be *sensibilium*, rather than, as every Etonian colleger used to know, *sensibile*. No scandalous slip, it is still the kind of loose thread that an intellectual dandy would no more care to see dangling than a participle.

The urgency in Ayer's polemic derives surely from a wish to deliver mankind from unwarranted deference to metaphysics, and from the religious and social consequences of unnecessary credulity. It is also elegantly phrased in a form which, he hopes, will secure some Tuscan applause. Ayer's formal style was calculated to delight the establishment whose morality he defied. Even his friend Isaiah Berlin, whose ascent to high places was by prudent – if not prudish – steps, was often shocked by Freddie's provocative conduct. He reacted rather as Lady Caroline Lamb who, when someone spoke of Byron's morals, remarked 'It's the first I've heard of them.'

Berlin's own style (personal and philosophical) was trim but unaggressive. An immigrant, however intelligent, was wise to advertise that he was never going to be fractious. Berlin had the attentive *disponibilité* of Jewish intellectuals such as Maimonides who ensured his position, for a time, by doubling as a physician under the Cordoban caliphate. Berlin could be puncturingly donnish in private – he once protested that, contrary to vile rumour, he had never called a certain trilingual professor 'a fraud'; he had actually called him 'a *genuine* fraud' – but his published work, however shrewd, cocked few noticeable snooks. Here he is in calm denunciation of

> the view... at the heart of much metaphysical rationalism... that all good things must be compatible, and that therefore freedom, order, knowledge, happiness, a closed future (and an open one?) must be at least compatible, and perhaps even entail one another, in a systematic fashion. But this proposition is not self-evidently true, if only on empirical grounds. Indeed, it is perhaps one of the least plausible beliefs ever entertained by profound and influential thinkers.'

The last sentence seems to swing a powerful hook, but its knockout effect is mitigated by the fact that the author has taken care to have no named champion in the ring with him. Berlin's speciality was to deal unvexedly with vexed issues. For instance, in his 1953 essay, 'Jewish Slavery and Emancipation', he considers whether assimilation is either a good or a possible course and of whether Jews 'should' emigrate to Israel in order to resolve their contradictions. Without denying his Jewishness, as Wittgenstein's family did, or rejecting it, as Karl Popper did, Berlin never seems personally involved in the question. It may be real, but it is not real for *him*: he asks 'What should *they* do?' rather than 'What should I do?' In his typical consultative mode, he seems professorially immune to the maladies which he diagnoses. Does this weaken his account of them or render it more likely to be correct? The perhaps facile, but honest, answer is: both.

While he appeared to go out of his way not to be offensive, and recommended himself to his hosts in such a way as to be honoured with the Order of Merit, as well as the statutory knighthood, Berlin was brave, or shrewd, enough to make his Jewishness an undenied part of his public personality. All the same, in his 1953 essay he likened the Jew to a hunchback and went further than he needed, or than we now need to accept, to depict Jews as *the* irremediable social exception. Ayer, by contrast, rarely if ever admitted openly to seeing the world from a Jewish perspective, whatever that might mean.

The second edition of *Language, Truth and Logic* came out in 1946. In the intervening ten years many millions had died, Jews and Gentiles, as the result of an ideology both vacuous and wicked. No trace of a direct reaction to these events is to be found in any Oxford philosopher of the post-war decade. Philosophy, Wittgenstein had said, leaves everything as it is; Ayer and his colleagues, friends or enemies, demonstrated that everything can also leave philosophy as it is. The British emerged from the war with their hegemony shattered, but their vanity intact. The Oxford style was still to discount European experience and so-called ideas, such as existentialism. The first decade after the war was a triumph of style over discontent: England was cold, diminished and complacent. The insular continuity of its philosophy was only one emblem, but a significant one, of a certain refusal to face the decline of Britannia's imperial and intellectual domination.

As Lucretius said of Epicurus, one man dared to be an exception. Even after he had mastered English, Karl Popper's style had a raspingly heterodox, not to say foreign tone. He did not ironise, he denounced; oh dear, it did all seem to matter to him so much. Though Popper somewhat resembled Ayer in advocating a science-based notion of meaning, he was more tolerant of certain kinds of metaphysics. Since he had neither been to Eton nor served in the Welsh Guards, he might have expected to be less acceptable than the native-born Ayer, but his manifest foreignness made him a character. His rudeness about Hegel and Marx was not uncongenial (it excused not having read them), and if he was cheeky about Plato, it was easy to whisper that he had not *quite* understood the Greek, or put it in context. For the rest, his programme appeared public-spirited enough, at least for red brick purposes:

We need studies based on methodological individualism... of the way in which new traditions can be created... our individualistic and institutionalist models of such collective entities as nations, or governments, or markets, will have to be supplemented by models of political situations as well as of social movements such as scientific and industrial progress...

This is unmistakably Popper, on account less of its style than of its earnestness. It is written in order to propose an adult curriculum. Although almost comically infuriated, in lecture-room practice, by the smallest criticism, Popper was, in principle at least, disposed to invite it. Compare this:

As far as we are concerned, the distinction between the kind of metaphysics that is produced by a philosopher who has been duped by grammar, and the kind that is produced by a mystic who is trying to express the inexpressible is of no great importance: what is important to us is to realise that even the utterances of the metaphysician who is attempting to expound a vision are literally senseless; so that henceforth we may pursue our philosophical researches with as little regard for them as for the more inglorious kind of metaphysics which comes from a failure to understand the workings of our language.

This passage, from the end of the first chapter of *Language, Truth and Logic*, is more arrogant than Popper, and markedly more dogmatic in the denunciation of dogma. When Popper says what 'we' need, he proposes joining institutions of common utility. Ayer's 'We' is the imperious first person plural which demands allegiance. Announcing the dissolution of the upper house of philosophy's governing body, he implies that the we of which he is the leading component will proceed in radical fashion. There is to be no appeal and there can be no exceptions. Ayer's policy is uncompromising and coercive. His domestic politics may have been typically English in their decorous socialism, but somewhere in the rhetoric of *Language, Truth and Logic* is the ruthlessness of a philosophical Robespierre. Why else did it appeal so thoroughly to the young?

The anti-Hegelian philosophy initiated, at the turn of the century, by Russell and Moore was an aspect, to say the least, of the vanity which world leadership seemed to authorise in the British style. Ayer's mid-century dismissal of Heidegger and Sartre was of a piece with this; wealth and power give men the assurance, and insurance, to say exactly what they think; so (at least for a time) does the illusion of them.

Positivism's advocacy of science was delivered by Ayer in the style of a Greats man. *Language, Truth and Logic* seems, on reflection, to be a travel book, written on returning from an intellectual Grand Tour. Like Colin Wilson's once notorious *The Outsider* of 1956, Ayer's book excited some and scandalised others, but even its post-war revision had less effect on the English humanities than Elizabeth David did on English cooking. The British intelligentsia, like the British in general, felt no great urge to think differently after 1945. Whatever the domestic inconveniences of a victory dearly bought, Hitler's defeat convinced the Establishment that pretty well everything they had thought and done was correct; there was no need for plan B.

On a petty level, Kingsley Amis's 1954 novel *Lucky Jim* had something of the same effect on literature as *Language, Truth and Logic* had on pre-war philosophy. It served notice that change was in the air, but did not immediately change anything. As a satire on academic life, *Lucky Jim* now seems jejune, and not particularly funny, but it remains a portent of something its author neither foresaw nor, in the long run, welcomed: the collapse of formal literary manners and of the social niceties which they lubricated. Amis might be an Oxford man (and a sporadic don), but he was never going to burn with a hard gem-like flame. The English style was about to lose its confidence, not through philosophical arguments, nor by Jim Dixon making funny faces at it, but by its losing last throw at Suez.

Within very little time, only Harold Macmillan's parodic patricianism kept the old style half-alive. Looking back in tranquillity, we can see that the new style of social comedy, as seen in John Osborne's plays, was soon as rueful as it was scornful. Osborne's clapped-out old comedian, Archie Rice, advised his audience not to laugh too loudly because we were in a very old building.

The symptom and, to some degree perhaps, the cause of post-Suez change in philosophy was Ernest Gellner's 1959 *Words and Things*. Once again, Victor Gollancz was the publisher of a volume which enraged the Oxford philosophers of whom Ayer himself was now, to some extent, a senior member. Gellner had been a scholar of Balliol (just as Stalin and Mikoyan had been seminarists), but he rebelled against what he satirised, unsmilingly, as the fruitless parlour games to which Austin, Ryle, and their epigoni were addicted. His other main target was Wittgenstein, which — no less than his arguments — earned him the endorsement of 'that old trouble-maker' Russell.

Gellner's style was without nuance or grace. He denounced and he lampooned. He looked back in anger and forward without sentiment.

He demanded a philosophy which took account of sociology and engaged with political issues. Hence Popper was spared his anathema, as was the author of *Language, Truth and Logic*, on account of its explicit candour. Gellner was enraged above all by what he called the Indian Rope Trick of the typical linguistic philosopher: he climbed up many ropes, Gellner jeered, but 'beware of trying to convince him that something must be supporting the rope'. Austin particularly infuriated him on account of his sardonic complacency: 'If you can make an analysis convince yourself... and you can get... cantankerous colleagues to agree with it, that's a pretty good criterion that there is something in it.' Austin's colleagues, Gellner said, sardonically, might be cantankerous *within* the method, but there were conspicuously un-cantankerous *about* it. The attack on élites, and their *élan*, has continued ever since and with it the implicit claim that we now know how to do definitive philosophy. Ayer had wanted to be a member of the club whose rules he scorned; Gellner had no such ambivalence: he wanted it closed.

Style in philosophy, as in literature, may not be a direct function of Marx's economic conditions, but a whole skein of unacknowledged and often unconscious social and political elements contribute to its formation and, self-evidently, to its traditions. The individuality of philosophers is reflected by the nuances of their styles as well as by the variety of their ideas, but *why* they write, or talk, as they do will always be something to do with the intellectual and social air they breathe and with the media in which they express themselves. It is a nice irony that Skidelski, in a few hundred words of journalistic debunking, accuses Ayer of sponsoring 'an amusing game'. The reaction to logical positivism, he says, 'led to Continental post-structuralism' and hence to a 'double assault' from which intellectual life is only now recovering. Ayer is thus declared responsible not only for what he thought but for what others said in violent, and obscurantist, reaction to it.

I am not being sarcastic when I declare myself an admirer of Robert Skidelski, but is there not something unnervingly similar in his attitude to Ayer and his intimation, in his biography of Oswald Mosley, that the Jews were to blame for the Fascists' anti-Semitism? This is the logic of the show-trial in which scapegoats are arraigned – in John Erickson's chilling phrase when describing Stalin's cynicism – 'before grinning judges'. The smirking judges in our society are newspaper editors and their Vishinskys are the columnists, out for their daily victims.

According to Skidelski, Ayer's success in popularising (?!) logical positivism was due to a 'lucidity which now seems merely hypnotic and to a personality and lifestyle which distance has robbed of most of their charm'. Humbug, however, will never lose its charm. Is the journalistic disparagement of dead men a marked improvement on the kind of rigour which, for all his supposed faults and errors, was Freddie Ayer's long professional habit? Must we accept that to have exchanged irony, elegance and the distrust of metaphysical nonsense for the crowd-pleasing glibness of knocking copy signals the advent of a new, more honest style in intellectual discourse? Jim Dixon might know just what kind of a face to make at that idea.

French and English

At my prep school, we used to play a game called French and English. Scampering from one safe area to another, the two sides attempted to tag each other on the way. Since there was no defining kit, it was never certain who was on whose side, still less which had won. However, the game worked off a lot of energy and passed the time. The Hundred Years War, which French and English fought from 1337 to 1453, had something in common with this game: it was extremely protracted; the two sides were never precisely defined (alliances were, to say the least, unreliable); and there was no clear winner, at least not until long after several generations of combatants had hung up their arms.

We have had to wait nine years for Jonathan Sumption's second, fat volume of what should prove to be a classic of sharp scholarship and dust-dispelling energy. This instalment begins – only ten years after the kick-off – in 1347, with Edward III confronting 'the problems of Victory'. It ends in 1369, with the seemingly triumphant English king's decision to alter his seals to add the arms of France to those of England.

This amalgamation was intended to symbolise Edward's irreversible vindication of his 'rights'. His son, the Black Prince, had defeated and captured the French King John II at Poitiers (1356, a date all schoolboys used to memorise with pride). After *very* long negotiations, the captive monarch – luxuriously humbled by enforced residence in London's Savoy Palace – had had to agree to abject conditions for his release. Game over? Not at all: soon after John's release, he died. His son, and heir, promptly found 'honourable' reasons to abrogate the treaty of the *fleur de lis*. Edward's subsequent proclamation of Anglo-French union, under one crown (his own), was little more than a gesture of fury at the understandable perfidy of the newly crowned Charles V.

Too much nonsense has been talked about the Middle Ages, glorifying their 'organic' societies, supposedly linked by a common faith in Christianity and not yet affected by what T.S. Eliot famously

Review of Jonathan Sumption, *Trial by Fire: The Hundred Years War*, vol. II, in the *Sunday Times*, 2000.

termed the 'dissociation of sensibility'. The latter, we were told, led to the anguished rootlessness of modern man and the apotheosis of Money, quite as if greed were a function only of Capitalism and lack of Faith.

Sumption's beady prose gives the lie to such sentimental readings of the Good Old Days. Few men in this history were good and fewer grew to be very old: war, plague, poison, the assassin's dagger, and the headsman's frequently clumsy axe saw to that. It was a time of living dangerously and perishing miserably. The codes of chivalry did apply, in theory, but they were tarnished by vanity and corrupted by avarice. Money was a constant preoccupation: the kings had to raise it in order to finance their armies; soldiers fought mainly in order to wrack it from their enemies.

The nobility typically cared more for their prisoners than for their cause. Huge ransoms could be extracted for classy captives. For the well-plumed, battles were not killing-fields, more places for a kind of upper-class strip-poker game. The defeated paid up and then scraped their barrels in order to stake themselves for another return to the charge. Common soldiers were likelier to be killed than their lords, since they had no cash value. In the spirit of *sauve qui peut*, they were inclined to switch sides if the transfer fees were right. The Middle Ages more often concerned what today's football writers call 'personal terms' rather than God, England or St George (whose cross was adopted, belatedly, to distinguish friends from foes who often wore the same gear and used the same language).

The Hundred Years War was never between cohesive nation-states, sure of their identities or fixed behind settled boundaries. It was a series of interlocking, internecine squabbles, feuds and affairs of honour which diplomats (often churchmen) sought intermittently to resolve. Pope Innocent VI's affectations of impartiality never convinced the English, but he and his legates did work to avoid bloodshed, seldom with success.

Innocent's successor, Urban V does, however, have the last laugh in the present volume. In 1364, Edward III pulled off what threatened to be a clinching coup: he arranged a marriage between his fifth son, Edmund Langley, and Margaret, the heiress of Louis de Male, whose lands included huge tracts of France. Like so many royals, the betrothed were closely related by blood. They could not be married without what was usually the easily obtained formality of a Vatican dispensation.

For once, however, His Holiness refused, on pious grounds, to sanction an alliance which would have led to the encirclement of France by the English crown. Margaret was immediately betrothed to Charles V's liegeman, Philip, Duke of Burgundy, to whom she was even more closely related by blood than she was to Langley. The Pope made no objection. Under the aegis of Rome, European unity was avoided; France survived to fight for many another day.

The course of innumerable campaigns in the vasty, often ravaged, fields of France is vividly traced. Switches of fortune, and allegiance, are unconfusingly analysed and, according to the lights of the time, justified. Rogue princes – not least the glamorous and shifty Charles of Navarre, a kingdom too pinched for his ambitions – change sides with an opportunism mirrored by the mercenary soldiers who rape, pillage and kill under the banner of whoever promises them the best wages.

The English common soldiers were better disciplined (because better paid) than French conscripts, but they were often tempted by circumstance – and the loss of earnings which followed victory – to become freebooters in the style of the Gascon *routiers* who were far from being as *sympa* (sympathetic) as modern *routiers* – the group name for today's French lorry drivers – claim to be. Their savage loyalty was first to their lord, then to their paymasters and, finally, perforce, to each other.

The richness of the French countryside, and its lack of reliable defenders, made it a plunderers' paradise. In the Limousin, in the central south-west, 'Murderers and robbers calling themselves English' controlled much of the open country. Rich, defenceless towns would buy off one set of raiders only to prompt the depredations of another. Bands of 'yobs' (a term used, if not coined, by the 'conservative Sir Thomas Gray') set off from England, like hooligans without tickets, to grab what they could from the demoralised French.

What the English did not filch, the Parisian authorities sought to tax. The French peasant's distrust of those who do not belong to his family has a long, bloody ancestry. When the French king debased the coinage, to raise revenue, it was the nobility's turn to cry foul (the lower classes rarely used coins). Defeat weakened the Crown and kindled class warfare. There were many mini-French revolutions before 1789.

The English nearly always determined when war should be waged. Their tactics were better and their society more stable. They enjoyed the security of the Channel which served them in the office of a wall, as long as their 'cogs' – little ships – controlled the seas. The possession of Calais gave Edward a permanent bridgehead. He could funnel troops into France more or less at will. The French tried only once, in 1360, to land on the south coast, whence they were repelled with heavy loss.

Throughout his vigorous narrative, Sumption displays an effortless command of sources. He writes with exemplary clarity and many neat turns of phrase (the odd misprint or omission is not, I suspect, his fault, though corrections are needed). Only the archaic term 'trailbaston' required me to reach for my Webster's. It refers to the tactics used by proto-VAT collectors to cudgel arrears from reluctant merchants. Sumption elucidates motives without slackening pace and spices the broad sweep with telling detail. His masterpiece is earning a place alongside Sir Steven Runciman's *History of the Crusades*. And – who knows? – after another six or seven volumes, we may be within earshot of the final whistle.

Some Talk of Alexandria

Boasting Irish origins, Lawrence Durrell was a product of the British Empire – he was born in India in 1912 and never lived for long in England – and of its more or less glorious decline. *The Alexandria Quartet*, his greatest (and only durable?) work of fiction, began to be published in 1957, by which time the world which it depicted had already been disassembled by *enosis* in Cyprus and by the fiasco of Suez.

Gamel Abdul Nasser's Egypt had no time, or place, for the polymorphous culture which Durrell had found, and garnished, in Alexandria. The 'wine-press of love' was purged by Arab nationalism: Jews and Greeks and francophone cosmopolitans ceased to rub shoulders, and other parts, with Copts and colonial administrators and mystagogues and double-agents of various stripes. The palimpsest lost its layered texts and became monotonous. What Durrell called 'apes in nightshirts' – the Arabic-speaking natives with whom he never consorted, even in his hottest dreams – took over the society whose club-sandwich of manners and morals had been his scrumptious subject.

Durrell's gorgeous impressions of the Med, just before and during the war which both vindicated British hegemony and presaged its end, were an obituary on a way of life, and privilege, which licensed curiosity and condescension unimaginable in today's Brits. Durrell's prose is swagged with arcane adjectival conceits and banded with colourful flourishes (it is no surprise that when he painted, it was in gouache); there can be nothing quite like it in the people's English of those who limit their horizons to today's trite little island.

Durrell celebrated the loss of the Mediterranean, as a British fief, somewhat as Evelyn Waugh, in *Brideshead Revisited*, overegged his sumptuous elegy in honour of the vanished supremacy of the Upper Classes. On his complacent travels, Waugh always had a return ticket; Durrell settled: he belonged to the tradition of Sir Richard Burton, though he never learned Arabic or went, in disguise, to Mecca. The Muslim world was as distasteful to him in the Middle East as it had

Review of Ian S. MacNiven, *Lawrence Durrell: A Biography*, in *The Spectator*, 1998.

been, I suspect, for the British in India, to whom Hindus, with their class system and their princely elegances, were more congenial. Durrell disguised himself only as a Foreign Office chap; his duplicity lay in giving honest service, especially in Cyprus, to a false, and losing, cause. Greek friends like George Seferis never forgave him for his hired loyalty to a policy which, as his creation Scobie would have said, reeked of 'la grande bogue'.

Durrell's childhood in India was comfortable, but not pampered. His father believed in being *pukka* but, as a railway executive, he was no *sahib*; the British have never much respected engineers and even later, when Durrell *père* was running a large corporation, he never got his feet in the top drawer. His honest partners were Sikhs, who were generous in buying him out when, hardly forty years old, he began to suffer the symptoms of the brain tumour which carried him off shortly afterwards. His wife, Louisa, and their younger children returned to England, where Larry had already been unhappily at school for some time. The family settled in exotic Bournemouth where a small fortune could be frittered away economically.

Entre deux guerres England proved a sharp spur to Larry's literary ambitions. His younger brother, Gerry, who filled the basins in the house with animal life, and with whom he was to have a lifelong sibling rivalry, could think of no more venomous expletive, when exasperated with Larry, than to say, 'You, you... you AUTHOR, YOU!'

Larry's early decision to be a man of letters did not entail preco-ciousness. Eager reader but wayward student, he can hardly be said to have failed to get into university, because he scarcely tried to do so. However, his later appetite for erudite ostentation and obscure doctrines (Gnosticism, Tarot, etc.) suggests that – like Michael Ayrton, whose Hellenic obsessions shadowed Durrell's – he was determined to outwit the dusty graduates who had studied Greece but never lived it.

Durrell's *nicest* book is *Prospero's Cell*, a more or less unadorned account of the years immediately before the war when he and his first wife, Nancy, lived on Corfu in the sunny simplicity which some of us were able to enjoy in the Cyclades as late as the early 1960s, before the six-packers spread their thick and loud blight on what had once been the inaccessible province of the Happy Few.

Durrell gives the impression that he and Nancy were alone except for the colourful local characters with whom he peopled all his southern landscapes. In fact, the whole Durrell clan was around for most of the time. Poverty was mitigated by Louisa's ill-managed liberalities. Larry's idea of the artist required him to write as if he were a free spirit, emancipated from the beastly bourgeoisie, cleaving only to the rampant Muse. In truth, he was always conscious of the need to keep pots boiling and lines of communication open to the literary market-place and the London *bourse* in which he hoped to be loudly quoted. His father's early death perhaps spared him a super-ego which might have limited his sexual recklessness or tempered his clowning garrulity, but he adopted other 'fathers': T.S. Eliot – to whom, as his poetic publisher *chez* Faber, he was servilely cheeky – and Henry Miller, whose erotic prolixity authorised the prosaic effusions and four-letter words that embarrassed Eliot when *The Black Book* was offered to him for publication by the pushy young poet who claimed third place behind TSE and Pound (ah modesty!).

Ian S. MacNiven evokes the apprentice Durrell – self-sufficient, dependent, swaggering, uncertain, opinionated, deferential – with convincing empathy. He captures the *feel* of pre-war England almost flawlessly, though he does refer to Sir Oswald Mosley as a 'peer' (for all Larry's right-wing style of being non-political, I warmed to his later refusal to admire 'Tom' Mosley on the grounds that he did not like people whose shoulder-flashes read 'Per Ardua ad Buchenwald').

Soon before the war, he and Nancy quit Corfu to spend time with Henry Miller and Anaïs Nin, at the Villa Seurat in Paris, but in the winter of 1939 they were back in Athens, where Larry was given his first official job (his first job of any kind) with the British Council. He was all but flat broke and the 'war work' which followed was not very demanding, or dangerous, until the German invasion drove the Durrells south, to Crete and then to Cairo and, finally, to Alexandria. He remained a servant of the Crown until success no longer obliged him to remain in the sphere of Antrobus, the hero of his not *that* funny series of stories about the Foreign Service.

Despite his Einsteinian celebration of it, Larry never liked Egypt or Egyptians. If he lived in Alexandria and enjoyed its sexual amenities, especially after Nancy had left him with their baby daughter, Penelope, his unboring account of the city was the fruit, in part, of his boredom in it. His knowledge of Cavafy's *polis* was revised and supplemented, when he came to write the *Quartet*, in the light of E.M. Forster's little book *Pharos and Pharillon* in which Cavafy is so sweetly commemorated in his modest apartment in the Rue Lepsius (known roguishly as the Rue Clapsius, on account of its brothel). MacNiven recalls that Cavafy lit candles for favoured visitors, such as Forster, for whom the whole room blazed with happy light. He fails to remark that Cavafy wrote a poem called 'Candles' in which he compared the spent stubs with the days of our life.

A biographer cannot follow every side alley, but I do not think that MacNiven is as interested in Durrell as an artist, or even in literature, as he is in the writer's erotic and social life, which was, God knows, frantic and fraught enough to fill some 700 pages. Durrell denied himself no carnal pleasure, though homosexuality was always unenticing to him. Perhaps he was never enough of a public schoolboy, though there was always something schoolboyish in his yah-boo-sucks style.

He was, however, accused – after his death – of having had an incestuous connection with his second daughter, Sappho, whom he had with Eve Cohen, the second of his three unhappy wives. Eve was a Tunisian Jewess and the main model for Justine. That so superstitious a man as Durrell should name his daughter after a suicidal lesbian poetess seems almost savage, though her name also advertised a verse play (of dubious merit) which he had composed with the same title. Sappho Durrell did indeed become a lesbian and she did commit suicide, poor girl, though she was not a poetess.

MacNiven is fond, but not uncritical, of his subject and gives a vivid enough account of his ups and down, ins and outs. Durrell was, inevitably, less tall then his stories (he measured only just over five feet), but he had an enviable capacity for seducing beautiful women. Where MacNiven fails is in giving us any indication of why Nancy, and most of the others, either left him or wished they had. Nor does he mention a significant remark of Larry's when he said, with regard to the English, something along the lines that they had made a crime of most of the nicest things you can do *to* a woman. The preposition is pertinent, I suspect, to why Larry's ladies did not often find him durably congenial: he lacked Robert Graves's '*meum–tuum* sense'. We are told that he was inclined to slap his women, but a certain *pudeur* covers his erotic habits. In so long a book and in the modern tell-all climate, this is a little mealy mouthed.

Larry was a remarkable landscapist, and grotesques often figure, like gargoyles, on his elaborate confections, but his *alter ego*/narrator, Darley, is a bit of a pill (and is meant to be?). The furniture of the Mediterranean appeals to him more than its humanity. Durrell was a narcissistic Odysseus without an Ithaka, restlessly seeking rest (and a reflective pool) in one idyllic place after another. A great writer? When you re-read the *Quartet*, as I did not long ago, after being invited to make a TV series of it, you find that there are no *scenes* between the characters, no *drama* but the scenes they make. The dialogue is skimpy and strained, but the word painting of the set-pieces is not to be forgotten. A certain kind of imposture plays an honourable part of fiction (sham and shaman come close together) and Durrell was, in that regard at least, a consummate performer.

Says Who?

Cyril Connolly once confessed to looking first in the index of his contemporaries' books to see if he was cited. It was better to be abused than ignored, above all by reference books designed for the ages. C.C. would be relieved to see that he outscores his old nemesis Frank Leavis (7 to 4) in this volume. The grumpy doctor would probably say that Oxford had looked after its own (never a Cambridge trait). Though the standards governing entry are not stipulated, the editors have honoured the programme of the American mayoral candidate who once promised 'I undertake to tread the narrow line between impartiality on the one hand and partiality on the other.' Lord Reith's unconscious gloss on this – 'When people feel deeply, impartiality is bias' – does something to explain why such a dictionary always excites a mixture of winks, nods and expression of incredulity: what is X doing here when Y was not invited? After scanning the entries, who is not tempted to echo the neglected Truewit (wasn't it?) in Ben Jonson's *Epicene*, when he murmured, after someone else got a laugh, 'I do say as good things every day, were they but taken down and recorded'?

The typical modern effort not to be biased in favour of the elegant or the clever is always likely to increase the number of those with grievances, since it sets no clear mark for admission. However, in view of being quoted as saying 'People like me were branded, pigeon-holed, a ceiling put on our ambitions' (*re* the 11-plus), John Prescott may conclude that he has got definitively into Oxford, though his self-trumpeting after the 1997 election – 'We did it! Let's wallow in our victory!' – is an apophthegm unlikely to outwear its brass. Such triumphalism is of a piece with Mrs Thatcher's 'Rejoice' (although only the audio version will do full justice to her baritone vibrato) and also with Mel Brooks's 'If you've got it, flaunt it!', from his ignored masterpiece *The Producers*, in which Zero Mostel utters a hardly less quotable cry of anguish, after an unwanted success, 'Where did we go right?'

Noël Coward is cited as saying, 'It would be nice if sometimes the

Review of *The Oxford Dictionary of Quotations*, in the *Times Literary Supplement*, 2000.

kind things I say were considered worthy of quotation… it's damned hard to be clever and quotable when you are singing someone's praises.' This is of a piece with Byron's unquoted instruction to a friend worried about how to review a poem he had admired (not by B.): 'Don't just praise him, praise him *well*!' His lordship is here for 'the isles of Greece' but not for having written to Lady Caroline Lamb, 'Remember me… thou false to him, thou fiend to me.' Nor is any clue given as to whether it was she or Claire Clairmont who, when someone asked what she thought of Byron's morals, retorted, 'It's the first I've heard of them.'

Gabriel Fielding's uncited 'Writing is a rat race in which you don't get to see the other rats' might serve as an epigraph to a volume, in which the competition, alive and dead, is spread out in common view 'like a patient etherized upon a table' (no marks for spotting the author, a fallen idol – where did Graham Greene get *that* phrase from? – here accused by Dr Leavis of 'self-contempt, well-founded').

If no one should be judged by his or her quotability, it is a lame author who never said anything whose source posterity might wish to check or whose wit a cadging scoundrel never sought to appropriate. The malice of writers is a seam that can never be fully mined, but surely Flaubert's 'Quel homme aurait été Balzac s'il eût su écrire!' is apt enough for some modern purposes to deserve space. And was it also the Fool of the Family who said that Balzac was a *feuilletoniste* who truffled his narrative with 'considérations générales pour faire bien'? We are not instructed, though Flaubert is here to say, 'It is splendid to be a great writer, to put men into the frying pan of your words and make them pop like chestnuts.'

Part of the purpose of such a dictionary as this must be to supply the correct phrasing (I could have sworn that the line was 'Bliss it was in that dawn…' whereas 'Bliss was it…' is what Wordsworth wrote) or to enable the head-scratcher to track down the author of 'Every man has two countries, his own and France' (the answer is not to be found here). If capricious eclecticism is tolerable, inaccuracy is not: Dorothy Parker's famous review of one of Channing Pollock's Broadway plays '*The House Beautiful* is, for me, the play lousy' is quoted without the definite articles, which is the taxonomy horrible.

This volume delivers Robert Benchley's telegram about Venice ('STREETS FULL OF WATER PLEASE ADVISE') but not his remark to Mrs Parker, after she had tried yet again to kill herself: 'Dotty, if you go on committing suicide like this, you're going to seriously damage your health.' Jean Genet's 'Nous ne sortirons jamais de ce bordel' (*Le Balcon*) is as good and useful a curtain line as Sartre's equally ignored 'Recommençons'. Hemingway's 'I walked back to the hotel in the rain' wins no place in the section of famous closures, nor among opening sentences does Willie Maugham's 'When someone telephones you and leaves a message that he needs to speak to you urgently, it is usually more urgent for him than it is for you', a reminder more relevant than ever in the age of voice-mail. Letitia, the mother of the great Napoleon, is not quoted for greeting her son's imperial elevation with 'Pourvu que ça dure', nor is Guizot's advice to the financially disenfranchised 'Enrichissez-vous', surely an invaluable pair of slogans for the age on which Jeffrey Archer and Al-('Call me Capone if you want to') Fayed have clapped their sordid stamp. And how can it be that Kitty Muggeridge's remark about (Sir) David Frost 'He rose without trace' is not available to tag on more of Our Betters?

While nit-picking, let me point out that George Mikes' and Sergio Leone's death dates are not given, nor is that of F.W. Harvey, who *may* be alive but who is said to have been born in 1888. 'From troubles of the world/I turn to ducks/ Beautiful comic things' should perhaps have been interred with his bones. Was Alfred Hayes not a novelist (*In Love, The Girl on the Via Flaminia*) as well as an 'American songwriter'? It is said that the description of some television programmes as 'chewing gum for the eyes' was an anonymous schoolboy, but my *Penguin International Thesaurus* ascribes it, rightly, to the quondam panellist of *Transatlantic Quiz*, John Mason Brown (1955). Richmal Crompton's Violet Elizabeth Bott did not only say 'I'll thcream and thcream and thcream until [surely not *till*?] I'm sick.' She added, as the editors do not, the clinching kicker: 'I *can*.' And should we not be told that Talleyrand's 'Surtout, Messieurs, point de zèle' was addressed to young diplomats before their first posting? By the same token, is there any sense in extracting 'Mud's sister, not himself, adorns my legs' from Housman's fragment of Greek tragedy without telling us that the messenger is alluding to dust?

Such lapses should be corrected but do not warrant another of Dorothy Parker's uncited, but handy, tartnesses: 'This is not a book to be cast aside lightly, it should be hurled with great force.' On the other hand, Mrs Parker's rival wit, Clare Booth Luce, surely merits more than a couple of squibs (neither from *The Women*), not least for, 'Why does he speak ill of me? I never did him a good turn.'

If Susan Sontag is being paraded as a remake of Dorothy Parker, her reputation for wit, or wisdom, is not markedly enhanced by 'What pornography is really about, ultimately, isn't sex but death.' Nothing qualifies an aphorism for oblivion better than a brace of superfluous adverbs, particularly if the point made is dull, and questionable. Rousseau's description of erotica as something designed to be read single-handed, is truer, pithier and unselected.

The presence of a large number of foreign authors marks a break with insularity, although there is no discoverable consistency in those who appear only in translation. We can understand this with Cavafy, despite the attendant loss of trenchancy, even when Keeley and Sherrard have done their usual expert work, but why select Peter Jay's version of Callimachus 2: 'Someone spoke of your death, Heraclitus. It brought me/ Tears, and I remembered how often together/We ran the sun down with talk', when we could have had 'They told me, Heraclitus, they told me you were dead/ They gave me bitter news to read and bitter tears to shed/ I wept as I remembered how often you and I/ Tired the sun with talking and sent him down the sky'? Jay's bathetic 'We ran the sun down with talk' suggests two literary men bitching about the popular press. Callimachus would certainly gnash his teeth at this fat volume, not least when anon. offers us 'A great book is like a great evil', as equivalent to 'mega biblion, mega kakon'. The Greek asyndeton delivers no kind of a simile, but simply states: 'Big book big mistake.'

French authors are given sometimes in the original, sometimes only in translation (Marshal Foch, for example). This is acceptable, though the gentle Diderot's 'Et des boyaux du dernier prêtre/Serrons le cou du dernier roi' is bathetically rendered as 'And with the guts of the last priest/Let's shake [??!] the neck of the last king'. *Serrer la main* may be to shake hands but how do you shake someone's neck? Diderot meant 'strangle' and only Oxford doesn't seem to know it. It seems odd, by the way, that not a single line either of Saint-Simon or of Greville's diaries gets noticed here, though Alan Clark's showily ignorant use of the word *actualité* is engraved for the ages.

Byron's unlisted request, in a letter from Venice to Douglas Kinnaird, to let him know 'Who's in and who's out' in the 'upper rogues' gallery' is, of course, something one asks of all such works as these. If Gertrude Stein is featured, very properly, for her 'remarks are not literature', she might not deny that they are the very stuff of modern culture. Some of the best of them have escaped the current cull, perhaps because they were uttered in an uncarrying voice. For instance, I recall our going to dine at Christopher Isherwood's house with George '*The Seven Year Itch*' Axelrod. Isherwood opened the door and said that he probably should have cancelled because he had a bad cold. 'My dear Christopher,' George retorted instantly, 'any cold of yours is a cold of mine.' Oscar Wilde (who, presumably for moral reasons, is not quoted once in my now antique edition of Bartlett) might have wished that he had said that. I should prefer to have had the nerve to have uttered the tersest, bravest entry of all: General Anthony McAuliffe's reply to the German call to surrender at Bastogne: 'Nuts!'

Among those passed over here, Sir John Foster's observation about a famously amorous lady 'She is like justice – not only done, but seen to be done' deserves a place, as does George Steiner's reproach to an announcement of apostasy (by the wife, I believe, of Moses Finley) 'Jewishness, in the twentieth century, is a club from which there can be no resignations.' Mordecai Richler is the wittiest author to be denied, even though he has reminded us that he is 'world-famous in Canada'. Nicholas Tomalin should surely be there for 'Zapping Charlie Cong', a headline which first alerted us to the turkey-shoot aspect of what was happening in Vietnam. Terry Southern's 'Gentlemen, you can't fight in here. This is the war room', from *Doctor Strangelove* is a line immeasurably superior to the three unresounding jokes from *Father Ted*.

Gary Player fails to make the cut with his highly quotable retort to someone who accused him of being lucky, 'Yes, and you know, the more I practise, the luckier I get'. A.H. Clough is properly appreci-ated, but Brian Clough might be understandably upset not to be on the team sheet for saying of Trevor Brooking, 'He floats like a butterfly, and stings like one too' (cf., of course, Mohammed Ali). President Eisenhower's neglected 1950s remark 'all isms are wasms' was not bad for a supposedly dull man, and his oracular warning about the power of 'the military-industrial complex' was surely in the pithy, Pythian class.

As for poetry, there is a lot of unmemorable stuff. Lighting a candle to Elton John's mawkishness leaves no place for, for example, 'In finesse of fiddles found I ecstasy'. William Plomer's 'A rose-red sissy half as old as time' is squeamishly not declared to be a description of Osbert Sitwell, who might have been more offended by the omission of 'Rat Week'. And who was it who described Sir Philip Sassoon as 'purée of white kid gloves'? Ah the oubliette, what memorable things it contains!

If the Seven Sages were alive today, they would be seven celebri-ties and their wisdom would, I suppose, be of the order of Jeremy Paxman's 'no government in history has been as obsessed with public relations as this one… Speaking for myself, if there is a message I want to be off it.' Let's hope TV's hard man was misquoted. The box does seem to bring people out in rashes of sententiousness. George Austin, Archbishop of York, cannot even make disloyalty amusing: 'We're paying the price for the Eighties and Lord Runcie's effete, liberal élitism among bishops which also spread into the theological colleges. There is now a big gap between the faith of those in the pulpit and those in the pews.' A heathen may be forgiven, or not, for asking whether that isn't why the former preach to the latter? Austin's verbiage would not be worth saving in a salvage drive. Can we be permitted to hope that it is included only out of malice?

How much sharper than any modern politician, and less canting, was A.J. Balfour! When Frank Harris said 'all the the faults of the age come from Christianity and journalism', Balfour replied 'Christianity, of course… but why journalism?' Major ('So right. OK. We lost'), Thatcher ('The lady's not for turning'), Callaghan ('You never reach the promised land') and Blair ('The People's Princess…') manage nothing between them but a compendium of the clumsy and the banal. As for today's ubiquitous cant about 'the people', I am reminded of Randolph Churchill's bellowed remark to a Stratford St Mary wine waiter who recommended a bottle on the grounds of its popularity: 'What makes you think I want to drink anything *popular*?'

That man of the people, Aneurin Bevan did better than any present pols when he said, 'I read the newspapers avidly. It is my one form of continuous fiction.' Wilde on the peerage was thus renovated by a man who thought Tories 'lower than vermin' but was old-style orator enough to emulate the style, and morals, of the toff.

The presence of a new category of Catchphrases testifies to the ecumenical nature of entry into Oxford these days. Bruce Forsyth's 'I'm in charge' gets the nod, as does Mrs Mopp's 'Can I do you now, sir?' though Mona Lott's 'It's being so cheerful as keeps me going' has gone. Is the *Goon Show*'s Bluebottle correctly reported as having said 'You rotten swines. I told you I'd be deaded'? My fallible mental files come up with 'You dirty rotten swine, you have deaded me.' Spike Milligan's genius is too copious to be fully, or worthily, celebrated: 'Underneath all those clothes, he's stark naked' and 'You can't get the wood, you know' have qualities more resonant than 'Let's be careful out there' (from *Hill Street Blues*).

It is always easy to say that there are too many chestnuts and not enough fire. However, a certain prudishness gives an unduly decorous tone to some reputations. 'More dined against than dining' is the only evidence of Maurice Bowra's legendary wit (we are spared his often dull scholarship), but did he not once say, of a colleague who announced his engagement to a plain woman, 'Buggers can't be choosers'? Churchill's growled comment on Sir Alfred Bossom, 'The fellow's neither one thing nor the other' might have served to remind us that he was not *all* statesman. Presumably in the interests of his canonisation, T.S. Eliot's much-cited 'the jew is underneath the lot' is expunged from his quotable quota.

The great well-spoken, nicely phrased, variously erudite and witty basis of our literary and social culture remains solidly in place. The classics have not been scamped and the genius of old masters still glows luminously. What is signally evident, however, is that Something Happened in the late 1950s or early 1960s which altered, very possibly forever, the tone and style of what qualifies for such pages as these. For bioptic analysis, try this, your starter for ten: 'His mouth had been used as a latrine by some small creature of the night, and then as its mausoleum.' Date and author? Not *very* difficult: the traces of old-fashioned posh-speak help to point to Kingsley Amis's 1954 semi-rupture with mandarin fiction in, yes, *Lucky Jim* (compare and contrast with *Lord Jim*, a dignity which Dixon may well by now have attained, in view of the hunger for *arrivistes* in today's Upper House), but had the author not *had* to be quoted, would such a laborious joke have amused the selectors?

If there is a surge of iconcoclasm and a liberating litter of four-lettered newspeak (Swift's Celia, Celia, Celia does not, however, shit in these pages), not a few modern mandarins are revealed in all their unblushing pomposity. Whoever it was who said 'Why write aphorisms? To help the mind lose weight' has not left a diet sheet for Saul Bellow, Polly Toynbee, Janet Street-Porter and any number of ponderous opinion-pedlars who have gained altogether too easy entrance alongside the masters, and mistresses, of unbuttoned wit, metric felicity or ageless intelligence.

The Pumpkinification of Stanley K.

When Roman emperors died, it was common for the Senate to decree their deification. In cases of conspicuous iniquity, vilification could be substituted for apotheosis. If (as was not unusual) the previous incumbent had been done away with by his successor, or by his sponsors, it was convenient to blacken the dead man's memory. In the case of the emperor Claudius, something more unusual, and two-faced, occurred. In public, he was granted divine status; in private, he became the target of ribaldry and ridicule which fell little short of diabolisation.

Claudius had been an improbable emperor. As a shambling and reclusive pedant, he was, during the previous reign, an avuncular figure of fun to his nephew and predecessor, the appalling but glamorous Caligula. When the latter was assassinated, after bingeing once too often on the blood of family and friends, Claudius was dragged into the open by the rampaging Praetorian guard. Instead of sharing Caligula's fate, he was elevated to the purple by those who he assumed had come to despatch him. As emperor *malgré lui*, he became a protractedly judicious Supreme Justice and a Commander-in-Chief who, seconded by efficient professional backup, managed to enjoy a Triumph (the Oscar, you might say, of Roman military achievement).

As for the downside, readers of Robert Graves' novels *I, Claudius* and *Claudius the God* will remember, Claudius was also notoriously cuckolded by his wife, Messalina (whose exploits might have furnished an early draft of *The Sexual Life of Catherine M.*). He made no friends among the aristocracy by preferring to trust in a secretariat of freedmen (liberated slaves). However, Claudius' posthumous reputation suffered most enduringly at the hands of the intellectual and dramatist Annaeus Seneca in the satire which bears the traditional title of the *Apocolocyntosis*, an unsubtle play on the word 'apotheosis'. Seneca's (now mutilated) squib was a lampoon deriding the late emperor's affectations of divinity. As with most powerful men, there was something to be said for Claudius, and not a little against. Seneca contrived to say both, in different contexts.

Areté, 2002.

The *Apocolcyntosis* was not written without spontaneity, nor without calculation. Seneca had bided his time, and had had time to do it. Having been charged with committing adultery with Caligula's sister, the Spanish-born *arriviste* had been banished to the island of Corsica by Claudius. For eight years, he petitioned dolefully for recall. Like some prosaic Ovid, he alternated philosophical resignation (he was a prominent Stoic) with grovelling flattery, not least of Polybius, Claudius' most influential freedman. So shameless was Seneca's *Consolatio ad Polybium* that, after Claudius' death, he sought to suppress it. He had by then been returned to favour and appointed tutor to the new, immature young emperor, Nero.

Written very early in Nero's reign, the *Apocolocyntosis* was at once appetisingly irreverent and implicitly didactic. Its farcical comedy had a moral for Nero: do not repeat Claudius' murderous mistakes. The young emperor laughed, but he did not learn his lesson. Seneca himself was ordered to commit suicide in the later, gory years of the emperor's reign. Favourites who entertain, or instruct, egomaniacs often imagine that they can be exceptions to the general rule of tyrannical ingratitude and vindictiveness. How many are right?

Apolocyntosis is routinely translated as 'The Pumpkinification (of Claudius)'. However, my late friend Professor John Sullivan remarked that it might as well be rendered 'The Transfiguration *of* a Pumpkinhead' as 'Transfiguration *into* a Pumpkin'. The satire would, in that case, be against a pulp-brained emperor fatuously aspiring to be a god. Once arrived on Olympus, Seneca's buffoon is judged by those he takes to be his peers, the presiding deities, and relegated, ignominiously, to The Other Place.

There is supplementary irony in the fact that, as well as secretly ridiculing Claudius, for Nero's imperial entertainment, Seneca had also composed the fulsome encomium which Nero pronounced at the late emperor's funeral (in AD 54). Seneca's ambitions warred with his Stoicism; his aptitude for both solemnity and skittishness reflected the split in his character, and his talents. Having it both ways, alternating aloof disdain with the urgent fulfilment of commissioned assignments, is a recurring feature of Seneca's life. Writers, some will say, are like that.

What has all this to do with Stanley Kubrick? It reminds us, at least, that when famous men die it is hardly unusual for their reputations to be reassessed upwards, or downwards, or both. Dominique Janicaud's two-volume *Heidegger en France* charts the ups and downs of that egregious savant's post-war reputation. Heidegger is regarded by some as the greatest philosopher of his era, by others as a time-serving obscurantist, indelibly tainted by his infatuation with Nazism. The fluctuations of the intellectual *bourse* reflect the influence of critical bulls and bears.[1] Kubrick's stock is similarly volatile. This is no argument for not attempting an evaluation or for regarding all opinions as equally valid (are all accountants equally trustworthy?). As Nietzsche remarked, 'You say there can be no argument about matters of taste? All life is an argument about matters of taste!'

When a patron has been quasi-omnipotent, his erstwhile clients find it difficult to accept that there are no longer favours to be culled by continued obsequiousness. Nor can they quite believe that no one need any longer be intimidated by the menace of the great man's disapproval or litigation. As for the promptness with which Seneca cocked a snook at Claudius' posthumous pretensions, Sullivan remarks, justly, that 'satire against those long-dead... tends to fall flat'. The same is true of memoirs as tactful as mine of Stanley Kubrick.

Eulogy also stales. Michael Herr's little pamphlet about Kubrick, and about me, deserves attention as an instance of the self-serving appropriation of a dead man's laurels and the preening assumption of, as the philosophers say, privileged access. Antony pulled the same trick in Shakespeare's *Julius Caesar*.

The reception of *Eyes Wide Open* (my short, truthful memoir) highlights the conflicting emotions, and hopes, of surviving courtiers, hucksters and *apparatchiks*. The last category brings to mind to a story told about the period immediately after Stalin's death. Since the cinema was a key aspect of his propaganda machine, the top Soviet screenwriters had always made sure that their scripts were as devout towards Stalin as if that atheist had already been blessed with divinity. They were so thoroughly institutionalised that they continued to write in the same vein after the tyrant's death.

At a meeting of the Politbureau, during which nervous moves towards deStalinisation were already being mooted (the first business on the agenda had been the execution of Laventri Beria[2] by his fellow-*mafiosi*), the Chief Screenwriter burst into the room waving a sheaf of

---

1   Who will now insist that Lucchino Visconti was a significant director? What was said, at the time, to be his sell-out film, *The Leopard*, is the only one I should care to see again, thanks to Burt Lancaster. Visconti's aristocratic air and social clout were the enforcers of his claim to artistic distinction.

2   In his memoirs, Beria's son, Serge, maintains that his father was much misunderstood (the same has been said, seriously, of Nero). Beria was a murderous secret

pages. 'I've done it,' he is said to have said, 'the first draft of the immortal Josef Vissarionovich's bio-pic! It's going to be great.'

Khruschev and his chums looked balefully at this obsolete enthusiast for the monster who had terrorised them, and Russia, for so many decades and whom they had been fortunate to survive. The script was not greenlighted (or should one say – recalling the red light that released the traffic in Bertolucci's *The Last Emperor* – red-lighted?). Changes of moral, and aesthetic, climate often follow the deaths of tyrants, great or petty, much more abruptly than their entourages can quite digest. What might once have seemed wanton, or treasonous, or self-destructively brave (like the anti-Stalin squib which sealed Osip Mandelstam's fate), becomes – in almost no time – hardly more than a mild footnote to the revision of an inflated reputation. There is no scandal in looking again at important figures; and little wisdom in merely repeating the kind of gush which ideology, or careerism, once demanded. What is more vacuous than certain critics' notion that they were Stanley Kubrick's confidants because he fed them, in private, with scraps which, in their articles, would fatten his fame?

If I began with a digression about Seneca, Claudius and Nero, it was not by chance. The intellectual, as instanced by Seneca, but never only by him, is both drawn to, and repelled by, the powerful: he craves advancement, but another side of him cannot wholly endorse his own worldly ambitions. It is typical of such a man, if he is creative, to project his apprehensions of unworthiness onto the crass milieu of politics, money, high society, business: Fellini's *La Dolce Vita* and many of Oliver Stone's 'socially conscious' movies manifest a no less furious duplicity. *Saeva indignatio* is often fuelled by desire for big bucks and (in Federico's case at least) big tits.

To direct films is a career unsuited to the squeamish or those with a suspicion that there may be better things to do than scheme, work and bluff your way to the top. Such halfway men, of whom Seneca was archetypal (he wrote lurid melodramas, one of which

---

policeman and a regular rapist, but his family saw a 'different man'. What is less astounding that the alleged 'paradox' that concentration camp guards were loving parents who hummed along with Mozart? Kubrick's family made much of not having 'authorised' my little book. What did they know of my working relationship with a man whom they, in a sense, had never met? Kubrick's domestic virtues, whatever they were, had nothing to do with his professional conduct. I never heard him say a single word about his beloved wife and children. He gave the impression of being an insomniac solitary, most at home with his computer. He slept, and died, alone.

Shakespeare cannibalised for *Titus Andronicus*), have been known to imagine themselves somewhat too fine for their own mundane good. That excellent scholar Erich Segal had the unusual strength of character to return to his cloister after a season of unscholastic fame, and fortune, as the author of *Love Story*. He never looked back, happy that he could now afford his own copy of Pauly-Wissowa's arcane, and very expensive, Classical Dictionary.

When Seneca saw that Nero was turning into something much more poisonous than a pumpkin, he excused himself from the court and went into rustic retirement. Having become a millionaire as Nero's intimate, the retiring philosopher thought it prudent to hand over his personal fortune to the emperor. In this way, he meant to advertise both his devotion to the man whom he now despised and his small appeal as a target for confiscatory greed (which, as Louis XIV's finance minister, Fouquet was to discover, often provokes the impeachment of ostentatiously well-heeled courtiers).

Seneca might as well have saved himself the trouble of jettisoning his profits. Proving more paranoid than avaricious, Nero harboured a long grudge against the man who preferred his own company to his emperor's. Detached intelligence is a virtue as little admired in courtiers as in screenwriters. When delivered from below, condescension can be a life- or livelihood-threatening luxury. Yet the better screenwriters are (and the more desirable to good directors), the less likely are they to be driven only by a servile appetite for promotion. As Bill Goldman's caustic rogueries regularly prove, even the best screenwriters swear no reliable allegiance to 'the Industry'.

After some time in retirement, Seneca was required to commit suicide for taking part in a putative plot against the fun-loving, spendthrift, sanguinary Nero. It says something about the latter's alleged fostering of the arts that both Petronius (Nero's *arbiter elegantiae* and author of the emperor-pleasing *Satyrica*) and the precocious young genius Lucan (author of the unfinished epic *Pharsalia*) were called upon to kill themselves at the same time. Admiration and jealousy alternate in the tyrant's mind; what he respects at once diminishes him, and must be cut down. Love entails hate, since it implies need or deficiency.

In the preface to my translation of *Satyrica* (Folio Society, 2003), I argue that Petronius's wilfully Epicurean suicide – which took the form of an all-night party – was intensely literary. Even as he died, Petronius was parodying Seneca's self-consciously Stoic response to Nero's last order to him. In such circumstances, writers can still be more interested in striking stylish attitudes than any reader (or publicity machine) can well imagine. It will be remembered that, as he received his deathblow, like a bad review, from a slave, Nero cried out 'Qualis artifex pereo': usually rendered as, 'What an artist dies with me!'. He had ensured that the best of his rivals were already dead. The desire to be unique knows no equals.

My Hollywood agent told me, not long ago, that I treated screen-writing as a 'hobby'. I had not checked every detail of a contract which I was paying him 10 per cent to vet and which he had counselled me to sign. No such accusation of dilettantism could ever be made against Stanley Kubrick. Carlyle's notion of genius as 'an infinite capacity for taking pains' fitted Stanley's obsessive personality to perfection. No less obsessively businesslike, especially when it came to inserting contractual conditions which put collaborators at a furtive disadvantage (ask Brian Aldiss), he added a capacity for *inflicting* pains to Carlyle's definition. By some clerical oversight,I was the only person he ever employed who was not embargoed from writing about his experiences with him. Achilles always has his heel. There is petty, mythic comedy, in this omission, although panicky executives and apprehensive acolytes did not see the joke. I had to be anathematised by the producers (I was not invited to the première) and consigned to oblivion by ranting *apparatchiks*, one of whom, in London, simul-taneously plagiarised my encomium on Kubrick in the BAFTA magazine. Cavafy's barbarians are not now at the gate; they are its salaried keepers.

*

The most frequent change which artists wish to bring about in any society is their own promotion in it. Such ambitions are often presaged by apparently high-minded critical manifestoes such as François Truffaut's notorious *Une Certaine Tendance dans le Cinema Français*. This seemingly selfless denunciation of dated aesthetics, and their practitioners in the *ancien régime* of French directors, was followed, in very short order, by the revelation that its author and his friends meant to replace the Old Guard with themselves and *their* (eventually perishable) aesthetics. The drive to direct is no more prin-cipled than Roman ambition for the principate.

We live in an age where immortals are wise to stay alive for as long as possible (even obituaries in the London *Times* have ceased always to speak well of the dead, though Stanley's never mentioned that he was – significantly? – a Jew). When people are conscripted to eulogy, or excoriated for honesty, in assessing a so-called artist, it is likely to be a consequence more of corporate policies than of private emotion.

Philip Bobbitt's brilliant new book, *The Shield of Achilles*, warns of a shift in international politics as a result of, as he puts it, the replacement of the 'nation-state' by the 'market-state'. The United States is the supreme instance of this phenomenon. The market-state is heralded by a revised notion of the essential aims of government. Social welfare is no longer a prime concern. Instead, the well-being of the citizens has to *follow* from the maximisation of commercial opportunity, and profits, even at the risk of individual citizens' security (in the street and with regard to pensions, Medicare, etc.). Corporate success alone is the determining evidence that the right targets are being addressed.

This new(ish) national ethos may not have a direct causal effect on morals, and on aesthetics, but – as Bobbit remarks – we do better to think of society as a 'field of forces', rather than as a pool table on which one ball has a measurable impact on whatever it hits. Our arts and our nexus of moralities are, *and* are not, transformed, if not pump-kinified, by revised economic conditions (Marx was right about most things, wrong only about the remedy).

Even gods are altered by new attitudes; the unchangeable changes too. Bobbit quotes a professorial colleague who, inspired by the emergent *zeitgeist*, recently, and straightfacedly, described Jesus as a 'moral entrepreneur'. The Sermon on the Mount has become a 'pitch' (Sinclair Lewis's Babbit can find a renovated home, in a better neighbourhood, in Bobbit's mercenary new world.) In an altered socio-economic climate, we can expect a modified morality and revised aesthetics. The best work of art in our brave newer world has to be the one which will raise the most revenue. Any attempt to attribute value to anything alien to the cash nexus is counter-revolutionary treason to the mercantile state, in whose interest the great corporations stand guard, inflexibly uniformed in righteous greed.

Political Correctness is one thing and Commercial Correctness is very nearly the same thing. We now find ourselves in thrall to a soft Stalinism which demands that we follow the party line, even when the Party is over. The Stalinist state demanded one hundred per cent endorsement by the electors; the market-state's ideal product solicits one hundred percent of consumers. Hence a film which is not intended, in theory, to appeal to *everyone* is – as the Stalinists would say if they were Free Enterprisers (and many now are) – counter-revo-

lutionary, unpatriotic and, oh, élitist (what else?). So far as the movies
are concerned, Political Correctness demands that no one be discrim-
inated against, even in speech (of which, in our society, advertising is
a key part), less because the previously excluded or undervalued
should be admitted as critics than because they are potential
customers. Any work of 'art' which has specific appeal (for instance,
to the literate, the intelligent or – as they used to say – the discrimi-
nating) must be suspected of commercial treason: it is (Newspeak)
undemocratic not to seek to appeal to *everyone*. A dated notion of
modernity claimed distinction for those who sought, by their show
of genius, to 'amputate the audience' (leaving only the initiates).
Postmodern art is interested primarily in the amplification of the audience, and the receipts (only the art can bear amputation). Kubrick's
duplicity, in being at once *of* Hollywood and not *in* Hollywood, was
at the heart of his attempt to retain the kudos of lonely genius without
losing his reputation as a man with the universally golden touch. His
films had, for that reason, to be both mainstream and, since he was
such a maverick, against the current. *Eyes Wide Shut* was his culminating effort to have things both ways. It was calculated to be a
shocker which shocked everyone into seeing it. The esoteric and the
erotic had always had affinities; they were now to become identical.
In the course of that assimilation, all the specifics of Schnitzler's *donnee*
were slowly whittled away. The Jewishness of 'Arthur's' hero was an
early erasure in this process. What was said (never by me) to be the
result of Stanley's 'self-hatred' as a Jew was, I am certain, the result
of an utterly *un*selfish, commercial decision by the producer, who just
happened to be Stanley Kubrick. If the film were to be about a Jewish
doctor, it would 'discriminate' against those who might otherwise
identify with its hero. The elimination of 'art' was pursued in the
systematic removal of any signs of wit (a function of class) in the
dialogue. Believe it or not, I say this without rancour: for a variety of
reasons, Stanley could not allow the sign of any mind, or art, but his
own to remain on the piece, and even this had to yield to the demands
for success on which his standing with the studio was postulated.
Kubrick had a curious creative intelligence, even for a director. His
work was at once idiosyncratic *and* impersonal. How much about the
'author' himself could a stranger deduce from his *oeuvre* except,
maybe, that he was obsessed with violence and killing? Could anyone
but a lover of paradox have concluded from the 'text' of his films that
Stanley was morbidly afraid of the dangers of flying, driving, seeing a
doctor and even leaving the precincts of his own house?

The work was an advertisement for an almost invisible man who hid, like the minotaur, at the centre of a maze which was, in Stanley's case, of his own devising. This almost superstitious self-effacement – which the old Flaubertian aesthetics deemed wholly proper in an artist – was accompanied by determination to advertise his name as often as possible, in as big letters as possible, on the work on which he left his hallmark, though it bore no palpable impression of the man himself. His name was that of a bigger character than he was. His style *was* Stanley Kubrick, but was Stanley Kubrick?

Let me establish something very clearly. Working with Stanley on *Eyes Wide Open* was the culmination of a youthful dream. It remains a marginal event in my life as a writer. To put it with convincing immodesty, my opinion of myself was not enhanced by becoming Kubrick's scribe. If I imagined very briefly that we were going to make a film 'together', I was experienced enough in the habits of sacred monsters to know that they have a tendency to consume all their collaborators. The greatest tribute Stalin could pay to the genius of his early comrades was to write them out of history and erase the smallest trace of their contribution to his achievements. The first evidence I had that Stanley was actually going to make the movie on which I had worked for so many months was an announcement in the Trades in which he claimed sole credit for the screenplay. Only when threats of legal action were made did his lawyer concede the justice of my complaint.

Kubrick's image as an artist was sustained by bully-boys, bluff and reticent braggadocio. It does not follow that it was unmerited. His greatest misfortune was that his last work, *Eyes Wide Shut*, was so nearly finished, and was at least *presentable* as such, at the moment of his death. The marketing machinery of Warner Brothers was thus able to maintain that the public, and the critics, were about to see a master-piece on which the Master had already put his *imprimatur*. Does any serious, or knowledgeable, person still maintain this?

Like most artists of painstaking quality, Kubrick was an obsessive tweaker. He died in March; his film came out in July. Had he lived, he would have cut, rearranged, perhaps re-shot, with maddening meticulousness (never forget the element of fear, Latin *metus*, at the root of that word). Those who were financially (very heavily) invested in *Eyes Wide Shut* were caught in a difficult fix. Had Kubrick not been marketed as a genius, some ruthless hand might well have put the scis-sors into his work. The score would have been radically revised and there would have been a lotta lotta editorial rejigging. Since Kubrick was Kubrick, no such ruthlessness could be sanctioned. His (alas) culminating work had to be declared what it was not: both finished and beyond criticism.

I sympathise with those who were forced to market the film *as though* it were everything they, and we, had hoped for. But now, when the commercial pressure is off, we (and probably they) can see its faults as well as its tantalising merits. Its main weakneses were not, I suspect, ever going to be susceptible of remedy, because they were present, very often, in the work which Stanley did complete to his own satisfaction, in so far as he was ever satisfied. If we look at the whole *oeuvre*, we can salute (or condemn) it as remarkably eclectic, as well as consistently wanting in humanity (there are no love scenes, not even any *recognition* of love, as opposed to *desire*, which is more photogenic).

The eclecticism is marked by a persistent recourse to, on the whole, classy source material; S.K. had no appetite for 'originals'. Plato once said that the degenerate form of an architect is a pastry-cook. Kubrick was more of a *charcutier*: he could make something delicious and seemingly exotic out of a pig of a subject. My friend, the painter and sculptor Michael Ayrton, had similarly protean gifts. If you went round an art gallery with him and stopped in front of something you seemed to admire, Michael would say, 'I can do you one of those'.

Like a cinematic decathlete, Stanley worked his way through most of the standard genres; since he never lived to work on *A.I.*, he never attempted any of them twice. He was probably wise to eschew the musical, but *Eyes Wide Shut* was to be his proof that he could do the erotic love story. It was also, as is widely known, the fulfilment of a bet with himself that the 'blue movie' could, under the right management, aspire to 'art' (a category of achievement to which Kubrick, a cynic in many regards, had naïve – dare one say good-Jewish-boyish? – aspirations).

He was hampered when it came to a love story, partly because (and this is not a criticism, and might even be praise) he abstained from sentiment ('as a director' is a qualification which is universally implicit, from now on, in what I am saying). The avoidance of *kitsch* is a 'noble' motive for such abstention, but the treatment of the couple in *Eyes Wide Shut* demanded a mastery of the nuances of what even the Viennese called 'love', in which, of course, there was more *eros* than *agape*. Schnitzler too would have thought it callow to speak of affection, but his novella becomes entirely lurid if there is no 'play' between the love which Fridolin feels for his wife and the vindictive lust by which he is simultaneously, or sequentially, possessed.

Kubrick's systematic refusal to invest his experience, as opposed to his expertise, in his work alarmed him when it came to dealing with marriage. He turned to me for an ability to dramatise the play between husband and wife, but my work was (maybe) too imprinted with a style that was not his, although he consented, at first, to admire it.

He then became fixed on the idea that a 'real' married couple would bring some automatic certificate of authenticity to his portrayal of the doctor and his wife. He might have thought that a *medical* husband would make the Cruise part even more authentic, but he did not. Not only did he choose a couple who, soon afterwards, turned out to have a marriage at least in part of convenience, but he gave them no reliable text to play, imagining – and here intelligence collapsed into unsuspected naïveté – that if they improvised chunks of their scenes something more valid would emerge. The result was the sorry sight and sound of the pink, nakedish Tom Cruise uttering shrill and improbable, unerringly platitudinous, reproaches to the over-actress who was supposed to be (but never was) the mother of his child. Nothing is less certain to produce authenticity than an actor bereft of an informative text (one which also gives form to the scene), relying on his own unactorly life to supply words and actions. What made Stanley yield to so misguided a method? The genre of Love Story was the one (apart from the musical) in which he was least practised, and – more important perhaps – with which he seems to have had little sense of touch.

It is neither my pleasure nor my purpose to go through the many symptoms of manifest inauthenticity which resulted from the casting of so coldly calculating a couple of careerists as Cruise and Kidman. The evidence of imaginative frigidity, as far as specific human beings are concerned, is of a piece with the general formality of the work. Kubrick made fables, not dramas; he toyed with generalities and their illustration by using grotesque and exaggerated puppets to people his pictures. This does not disqualify him from high regard, nor make him unworthy of serious attention, but there it certainly is: he was afraid of human beings, their feelings, their violence, their savagery, their mortality and he would not, perhaps could not, invest himself in them. In a metaphorical sense, he was impotent: he had to be externally empowered by his clout, his skill, his ingenuity, his wilfulness, his acumen, but he took no personal joy *as an artist* (if you want to call him that) in humanity. It was not foolish of him, nor was it shameful, but it was sad. The genre he chose to prove how polyvalent he was, to convince himself that there was nothing he could not do, was one he tried when his physical energy was waning and which his imagination was incapable of inhabiting. There are clever and 'typical' sequences in *Eyes Wide Shut*; neither passion nor even the erotic scandal are realised. D.H. Lawrence's 'sex in the head' was as near as Kubrick came to the heart of the matter. It would be nice to think that, given time to tinker and eliminate and re-jig, something superb could have been contrived, but I am not so sure. He did not necessarily get the recipe wrong but, on this occasion, the *charcutier* misjudged his pig.

Warner Brothers' corporate determination to insist on Stanley's *apotheosis* was always likely, with time, to look excessive. His qualities were rare, but they were not unbounded. He too tried, like Seneca and Petronius, both to be a force in the world and to be above mundane considerations. This does make a pumpkin of him, but it must cast doubt on claims to divinity.

The Benefits of Doubt

Suppose I say that the body will rot, and another says, 'No. Particles will rejoin in a thousand years and there will be a Resurrection of you.'

If someone said, 'Wittgenstein, do you believe in this?' I'd say, 'No.' 'Do you contradict this man?' I'd say, 'No.'

If you say this, the contradiction already lies in this.

Would you say: 'I believe the opposite,' or 'There's no reason to suppose such a thing?' I'd say neither.

Ludwig Wittgenstein, Lectures on Religious Belief

Tautologies have no appetite; they are satisfied by themselves. The Jewish God is said to have announced Himself, on at least one occasion, as 'I Am That I Am', a statement which, in English at least, makes Him hard to distinguish, logically, from the Aristotelian deity whose only worthy object of contemplation is himself. In much the same way, the Christian version of the unmoved mover has, in view of his ubiquity, nowhere he could conceivably go. Thales' remark, 'The world is full of gods' has a monotheistic corollary which is best, if uncomfortingly, declared in Spinoza's economic *deus sive natura* which asserts the synonymity of God and Nature. On this reading, God is full of the world, in the sense of Creation, and the Creation *is* God (an argument which sanctifies ecology).

However, Thales' declaration was a prelude not to the kind of superstition still current when Theophrastus satirised it two or three centuries later, but rather to a 'rational' discounting of theological explanations of natural phenomena: since there were gods everywhere, nothing specific could be attributed to their presence. In Wittgenstein's terms, one could 'divide through by divinities' and still have the same natural world and events for which to provide explanations. If 'a god, or gods, is/are in (or behind) it' were true of everything, it was also irrelevant.

All systems which explain everything also explain nothing: 'God's mercy' like 'Allah's will' covers both life and death, but promises

Contribution to the symposium 'Two Cheers for Secularism', 2000.

neither. Thales' assertion of a multiplicity of gods was at once a preambulatory acknowledgement of divinities' existence and signalled a pious disinclination to include them in practical considerations. The word 'consideration' has, at its root, the idea of stargazing, of evaluating heavenly prospects, which illustrates quite prettily how hard, if not impossible, it is to find forms of language untainted by implications which subvert the supposed clarity of their expression.

When Einstein said that God did not play dice with His creation, he did not assert the futility of science, but its God-backed dependability; what could be depended on was that God did not monkey with the machinery or, so to speak, fiddle the books by arbitrarily altering the balances. The pious may take what comfort they choose from this, but the amusing solemnity of Einstein's remark hardly endorses any specific creed; God here might as well be another name for the governing principle of the universe as for a loving, or moral, Father: *deus sive natura* rides again. Einstein's evident (and very Spinozistic) intention was to fortify human reliance on intelligence, not to sponsor credulity in, for example, omens, miracles or the hope of divine intervention.

In this he had much in common with Descartes' rather desperate attempt to find a way back from the extreme scepticism into which reason had led him. He found a bridge back to the reliability of the sensible world by maintaining that God would not allow man to be systematically misled. This 'proved' that the material world did indeed exist, even though there could be no proof that it did so. He thus avoided both palpable absurdity and incendiary problems with the Catholic Church. Descartes retrieved the world's reality more or less as Berkeleians did when they made God the eternal observer who, by unsleeping vigilance, made sure that the tree in the quad did not disappear when no mortal happened to be looking at it, a risk which seemed implicit in Berkeley's claim that objects consist only of what we see and feel when we observe or bump into them.

All dogmatic dismissals of God have a way of preparing His return; it is for this reason that Wittgenstein's remarks, cited above, have a steady place in the logic of what might be called 'God-talk'. At the simplest level, it is a notorious truth that the non-existence of God can no more be proved than can His existence. Nor, of course, can the non-existence of the Devil or of the vocal but invisible Virgil to whose views, at critical moments, the classical scholar Jackson Knight had the privilege of listening, thus gaining incontrovertible evidence of what the *Aeneid* was meant to mean.

As E.R. Dodds pointed out, in *The Greeks and the Irrational*, the Greek 'invention' of reason did not mean that they no longer 'believed in' a supernatural dimension to their world, still less that, at the culmination of their civilisation, they became the apostles of Reason. The cult of rationality makes its keenest appeal in the light of a consciousness of the danger, and charm, of the irrational. We are reasonable, if we are, *as if we were*; it is both the strength and the hypocrisy of logic and of constitutions, of justice and of compromise, that we *take them to be* valid.

Dodds's example of the stand-off between civility and savagery, between the uses of reason and the seductions of what lay outside it, was Euripides' *Bacchae*, that terrifyingly sane dramatisation of supernaturally inspired, and frighteningly uncivil madness. It is part of the comedy of scholarship that Euripides' modern fame began with his reputation as a 'rationalist'. He might better be called an ironist. What is most truly modern about him is his (perhaps appalled) recognition of the intimidating forces of powers which merely reasonable men cannot accommodate in any comprehensive scheme of political management.

The ultimate 'reasonable' vestige of this kind of uncontrolled force is 'the market', to which Thatcherites incited us to bow in pious impotence. One cannot easily attribute virtue to the market, but its acolytes urge us to yield to its wisdom; it knows best when prices should rise or fall and those who seek to oppose its course, up or down, pay for their impiety with ruin. A society without a moral scheme is bound to result, for better or worse, from a ruling principle in which wisdom and virtue have no necessary community. Accountancy replaces morals; accountants casuists.

It is a small step, as totalitarian schemes have proved, from a belief in inevitabilities (which are, at their 'truest', another species of tautology) to callous determination to be on their side. Social Darwinism and Marxism seek to curry favour with the Future by being its deputies and sponsors. In this way, we arrive at a paradox: it may be true that nothing can stop what cannot be stopped, if only because it cannot be false, but it does not follow that man has a *moral* obligation to be its partisan. If man's morality is anything of value, it involves the *construction* of generosities which are not necessarily to be found in God or nature.

The myth of Prometheus, as Shelley perceived, is an argument on precisely this topic. Dismay that 'the world' is not systematically moral makes all things permissible, as Dostoevsky lamented, perhaps unduly: cannot moral conduct become one of the available options? A godless world does not make good behaviour improper or unnatural, even though it may deprive it, depressingly perhaps, of supernatural rewards or sublime music.

If man were *only* one more inhabitant of the earth, like the fox, he would have no conceivable duty to preserve it or to control his own appetites, including that for destruction and cruelty; he could not even imagine that he had such a duty. If it is true that Nature is synonymous with God, man is the only unnatural mundane being: his uniqueness lies in being the only creature able to postulate, and perhaps realise, a world other than the one he came into. One way or another, we are on our own. Does a godless world imply that selfishness is more 'natural' than the altruism on which communal religions tend to place such emphasis, as if unselfishness were impossible without them, although it has not always been their defining feature? In the Authorized Version, Jesus himself asked only that we love our neighbour *as ourselves*, which implies that the model of concern for others is the degree to which we care for ourselves. Why not? 'Suffer the little children to come unto me' is not the remark of someone with markedly low self-esteem.

Those, such as Iris Murdoch, who make programmatic demands for 'more religion' seem always to imagine, with more or less intelligence and honesty, that the young can receive salutary injections of religion, in modest doses, as a result of which they will be vaccinated against wickedness, not least against teenage pregnancy, without becoming tiresomely chaste. The aversion from extremism (especially the Muslim strain) on the part of those who advocate the inculcation of religion is as comic – in its presumption that the love of God can be administered in controlled quantities – as was Pentheus' repudiation of Dionysos in *Bacchae*. It is possible both to sympathise with those who lament the lost good effects of religion and to find them them laughably oblivious of the immoderate devotion which gods regularly demand of their adherents. To give children a little bit of religion is not unlike making a woman a little bit pregnant, But to give them none, what is that?

Bacchae is a cool account of the dangers of repression. The young King Pentheus of Thebes ridicules the pretensions of the 'hippy' vagabond, of ambiguous sexuality, who announces himself to be the god Dionysos. Just as Stalin discounted the influence of the Pope, by asking how many divisions he had, so Pentheus mocks the effete youth who is foolish enough to threaten him. After a period of dangerous patience, the god responds by releasing forces which not only rock the seven-gated city's foundations but later delude King Pentheus himself into putting on drag in order to spy on the orgiastic rituals to which the fugitive women of Thebes have been so thrillingly seduced. Finally Pentheus becomes their prey; mistaken for a wild beast, he is torn to pieces by a female hunting party led by his own mother, after which 'sanity' returns to the city and Dionysos goes calmly, unremorsefully, on his way. His divinity has been validated by the ruin he has brought.

It is part of Euripides' perceptive wit that he makes Tiresias – T.S. Eliot's 'old man with wrinkled dugs', the prophet with sexual experience both as a man and as a woman – and Kadmos (the superannuated grandfather of the reigning prince) the advocates of caution, tolerance and, so to speak, elasticity; they advise Pentheus against violent response to Dionysos' early demands that his cult be honoured in the city where his mother, Semele, was born. Pentheus dismisses their prudence and, like any young fogey, announces himself the vessel of an incautious conservatism, contemptuous of the new. Refusal to believe that there can be anything which is not subject to his arbitrary rule brings disaster on the king and on his city. To insist on the *status quo*, we infer, is always a form of tyranny. The exclusion of the Other, of which Dionysos was the apotheosis, leads to the collapse of the Self. Unable to see the divinity of the androgynous hippy who is in front of him, Pentheus contrives to have both his kingdom and himself ripped apart.

It would be imprudent to draw precise moral or theological conclusions from a play whose 'argument' contains so much irony and is itself a blend of the hot and the cold, or cool. As every schoolboy used to know, Euripides wrote *Bacchae* – usually said to be his last play – after he, like Anaxagoras before him, had been exiled from Athens for flagrant heterodoxy. *Bacchae* may ridicule the vanities of a young king, but it is certainly not an unalloyed advertisement for Dionysos, still less an assertion of the 'truth' of the Olympian religion (the Greek had no more notion of a formal theology than did the Jews).

If Euripides cannot be proved to have written *Bacchae* with any purpose but to enjoy himself, perhaps to flaunt his now unbridled genius to the Athenians who had expelled him, it is not foolish to contrast his play with Plato's *Republic*, on which it offers incidentally sarcastic comment. In *his* masterpiece, Plato implicitly criticised the Olympian gods – even those of unquestionable title in the Greek pantheon – for their immorality, even though he was slyly tactful enough to attack Homer and Aeschylus for their irresponsible portraits of the Olympians rather than directly to reproach the gods themselves.

In his denunciation of irresponsible art, Plato maintained that the ideal polity could not allow gods to be portrayed as lecherous, drunk or dishonest; a revised version of their personal histories would have to be promulgated. This has become a regular part of (often belated) attempts to make divinities logically consistent and loin-clothed. Are not Christians sometimes embarrassed by the story that Jesus blasted a fig tree in what seems like a fit of all-too-human petulance? It is easier to declare the story apocryphal than to concede that Jesus lost his temper. The notion of free will, granted to man as a kind of generosity, is more useful in protecting God, from accusations of failing benignly to intervene in human affairs, than in supplying evidence of His love of His creation. The Platonic demand that the gods behave themselves perfectly in all published texts was expressed in a refusal to allow that they could do anything else. Since logically they were incapable of bad behaviour, they must have been misreported by the poets whose presence in the Ideal Polity was as undesirable to Plato as Dionysos' was to Pentheus (or that of 'free-thinking Jews' was to Mr Eliot, when he considered the form which his ideal Christian community might take). The more that men seek to enact what behaviour is acceptably to be attributed to the gods, and the more they interdict any dissident voice, the more palpably they have ceased to fear God and the more determined they seem to have become to create their creator.

What distinguished the Greek writers of the fifth and fourth centuries was the development of a language – evolving from that of myth – sufficiently commodious both to respect and to question (and satirise) the heroes and gods who supplied the *dramatis personae* of the Greek imagination. This observation may be something of a commonplace; it is less common to point out with what more or less assertive tact Euripides and his contemporaries, including Plato, incorporated what more artless writers might simply have junked. As Wittgenstein recommended, in another context, they 'said the new thing in the old language'; in this way, they sustained the complex continuities of their culture. The road was resurfaced, and somewhat redirected, while traffic continued to flow along it.

The Greek 'intellectuals' rationalised and humanised what Seferis recognised, more than twenty centuries later, as 'the Greek style' without jettisoning its ballast of unreason and even of savagery.

Imperfection is part of vitality; division sustains. The Jews, in a not wholly different way, preserved the lineaments of community, even after the catastrophe of Trajan, by distinguishing the specificity of quotidian law from the apolcalyptic tradition of the prophets: reason and the irrational are married by their divorce. Defeated Athens and desecrated Jerusalem thus remained, and remain, the poles of European thought for *and against* God or gods.

To humanise is not to disarm; quite the contrary. The late Gillian Rose's retrieval of violence *within* ethics, within 'polite' (urban/ urbane) morality, was an attempt to restore the dangerous complexity (and complicity) which 'modernism' disparaged; her awkward, knotty language was the linguistic correlative of the violence which, like Dionysos, had to be admitted into the human audit if it was to render a full inventory of our prospects. The New Testament parable of the seven devils warns of the futility of supposing that we can eliminate the diabolical from human life. Jung maintained that the great mistake of Christian theology was the eviction of the Devil from the Godhead. Those who suppose that they have purged their society of 'the one thing' which threatens its tranquillity procure the circumstances for even greater horrors.

Did T.S. Eliot understand the relevance of this warning to his plans for a Christian society? As Freud also implies, the unfathomable, the scandalous, is part of what we are; as the pun and the slip of the tongue remind us, the inadmissible will always find a way in. The notion of a homogeneous and virtuous society sponsors the seven devils – cruelty, superstition, ignorance, vanity, immobilism, exclusivity and self-righteousness – which will come to replace the domestic devil of, let us say, *dirt*. The 'Victorian' eviction of dirt, in the sexual sense, has given the notion of 'expressing one's sexuality' the commanding significance which, in our time, has sanctioned it to become a, if not *the*, form of mundane salvation. As any ironist might have guessed, the triumph of the pleasure principle leaves people wondering why they cannot be happier still. There is always the question, as Jean Baudrillard put it, 'What are you doing *after* the orgy?'

So what is all this about? It amounts, I suppose, to a sort of declarative dodge on my part. I have tried, in the form of a discursive intellectual parable, to show how difficult it is for man – let alone *this* man – to find a reasonable language in which to consider (ah!) what God means, or should mean to him. The naïve atheist, who sees no reason to believe in a Being who never manifests those qualities of goodness or love for which He is so regularly applauded (and

a Jew, it is less because I feel myself to belong to a community of beliefs or practices than because 'denial' would be either contemptible or require apostate allegiance to a religion incompatible with being a Jew. The Jewishness of – for easy instance – Spinoza, of Raymond Aron, of Italo Svevo, of Freud, of Menuhin, even of Wittgenstein, was never in question, but their lives were conducted in a more or less entirely secular and certainly an intellectually and artistically open-minded manner. Good and useful lives can be lived within an Orthodox scheme, but there is no evidence that the only valid Jew must be certified by any religious body (or Israeli official). That Cardinal Lustiger, the Archbishop of Paris, could say that he was *still* a Jew suggests how far it is possible to go without (in one's own view at least) having left.

A critic is still at liberty to maintain that I am the kind of man whom St Paul derided as blowing neither hot nor cold, but then I am the kind of man who might choose to deride the saint, precisely because he tried to resolve his contradictions by advocating a religion which is itself sublimely confused: *credo quia impossibile* is, to a heathen mind, a curiously frantic boast. The reluctance to engage in dialogue – why else would it be discussed so often? – to be found in Christianity is closely linked with the apostolic fervour which requires conversion, not accommodation.

What could be less congenial to the Christian approach to life than the kind of drama which Greek religion sponsored, in which dialogue constantly revises and challenges the view taken of, and even by, the gods? The Jewish tradition seems hardly less unamenable to question, but the Talmud and the yeshivas (in which the rabbis were teachers – however severe – and never priests) testify to a history of question and response, challenge and compromise which the Christian churches seldom match.

We are left with a serviceable scepticism which avoids the dogmatic futility of God-denial but insists on distinguishing law from prophets and – conscious of the limitations, and even of the comedy of a merely reasonable interest in religion – is disinclined to allow metaphysics to infect, still less to determine, mundane practice.

Something very simple, and perhaps very English, follows from this: without the wish to deprive anyone of his or her right to worship God, in whatever form seems good to them, I believe (if that is the right verb) in the sacredness of the profane, in the necessity of a middle ground of common citizenship in which no unproved and unprovable notion of rectitude – however admirable – gives a warrant for uncivil coercion, still less for social disqualification or religiously sanctioned murder.

Only a fool fails to recognise the limitations of a secular society, based on a system of interpenetrating uncertainties; only a villain proposes that there is anything better in prospect for so systematically duplicitous a creature as man. The paradox seems to be that scepticism leads to an adaptable and free society, while certainty, however licensed, limits human intelligence, destroys individuality, and incites the ruinous triumph of intolerance.

Bertrand Russell once argued (only once) that if it could be proved that the destruction of the Jews could secure God's promise of heaven on earth, there could be no reasonable argument against it. He was wrong; not even God's promise *necessarily* warrants committing a crime. Still less, it seems to me, does the attribution of the scriptural doctrines of *any* religion to His personal dictation justify the enactment of cruelty or murder. If someone asks me who on earth thinks otherwise, I can only invite him to look at the absurd world in which we live and to which, as Jean Genet promised and threatened, there is no viable alternative. To regard the human condition without excessive hope, but not to despair of it, remains the sceptic's warily optimistic recipe. As someone once said, 'The man who has all the answers has not heard all the questions.' To be confident that one has more questions than answers is not the least of the benefits of doubt.

Index